The Life of Haydn
in a Series of Letters Written at Vienna
followed by
The Life of Mozart
with Observations on Metastasio,
and on the Present State
of Music in France and Italy

STENDHAL

CAMBRIDGE UNIVERSITY PRESS

Cambridge, New York, Melbourne, Madrid, Cape Town,
Singapore, São Paolo, Delhi, Mexico City

Published in the United States of America by Cambridge University Press, New York

www.cambridge.org
Information on this title: www.cambridge.org/9781108061971

© in this compilation Cambridge University Press 2013

This edition first published 1817
This digitally printed version 2013

ISBN 978-1-108-06197-1 Paperback

This book reproduces the text of the original edition. The content and language reflect
the beliefs, practices and terminology of their time, and have not been updated.

Cambridge University Press wishes to make clear that the book, unless originally published
by Cambridge, is not being republished by, in association or collaboration with, or
with the endorsement or approval of, the original publisher or its successors in title.

CAMBRIDGE LIBRARY COLLECTION
Books of enduring scholarly value

Music

The systematic academic study of music gave rise to works of description, analysis and criticism, by composers and performers, philosophers and anthropologists, historians and teachers, and by a new kind of scholar - the musicologist. This series makes available a range of significant works encompassing all aspects of the developing discipline.

The Life of Haydn and The Life of Mozart

Marie-Henri Beyle (1783–1842), better known by his pen name Stendhal, is remembered today for such novels as *Le Rouge et le Noir*. In his lifetime, he wrote in a variety of literary genres and under a multitude of names. Louis-Alexandre-César Bombet was his choice of pseudonym for these early works, originally published in French in 1814. His lives of Haydn and Mozart were substantially derived from works by Giuseppe Carpani and Théophile Winckler respectively. Despite this audacious plagiarism, Stendhal's passion for music is evident, especially for Mozart, whose *Clemenza di Tito* he had enjoyed in Königsberg during the winter of 1812 whilst serving in Napoleon's army. Of especial interest to the modern reader are Stendhal's frequent digressions expressing his forthright opinions on the issues and figures of his day. This reissue is of Robert Brewin's English translation of 1817, with additional notes by the composer William Gardiner.

Cambridge University Press has long been a pioneer in the reissuing of out-of-print titles from its own backlist, producing digital reprints of books that are still sought after by scholars and students but could not be reprinted economically using traditional technology. The Cambridge Library Collection extends this activity to a wider range of books which are still of importance to researchers and professionals, either for the source material they contain, or as landmarks in the history of their academic discipline.

Drawing from the world-renowned collections in the Cambridge University Library and other partner libraries, and guided by the advice of experts in each subject area, Cambridge University Press is using state-of-the-art scanning machines in its own Printing House to capture the content of each book selected for inclusion. The files are processed to give a consistently clear, crisp image, and the books finished to the high quality standard for which the Press is recognised around the world. The latest print-on-demand technology ensures that the books will remain available indefinitely, and that orders for single or multiple copies can quickly be supplied.

The Cambridge Library Collection brings back to life books of enduring scholarly value (including out-of-copyright works originally issued by other publishers) across a wide range of disciplines in the humanities and social sciences and in science and technology.

THE

LIFE OF HAYDN,

IN A SERIES OF

LETTERS WRITTEN AT VIENNA.

FOLLOWED BY

THE LIFE OF MOZART,

WITH

OBSERVATIONS

ON

METASTASIO,

AND ON

THE PRESENT STATE

OF

MUSIC IN FRANCE AND ITALY.

TRANSLATED FROM THE FRENCH OF

L. A. C. BOMBET.

WITH NOTES

BY

THE AUTHOR OF THE SACRED MELODIES.

LONDON:

JOHN MURRAY, ALBEMARLE-STREET.

1817.

Printed by W. Lewis, St. John's-square, London.

TABLE OF CONTENTS.

TRANSLATOR'S Preface.
Author's Preface.

LETTER I.

DESCRIPTION of Haydn's residence; — of his appearance in his old age;—of Vienna, and the Prater;—character of the society of Vienna;—of the women;—political discussion prohibited by the government;—general state of manners favourable to music.

LETTER II.

SOURCES of the author's information;—vocal music chiefly studied before Haydn;—Lulli first introduces Overtures;—Ancient Instruments in the *Cena di San Giorgio* by Paul Veronese;—Troubadours;—Viadana;—Orchestra of the Odeon;—Rameau;—Bad taste in music and Painting;—Remark of Montesquieu on the connoisseurs;—French authors of the present day aim at singularity;—their music tiresome;—different character of the Italian;—Scarlatti's overtures, imitated by Corelli, Porpora, and others;—improved by San Martini, Jomelli and others;—Quartetts of Corelli, and Gassman; — Pleyel; — Beethoven; — and Mozart.

LETTER III.

BIRTH of Haydn;—his father a cart-wright, and sexton of the village;—their family concerts;—Haydn's first instructor, Frank;—learns to play on the tambourine;—sings at the parish church;—visit of Reüter;—Haydn learns to shake;—anecdote of the cherries;—goes with Reüter to Vienna;—his early application and fondness for music;—advantages of the musical composer;—amateurs;—advice to sentimental ladies;—Italian sensibility to music;—Pacchiaroti;—anecdote.

LETTER IV.

CONCERTOS censured;—Haydn's first mass;—his extreme poverty;—Courses of Literature;—Haydn teaches himself counterpoint;—Porpora;—Haydn seeks to ingratiate himself with him—learns from Porpora the Italian style of singing—gradual developement of his genius.

LETTER V.

HAYDN expelled from St. Stephen's;—is received by Keller, the peruke-maker;—engages to his daughter;—his first productions;—nocturnal serenades;—adventure with Curtz; tempest in the Diable Boiteux;—composes six trios;—clamour raised against them;—lodges in the same house with Metastasio;—enters the service of count Mortzin;—introduction to prince Esterhazy;—is engaged by him;—composes for the baryton;—marries Ann Keller;—mademoiselle Boselli.

LETTER VI.

REGULAR distribution of Haydn's time;—character of his works; —his quartetts—compared to a conversation;—his symphonies— andantes—allegros— minuets;— remark of Mozart on modern comic operas;—reason why the French do not excel in music.

CONTENTS.

LETTER VII.

ANECDOTE of the young Italian at the Borromean isles;—comparison of the French, and Italian character;—French conversation;— café de Foi;— saloon of madame du Deffant;— French colonists;—difference between the Frenchman and the Italian.

LETTER VIII.

SITUATION of the author;—instrumental music more cultivated than vocal;—a taste for the fine arts may be acquired;—anecdote;—Haydn's opinion of the importance of melody;—hymn sung by the charity-children at St. Paul's;—madame Barilli;—Lazzaroni;—good singing difficult to be defined;—use of discords;—first discovered by Monteverde, and Scarlatti;—Mozart too free in his modulations;—discords in music like chiaro-scuro in painting;—Haydn collects the national airs of different countries;—strolling Neapolitan musicians;—Lionardo da Vinci;—Haydn's mode of composition;—his attention to his dress;—neatness with which he wrote;—takes some little history as the subject of his symphonies;—Haydn compared to Titian;—scene of Orestes, in Gluck's Iphigenia:—San Martini;—Haydn's secret of composition;—Sarti.

LETTER IX.

ANECDOTE of Jomelli;— the abbé Speranza;— Zingarelli;— Haydn's style;—advantages of instrumental music over vocal;— Gluck's Orpheus and Eurydice;—ballet of Prometheus;—Paesiello and Sarti;—judicious distribution of the parts in a symphony, like harmony of colouring in painting;—Correggio—Carravaggio—Caracci—Mozart the La Fontaine of music.

LETTER X.

THE Seven Words;—ceremony of the *entierro*, at Madrid;—Michael Haydn;—sacred symphonies;—Correggio the inventor of chiaro-scuro.

LETTER XI.

HAYDN naturally gay and lively;—different habits of society at Paris and at Vienna;—comic music;—Merula;—Marcello—Jomelli—Galuppi—FatherMartini—Clementi—Porpora;—trills;—Haydn's comic pieces;—the departure;—the toy symphony;—the surprise.

LETTER XII.

HAYDN'S vocal music;—his operas;—inferior in the department of melody to other masters;—character of his genius;—Haydn the Claude Lorraine of music;—Cimarosa the Raphael;—pleasure given by music, different from that derived from painting;—in what respects.

LETTER XIII.

MELODY;—Matrimonio segreto;—Melody the test of genius in music;—Gluck;—scene of Orestes and the Furies;—Corneille's *qu'il mourut*;—Naples the country of all the great melodists;—character of the music of Germany;—of Flanders;—of France;—of England;—of Russia;—of Spain;—of the East;—of Italy;—the instrumental part subordinate to the vocal in the operas of that country;—operas of Haydn deficient in melody;—the harmonist ranked with the landscape-painter;—the melodist with the painter of history;—Claude Lorraine and Raphael.

CONTENTS.

LETTER XIV.

THE Neapolitan school of music;—Scarlatti;—Porpora;—Leo;—Durante;—Vinci;—Pergolese;—Hasse;—Jomelli;—Perez;—Traetta;—Sacchini;—Bach;—Piccini;—Paesiello;—Guglielmi;—Anfossi;—epochas of the principal composers.

LETTER XV.

VENERATION due to departed genius;—Petrarch;—Cimarosa;—Haydn composed with difficulty;—similar in this respect to Ariosto;—singular arrangements made by several composers;—by Gluck;—by Sarti;—Cimarosa;—Sacchini;—Paesiello;—Zingarelli;—Haydn;—death of prince Nicholas Esterhazy;—pieces of Lulli and Rameau sent to Haydn as models by a Parisian amateur;—death of mademoiselle Boselli;—Haydn's first visit to London, in 1790;—anecdotes of his residence there;—ancient concert;—second journey of Haydn to London, in 1794;—his engagement with Gallini;—Mrs. Billington;—his portrait taken by Reynolds;—receives a diploma from Oxford:—Canon cancrizans;—Haydn returns home;—state of his fortune.

LETTER XVI.

MASSES of Haydn;—Gregorian and Ambrosian chants;—Guido Aretino;—Palestrina;—early authors in music and painting superior in genius to many who have produced more pleasing works;—Durante;—Haydn observes a medium in his sacred music between the ancient and the modern Italian style;—French sentiment;—anecdote of Farinelli and Senesino;—musical sheep of the Borromean isles;—character of Haydn's masses;—true object of sacred music;—attained by Haydn.

LETTER XVII.

INTRODUCTION to the Creation.

LETTER XVIII.

SUBLIME geniusses compared to lofty mountains;—Moliere;—oratorio of Tobias;—Haydn's veneration for Handel;—character of Handel's music;—details respecting the oratorio;—Zingarelli's Destruction of Jerusalem;—baron Von Swieten;—first performance of the Creation, in 1798, at prince Schwartzenberg's;—on the *physical* imitation of nature by music;—Melani's Padestà di Coloniola;—Gluck's Pilgrim of Mecca;—Marcello's Calisto;—sentimental imitation;—Matrimonio segreto;—Letter of Othilia, from Goethe;—descriptive music;—Critique on the Creation;—Chaos;—creation of light;—fall of the angels;—creation of the thunder, hail, snow, &c.—creation of the waters;—of the plants, &c.;—rising of the sun;—of the moon;—finale of the first part;—creation of the birds;—of the animals;—of Adam;—of Eve;—last part of the Creation.

LETTER XIX.

SUCCESS of the Creation;—explosion of the infernal machine at Paris;—translations of the text of the Creation;—critique of it continued;—number of instruments and voices necessary to give a proper idea of it;—taste in music dependant on our associations;—moments of the most lively pleasure, or pain, leave no distinct traces in the memory;—illustrations of this idea;—of beauty in music, and of ideal beauty in general;—melody the department of genius;—harmony less affected by the changes of public taste;—citation from the Spectator;—the German and Italian contrasted;—Dutch taste in female beauty;—Parisian taste;—change in the French character during the last thirty years.

CONTENTS.

Fragment of the Reply to the preceding.

SUBJECT of ideal beauty continued ;—Canova ;—advantages enjoyed by the scupltor over the musician ;—Italy the most favoured country for music.

LETTER XX.

ORATORIO of the Four Seasons ;—advantages arising from the variations of taste in different countries ;—modern French drama ;—critical examination of the Four Seasons ;—Haydn's own remark upon this work ;—adventures of Stradella and Hortensia ;—comparison of the principal musicians and painters.

LETTER XXI.

LAST years of Haydn ;—mass performed for him by the French institute ;—celebration of his birth-day at the house of prince Lobkowitz ;—affecting circumstances attending it ;—he takes a final leave of the public.

LETTER XXII.

EXTREME weakness of Haydn in his 78th year ;—siege of Vienna by the French ;—death of Haydn ;—his religious feeling ;—his heir ;—his epitaph ;—composers of the present day.

CATALOGUE of Haydn's Works.

THE Life of Mozart.

LETTER on the Genius of Metastasio.

ON the present State of Music in Italy.

ADDITIONAL NOTES.

On Melody, 200.
On thorough Bass, 51. 348.
On the Human Voice, 124.
On the Instinctive Tones, 221.
On Singing, 464.
On Accent, 359.
On the different Keys, 98.
On the Colour of the Instruments, 255.
On the Powers of the Orchestra, 230.
On the Italian and German Music, 252.
On English Music, 165.
On a National School, 171.
On the Philharmonic Society, 35. 192.
On the Improvement of the Art, 2.
On the Trombone, 15.
On the Piano-forte, 106.
Description of Haydn's Canzonetts, 150.
——————————— Creation, 103. 261.
——————————— Chaos, 247.
——————————— Rising of the Sun, 256.
——————————— Leviathan, 258.
——————————— Wild Beasts, 265.
——————————— Sinfonias, 186.
——————————— Comic ditto, 144.
——————————— Ariadne, 153.
——————————— Orpheus, 194.
——————————— Masses, 215.
——————————— Beethoven's Sinfonia, 115.
——————————— Quartetts, 64.
——————————— Mount of Olives, 205.
——————————— Mozart's Operas, 301.
——————————— Requiem, 403.

TRANSLATOR'S PREFACE.

THE Public are here presented with a work for their amusement. Independently of the interest with which musical men will always regard whatever relates to names so eminent in their art as those of Mozart and Haydn, the general reader will find, in the following pages, a variety of anecdote, and an elegance of criticism, on all subjects connected with the fine arts, which can scarcely fail to gratify him.

The epistolary form of the work is stated, in the short preface which precedes it, to have arisen from its having been originally written to satisfy the enquiries of a friend at Paris, without any intention of publication; as the frequent allusions to the private circumstances and feelings of the author, and the numerous digressions and criticisms in which he indulges, sufficiently shew He appears to have been driven from France by the storms of the Revolution, and to have resided in Germany and Italy, during an exile of twenty years. He asserts, at the commencement of Letter II., that he received the information which he has given respecting Haydn, from his own lips, or from those of his intimate friends; and in a note at the close of his narrative, (page 117) he declares that he is prepared to verify his statements, if called in question.

It may be further satisfactory to the reader to state that, in all the principal facts, his relation agrees with the Historical Notice of the Life and Works of Haydn, read before the French Institute, October 6, 1810, by M. Le Breton.

The Memoir on Mozart was originally published in Germany, where the accuracy of the facts referred to, must have been generally known.

The Translator is not aware that any equally authentic account of these celebrated composers has yet appeared in this country.

The object of the Letter on the Genius of

Metastasio is to shew that the merits of the Poet of Music have not been duly appreciated. In the opinion of his superiority to Petrarch, the author is supported by M. Sismondi; but it will probably be thought that his enthusiasm has carried him too far, when he asserts that his favourite has occasionally surpassed Anacreon, and Horace.

The letter on the present state of music in France and Italy, contains a brief account of the most distinguished composers, and vocal performers, of the present day, and is further interesting from the observations made on the different character of the two nations, in the same style of lively and judicious criticism, as prevails in the former part of the work.

Of the Notes, such as are without signature are found in the original. To these the Translator has added others, marked by the letter T, which are for the most part explanatory, though he has occasionally animadverted on certain opinions of the author, which appeared to him erroneous.

But the greater part are by a gentleman, whose taste in music has already been exhibited to the public in the "SACRED MELODIES;" a work, published under the most illustrious patronage, and which, it is to be hoped, will, ere long, succeed in its object of banishing the barbarous ditties of Sternhold and Hopkins from our churches. Of the subjects of many of these Notes, the Translator is not a competent judge; but to those who, like himself, find great pleasure in music, without much practical acquaintance with it, he presumes they will often be found to convey useful information; and to those possessing a more scientific knowledge of it, they will, occasionally, supply materials for curious and amusing speculation. To all these the initial letter G is attached.

The Translator is sensible that the office he has undertaken is one, which, while it is exposed equally with the higher branches of literary occupation, to criticism, is attended with little credit, even when successful. The knowledge of the French language is now so generally diffused in this country, that some persons may be disposed to question the necessity of a translation, altogether. But there are many, who, though they possess a general acquaintance with the language, are not sufficiently familiar with its musical phraseology, to read a work on that subject with pleasure. There are, also, a still greater number, in the middle class of society, with whom music is rather an amusement, than an accomplishment, and whose information in the other branches of polite education is by no means in the same proportion; while those who are professedly devoted to the art, are commonly so absorbed by it, as comparatively to neglect all other subjects.

It was for one of these *Pazzi per Musica*, that the present work was translated, and it is now published, merely because it is presumed to contain more musical information, in a popular form, than is to be met with in any other book of a size equally moderate.

THE AUTHOR'S PREFACE.

I was at Vienna in 1808, whence I wrote to a friend some letters respecting the celebrated Haydn, whose acquaintance an accidental occurrence had fortunately procured for me, eight or ten years before. On my return to Paris, I found that my lettters had acquired some celebrity; and that pains had been taken to obtain copies of them. I am thus tempted to become an author, and fairly to shew myself in print. I accordingly add a few illustrations, I remove some repetitions, and present myself to the friends of music, in the form of a small octavo.

LETTERS

ON

THE CELEBRATED COMPOSER

HAYDN.

LETTER I.

To M. Louis de Lech...

My Friend, *Vienna, April 5, 1808.*

Your favourite Haydn, that great man, whose name sheds so bright a splendour in the temple of harmony, is still living; but he exists no longer as an artist. At the extremity of one of the suburbs of Vienna, on the side of the imperial park of Schönbrunn, you find, near the barrier of *Maria Hilff*, a small unpaved street, so little frequented that it is covered with grass. About the middle of this street rises an humble dwelling, surrounded by perpetual silence: it is there, and not in the palace Esterhazy, as you suppose, and as in fact he might if he wished, that the father of instrumental music resides;—one of the men of genius of the eighteenth century, the golden age of music.

Cimarosa, Haydn, and Mozart, have but just quitted the scene of the world. Their immortal works are still performed, but soon will they be laid aside: other musicians will be in fashion, and we shall fall altogether into the darkness of mediocrity.*

We by no means coincide in this opinion with our author; on the contrary, we consider the modern music to be formed upon principles, which will ever preserve it from the oblivion which he apprehends. It is the fate of the arts to have their ages of mediocrity. Men of inferior talent may dazzle for a time, but they disappear, and exhibit true genius in greater splendour.

Haydn is unquestionably the greatest musical genius that has ever appeared. He is not only the founder of the modern art, but the most perfect of all modern authors. His peculiar excellence lies in that unity of design, and felicity of execution, which we look for in vain in other

These ideas always occupy my mind when I approach the peaceful dwelling where Haydn reposes. You knock at the door: it is opened to you with a cheerful smile by a worthy little old woman, his housekeeper; you ascend a short flight of wooden stairs, and find in the

composers. In his works we meet with nothing which we wish to remove, or amend. Though learned, he is always intelligible, and the impassioned melody which pervades his compositions, never fails powerfully to interest the feelings. In short, it is from him that we acquire the most correct ideas of musical taste, and perfection; and as his music is founded upon the *instinctive tones* of our nature, (see note, Letter XVI.) we have no fear that it will ever be lost, while human feelings remain.

Nor can we imagine the art is on the decline, while so great a genius as Beethoven lives. This author, though less perfect in other respects than Haydn, exceeds him in power of imagination; and, from recent specimens of his unbounded fancy, it is to be expected that he will extend the art in a way never contemplated even by Haydn or Mozart. If we were inclined to push our speculations farther upon this point, we might refer to the very extraordinary discoveries that are now making in Russia, in the department of instrumental music. In the course of twenty years it is probable that such effects will be produced in that country as will lead to the most important results in the science of sounds.   G.

second chamber of a very simple apartment, a tranquil old man, sitting at a desk, absorbed in the melancholy sentiment that life is escaping from him, and so complete a nonentity with respect to every thing besides, that he stands in need of visitors to recall to him what he has once been. When he sees any one enter, a pleasing smile appears upon his lips, a tear moistens his eyes, his countenance recovers its animation, his voice becomes clear, he recognizes his guest, and talks to him of his early years, of which he has a much better recollection than of his later ones: you think that the artist still exists; but, soon, he relapses before your eyes into his habitual state of lethargy and sadness.

The Haydn all fire, so exuberant and original, who, when seated at his piano-forte created musical wonders, and in a few moments warmed and transported every heart with delicious sensations—has disappeared from the world. The butterfly, of which Plato speaks, has spread its bright wings to heaven, and has left here below only the gross larva, under which it appeared to our eyes.

I go, from time to time, to visit these cherished remains of a great man, to stir these ashes, still warm with the fire of Apollo ; and, if I succeed in discovering some spark not yet entirely extinct, I go away with a mind filled with emotion and melancholy. This, then, is all that remains of one of the greatest geniuses that have existed !

> Cadono le città, cadono i regni,
> E l'uom d'esser mortale par che si sdegni.

This, my dear Louis, is all I can tell you, with truth, of the celebrated man, respecting whom you make such urgent enquiries. But to you, who love the music of Haydn, and who are desirous of knowing it, I can give other details than those which relate merely to his person. My residence here, and the society which I see, give me also a further opportunity of writing to you at length concerning this distinguished composer, whose music is performed at this day, from Mexico to Calcutta, from Naples to London, from the suburb of Pera to the saloons of Paris.

Vienna is a charming city. Represent to yourself an assemblage of palaces, and very neat houses, inhabited by the most opulent families of one of the greatest monarchies of Europe; by the only *noblemen* to whom that title may still be with justice applied. The city of Vienna, properly so called, contains seventy-two thousand inhabitants, and is surrounded by fortifications which now serve only as agreeable walks: but, fortunately, in order to leave room for the effect of cannon, which are no longer to be found, a space of twelve hundred yards has been reserved all round the town, on which it has been prohibited to build. This space, as you may suppose, is covered with turf, and with avenues of trees crossing each other in all directions. Beyond this verdant inclosure are the thirty-two fauxbourgs of Vienna, in which live one hundred and seventy thousand inhabitants of all classes. The majestic Danube borders the central town on one side, and separates it from the fauxbourg of Leopoldstadt. In one of its islands is situated the famous *Prater*, the finest promenade in the world, which, when compared with the Tuilleries, with Hyde Park, or with the Prado of Madrid, is what the view of the

Bay of Naples from the house of the hermit on Mount Vesuvius is, in comparison with all the other prospects that are boasted of elsewhere. The isle of the Prater, fertile as are all the islands of large rivers, is covered with superb trees, which appear still more noble from their situation. This island, which every where displays nature in all her majesty, presents you at one time with avenues of chesnut-trees in magnificent lines; and, at another, with the wild aspects of the most solitary forests. It is traversed by a hundred winding paths, and when you arrive on the banks of the Danube, which you suddenly find under your feet, the eye is again charmed by the Leopoldsberg, the Kalemberg, and other picturesque elevations which appear in the distance. This garden of Vienna, the effect of which is not injured by the presence of any of the labours of mechanic industry painfully occupied in the pursuit of gain, and where the forest is only occasionally broken by a few meadows, is six miles long and four and a half broad. I know not whether the idea be singular, but to me, this superb Prater has always appeared an apt image of the genius of Haydn.

In this central Vienna, the winter residence of the Esterhazys, the Palfys, the Trautmansdorffs, and of so many other noble families, surrounded by an almost regal pomp, there is not that brilliant display of mind, which was to be found in the saloons of Paris before our stupid revolution ; nor has reason raised her altars there as at London. A certain restraint, which forms a part of the prudent policy of the house of Austria, has inclined the people to pleasures of a more sensual kind, which are less troublesome to a government.

The house of Austria has had frequent relations with Italy, a part of which it possesses, and many of its princes have been born there. All the nobility of Lombardy repair to Vienna to solicit employments, and music is become the ruling passion of its inhabitants. Metastasio lived fifty years among them ;* it was for them that he composed

---

* Metastasio was born in 1698. He went to Vienna in 1730, and lived there till 1782.

those charming operas, which our petty literati of the school of La Harpe, take for imperfect tragedies. The women here are attractive; a brilliant complexion adorns an elegant form: the natural, but sometimes languishing and tiresome air of the ladies of the north of Germany, is here mingled with a little coquetry and address, the effect of the presence of a numerous court. In a word, at Vienna, as at Venice in former times, politics, and abstract reasoning on possible improvements, being prohibited, pleasure has taken possession of every heart. I know not whether that *interest of manners,* of which so much is said, finds its account in this; but it is certain, that nothing can be more favourable to music.* The enchantress has pre-

---

This observation only goes to prove generally, that where the higher objects of human pursuit are withdrawn, inferior ones will be sought after in their stead. We should be sorry to believe that depravity of morals is necessarily connected with a good taste in music; nor do we apprehend any such result in this country, so long as Englishmen maintain, with watchful jealousy, those political rights by which they have been far more gloriously

vailed here, even over German hauteur. The most distinguished of the nobility are directors of the three theatres where music is performed. It is they, likewise, who are at the head of the Musical Society, and some of them expend from eight to ten thousand francs a year, in promoting the interest of the arts. The Italians may be more sensible to the fine arts, but it must be confessed that they are far from meeting with such encouragement amongst them. Accordingly, a village, a few leagues distant from Vienna, produced Haydn: Mozart was born at a little distance farther, towards the mountains of the Tyrol; and it was at Prague, that Cimarosa composed his *Matrimonio segreto.*

---

distinguished, than by any splendour which music or painting can bestow. Reason, we trust, will still have her altars, not only in the metropolis, but in every part of the island; nor shall we forget, that however delightful the fine arts may be as ornaments, they are miserable substitutes for freedom and virtue.   T.

LETTER II.

Vienna, April 15, 1808.

THANK heaven, my dear Louis, I pass much of my time in the musical parties, which are so frequent here. It is the union of the agreeable circumstances mentioned in my last, which has at length fixed my wandering lot at Vienna, and conducted to the port

> Me peregrino errante, e fra gli scogli,
> E fra l'onde agitato, e quasi assorto.

I have good authorities for every thing that I may say to you respecting Haydn. I have received his history in the first instance from himself, and, in the next, from persons who have associated most with him during the different periods of his life. I will mention the baron *Von-Swieten,* professor *Fribert,* professor *Pichl,* the violoncello *Bertoja,* counsellor *Griesenger,* professor *Weigl,* M. *Martinez,* and mademoiselle de *Kurtzberg,* the intelligent pupil and friend of Haydn, and the faithful copyist of his music. You will pardon these details; they relate to one of those geniuses, whose powers have been exclusively employed in increasing the pleasures of the world, and in furnishing additional recreations from its sufferings; geniuses truly sublime, yet to whom the stupid crowd prefer men, who gain to themselves a reputation, by setting some thousands of these miserable fools by the ears.

The musical Parnassus already reckoned upon its lists a great number of celebrated composers, when an Austrian village gave birth to the creator of symphony. The genius and studies of the predecessors of Haydn, had been directed to the vocal part, which, in fact, forms the basis of the pleasures which music affords; they employed instruments only as an agreeable accessory: like the landscape parts of an historical picture, or the ornaments in architecture.

Music was a monarchy: the air reigned absolute; the accompaniments were only subjects. That description of music into which the human voice does not enter, that republic of different yet connected sounds, in which each instrument in turn attracts the attention, was scarcely known at the end of the seventeenth century. It was Lulli, I think, who invented the symphonies which we call *overtures:* but even in these symphonies, as soon as the *fugued* passage* ceased, the monarchy was again perceived.

The violin part contained the whole of the air, and the other instruments served as an accompaniment, as they are still used in vocal music with respect to the *soprano,*

---

* The *fugue* is a species of music, in which an air, called the *subject,* is treated according to certain rules, by making it to pass successively, and alternately, from one part to another, as in the well-known canon of *Non nobis Domine.*

Every body has heard Dussek play on the piano the variations of *Marlbroug,* or of the air *Charmante Gabrielle.* In this inferior sort of music, the primitive air, which is spoiled by so much pretension, is what is called the *theme,* the *subject,* the *motif.* It is in this sense that the words are employed here.

the *tenore*, and the *contralto*. to which alone the musical idea, or the melody, is confided.

Symphonies, therefore, were only an air played by the violin, instead of being sung by an actor. The learned will tell you that the Greeks, and afterwards the Romans, had no other instrumental music: at least, it is certain, that none was known in Europe, before the symphonies of Lulli, but that which is necessary for dancing; and even this imperfect music, in which one part only executed the melody, was performed in Italy with but a small number of instruments. Paul Veronese has preserved to us the form of those which were in use in his time, in the famous "*Cena di San Giorgio,*" which is at once the largest, and the most pleasing picture in the Museum of Paris. In the foreground, in the vacant space of the semi-circle formed by the table, at which the guests of the marriage of Cana are seated, Titian is playing on the double bass, Paul Veronese and Tintoret on the violoncello, a man with a cross on his breast is playing on the violin,

Bassano is blowing the flute, and a Turkish slave the sackbut.*

When the composer desired a louder music, he added to these instruments straight trumpets. The organ was generally played by itself. The greater part of the instruments employed by the Troubadours of Provence, were never known out of France, and did not survive the fifteenth century. At length, Viadana,† having discovered thorough

---

* This ancient instrument, which is frequently mentioned in the sacred writings, might have been lost to us for ever, had it not been preserved in the ashes of Mount Vesuvius, to give force and energy to the music of modern times. When the cities of Herculaneum and Pompeii were discovered, one of these instruments was dug up, after having been buried nearly two thousand years by that dreadful catastrophe. The lower part of it is made of bronze, and the upper, with the mouth-piece, of solid gold. The King of Naples made a present of it to his present majesty; and from this antique, the instruments, now called by the Italians *Tromboni*, have been fashioned. In quality of tone it has not been equalled by any of modern make; and perhaps it has done more towards augmenting the sublime effects of the orchestra, than any one of the known instruments. G.

† Born at Lodi, in the Milanese; he was *maitre de chapelle* at Mantua, in 1644.

bass, and music making daily progress in Italy, violins, then called *viols*, gradually superseded the other instruments; and, about the middle of the seventeenth century, the composition of the orchestra was the same as at the present day.

Doubtless, at this period, those whose feelings were most alive to music, did not imagine, even in their most delightful reveries, such an assemblage as the admirable orchestra of the *Odeon*, formed of so great a number of instruments, all yielding sounds graduated in a manner so gratifying to the ear, and played with such complete unity of effect. The finest overture of Lulli, as performed before Louis XIV., surrounded by his court, would make you run to the other end of Paris. This brings to my mind some German and French composers, who have attempted, in our day, to give us the same sort of pleasure, by the beating of kettle-drums; but this is no longer the fault of the orchestra. Each of the performers who compose that of the opera, taken individually, plays very well; they are only too skilful; it is this which gives these barbarous composers the power of tormenting our ears.

These authors forget, that in the arts nothing endures but that which always pleases. It was easy for them to seduce that numerous portion of the public who find no direct enjoyment in music, and who only seek in it, as in the other fine arts, for an opportunity of speechifying and going into extasies. These insensible fine-talkers have misled some real amateurs; but all this episode in the history of music, will soon return to the oblivion which it merits, and the works of the great masters of the present day will, in fifty years, keep faithful company with those of Rameau, whom, fifty years since, we admired so much: and yet Rameau had pilfered, in Italy, a considerable number of charming airs, which were not entirely smothered by his barbarous art.

For the rest, the sect of musicians who torment you at Paris, and of whom you complain so loudly in your letter, has existed from remote antiquity: it is the natural product of much patience, joined to a cold heart, and an unlucky notion of applying to the arts. The same description of people annoy painting: it was they, who, after *Vasari,* inundated Florence with cold designers, and who are the pest of your school of the present day. In the time of Metastasio, the German musicians sought to overpower the singers by the instruments: and these again, desirous of recovering their empire, set themselves to make *vocal concertos,* as that great poet was wont to say. It was thus, that, by a total perversion of taste, the voices, imitating the instruments which sought to overpower them, we heard *Agujari, Marchesi,** *Marsa, Gabrielli,*† *Danzi,* Mrs. *Billington,* and other singers of great talent, transform their voices into a flageolet, set the instruments at defi-

---

* The divine Marchesi, born at Milan, about 1755. Never again will Sarti's rondeau, " *Mia Speranza,*" be sung as he sang it.

† The Gabrielli, born at Rome in 1730, a pupil of Porpora and Metastasio, so noted for her astonishing *capricci.* When I was young, the old people still talked of the style in which she sung at Lucca, in 1745, with Guadagni, who was then her lover.

ance, and surpass them in the difficulty and singularity of their passages. The poor amateurs were obliged to wait for their gratification, till these divine talents were tired of shewing off. Pursued by the instruments, their singing in the *bravura* airs possessed only one of two things which are essential to the fine arts, to please in which, it is necessary that the imitation of impassioned nature should be united in the spectator, with a feeling of the difficulty overcome. When the last alone is displayed, the minds of the audience remain unmoved, and though they may be incited for a moment, by the vanity of appearing connoisseurs in music, they are like those good-natured people of whom Montesquieu speaks, who, while yawning enough to dislocate their jaws, pulled each other by the sleeve, to say, " Heavens, how we are amused! how fine that is!"* It is owing to beauties of this kind that our music is in a state of such rapid declension.

---

* Lettres Persannes.

In France, in music, as well as in literature, it is the pride of an author to astonish by an uncommon phrase: the good folks do not perceive that the author has said nothing: think there is something singular in the thing, and applaud; but after having duly applauded two or three of these singularities, they begin to gape; and, in this melancholy mood, end all our concerts.

Hence arises the opinion which prevails in countries where the music is bad, that it is impossible to listen to any for more than two hours together, without being tired to death. At Naples,—at Rome, amongst genuine amateurs, where the music is well chosen, it charms without difficulty for a whole evening. I have only to refer to the agreeable concerts of Madame la D. L....; and I am sure of being supported in my assertion by all those who have had the happiness to be admitted to them.

To return to the rather dry history of instrumental music, I would remind you, that the invention of *Lulli*, though well suited to the object which he had in view, which was to open, with pomp, a theatrical representation, had so few imitators, that, for a length of time, his symphonies were performed in Italy before the operas of the greatest masters, who were not willing to take the trouble of composing overtures; and these masters were *Vinci, Leo,* and the divine *Pergolesi.* Old Scarlatti was the first who brought out overtures in his way: they had great success, and he was imitated by *Corelli, Perez, Porpora, Carcano, Bononcini,* &c. All these symphonies, like those of *Lulli,* were composed of a violin part, a bass, and nothing more. The first who introduced three parts, were *Sammartini, Palladini,* old *Bach*, *Gasparini, Tartini,* and *Jomelli.* It was only occasionally that they attempted not to give movement to all the parts.

Such were the faint gleams which announced to the world the sun of instrumental music. *Corelli* had composed duets, *Gassmann* quatuors; but a cursory glance at these stiff, learned, and ice-cold compositions, will be sufficient to satisfy us, that Haydn is the true inventor of *symphony:* and not only did he invent this kind of music, but he carried it to such a degree of perfection, that his sucessors must avail themselves of his labours, or relapse into barbarism.

Experience has already shewn the truth of this bold assertion.

Pleyel has diminished the number of chords, and been sparing of transitions; his works are deficient in strength and dignity.

When *Beethoven* and *Mozart* himself have accumulated notes and ideas; when they have sought after variety and singularity of modulation, their learned symphonies, full of research, have produced no effect; but when they have followed the steps of Haydn, they have touched every heart.

LETTER III.

Natura il fece, e poi ruppi la stampa.
Nature made him, and then broke the mould.
ARIOSTO.

Vienna, May 24, 1808.

FRANCIS JOSEPH HAYDN was born on the last day of March, 1732, at *Rohrau,* a small town, fifteen leagues distant from Vienna. His father was a cartwright; and his mother, before her marriage, had been cook in the family of Count Harrach, the lord of the village.

The father of Haydn united to his trade of a cartwright, the office of parish sexton. He had a fine tenor voice, was fond of his organ, and of music in general. On one of those journies, which the artisans of Germany often undertake, being at Frankfort-on-the-Mayne, he learned to play a little on the harp: and in bolidays, after church, he used to take his instrument, and his wife sung. The birth of Joseph did not alter the habits of this peaceful family. The little domestic concert returned every week, and the child, standing before his parents, with two pieces of wood in his hands, one of which served him as a violin, and the other as a bow, constantly accompanied his mother's voice. Haydn, loaded with years and with glory, has often, in my presence, recalled the simple airs which she sung; so deep an impression had these first melodies made on this soul, which was all music! A cousin of the cartwright, whose name was *Frank*, a schoolmaster at *Haimburg*, came to *Rohrau*, one Sunday, and assisted at the *trio*. He remarked, that the child, then scarcely six years old, beat the time with astonishing exactitude and precision. This *Frank* was well acquainted with music, and proposed to his relations to take little Joseph to his house, and to teach him. They accepted the offer with joy, hoping to succeed more easily in getting Joseph into holy orders, if he should understand music.

 He set out accordingly for Haimbourg. He had been there only a few weeks, when he discovered in his cousin's house two tambourines. By dint of trials and perseverance, he succeeded in forming on this instrument, which has but two tones, a kind of air, which attracted the attention of all who came to the school-house.

It must be confessed, my friend, that in France, amongst a class of people so poor as the family of Haydn, music is never thought of.

Nature had bestowed upon Haydn, a sonorous and delicate voice. In Italy, at this period, such an advantage might have been fatal to the young peasant: perhaps *Marchesi* might have had a rival worthy of him, but Europe would have lost her symphonist. *Frank*, who gave his young cousin, to use Haydn's own expressions, more cuffs than gingerbread, soon rendered the young tambourist able not only to play on the violin and other instruments, but also to understand Latin, and to sing at the parish-desk, in a style which spread his reputation through the canton.

Chance brought to Frank's house, *Reüter*,

Maitre de Chapelle of St. Stephen's, the cathedral church of Vienna. He was in search of to recruit his children of the choir. The schoolmaster soon proposed his little relative to him; he came; *Reüter* gave him a *canon* to sing at sight.

The precision, the purity of tone, the spirit with which the child executed it, surprised him; but he was more especially charmed with the beauty of his voice. He only remarked, that he did not *shake*, and asked him the reason, with a smile. The child smartly replied, " How should you expect me to shake, when my cousin does not know how himself?" " Come here," says *Reüter*, " I will teach you." He took him between his knees, shewed him how he should rapidly bring together two notes, hold his breath, and agitate the palate. The child immediately made a good shake. *Reüter*, enchanted with the success of his scholar, took a plate of fine cherries, which Frank had caused to be brought for his illustrious brother professor, and emptied them all into the child's pocket. His delight may be readily conceived. Haydn has often mentioned this anecdote to me, and he added, laughing, that whenever he happened to shake, he still thought he saw these beautiful cherries.

It will be easily supposed that *Reüter* did not return alone to Vienna; he took the young *shaker* along with him, then about eight years old. In his low fortune, we find no unmerited advancement, nothing effected by the patronage of any rich man. It was because the people of Germany are fond of music, that the father of Haydn taught it to his son; that his cousin *Frank* instructed him still farther; and that, at length, he was chosen by the *maitre de chapelle* of the first church in the empire. These were natural consequences of the habits of the country relative to the art which we admire.

Haydn has told me, that dating from this period, he did not recollect to have passed a single day without practising sixteen hours, and sometimes eighteen. It should be observed, that he was always his own master, and that at St. Stephen's, the children of the choir were only obliged to practice two hours. We conversed together respecting the cause of this astonishing application. He told me, that, from his most tender age, music had given him unusual pleasure. At any time, he would rather listen to any instrument whatever, than run about with his little companions. When at play with them in the square, near St. Stephen's, as soon as he heard the organ, he quickly left them, and went into the church. Arrived at the age of composition, the habit of application was already acquired: besides, the composer of music has advantages over other artists; his productions are finished as soon as imagined.

Haydn, who abounded in such beautiful ideas, incessantly enjoyed the pleasure of creation, which is, doubtless, one of the highest gratifications which man can possess. The poet shares this advantage with the composer; but the musician can work faster. A beautiful ode, a beautiful symphony, need only to be imagined to cause in the mind of the author that secret admiration, which is the life and soul of artists. But in the studies of the military man, of the architect, the sculptor, the painter, there is not invention enough for them to be fully satisfied with themselves; further labours are necessary. The best planned enterprize may fail in the execution; the best conceived picture may be ill painted; all this leaves in the mind of the inventor, an obscurity, a feeling of uncertainty, which renders the pleasure of creation less complete. Haydn, on the contrary, in imagining a symphony was perfectly happy; there only remained the physical pleasure of hearing it performed, and the moral pleasure of seeing it applauded. I have often seen him, when he was beating the time to his own music, unable to refrain from smiling at the approach of a passage which he was pleased with. I have also seen, at the great concerts which are given at Vienna, at certain periods, some of those amateurs, who only want the faculty of feeling, dexterously place themselves in a situation where they could see Haydn, and regulate, by his smile, the extatic applauses by which they testified to their neighbours the extent of their rapture. Ridiculous exhibitions! These people are so far from feeling what is fine in the arts, that they never even suspect that there is a modesty belonging to sensibility. This is a little piece of truth, which our sentimental ladies will doubtless feel obliged to me for having taught them. I will add an anecdote which may serve both as a model in the art of extatics, and as an excuse, if any frozen fellow should think proper to be ironical, and indulge in ill-timed pleasantry.

The *Artaxerxes* of Metastasio was performed in one of the first theatres of Rome, with the music of *Bertoni*; the inimitable *Pacchiarotti*,* if I am not mistaken, executed the part of Arbaces. During the third representation, at the famous judgment-scene, in which the author had placed a short symphony after the words

'Eppur sono innocente,'

---

* Pacchiarotti, born near Rome, in 1750, excelled in the pathetic —I believe he is still living in retirement at Padua.

the beauty of the situation, the music, the expression of the singer, had so enraptured the musicians, that *Pacchiarotti* perceived, that after he had uttered these words, the orchestra did not proceed. Displeased, he turned angrily to the leader—" What are you about?" The leader, as if waked from a trance, sobbed out with great simplicity, " We are crying." In fact, not one of the performers had thought of the passage, and all had their eyes filled with tears, fixed on the singer.

I saw, at Brescia, in 1790, a man, of all Italy perhaps the most affected by music. He passed his life in hearing it: when it pleased him, he slipped off his shoes without being aware of it; and if the pathetic was carried to its height, he was accustomed to throw them over his head upon the spectators.

Adieu.—I am frightened at the length of my letter; the matter increases under my pen : I thought I should write you three or four letters at most, and I am becoming endless. I profit by the obliging offer of

M. de C. who will transmit my letters to you, at Paris, free of postage, beginning with the present.

I am glad of this. If you were to receive by the post these enormous packets from abroad, it might be supposed that we were occupied in things of more importance; and in order to be happy, when one has a heart, it is necessary to withdraw ones-self from notice.

Vale et me ama.

LETTER IV.

Baden, June 20, 1808.

IN faith, my dear Louis, I seem to be no longer fond of music. I am just come from a concert, which has been given on the opening of the handsome room at Baden. You know that I have given pretty good proof of my patience: I have gone through a regular attendance on the sittings of a deliberative assembly; I have endured, in the midst of the most agreeable society, the friendship with which, for my sins, I was honoured by a stupid man in power, with whom you have some acquaintance; but I must confess, that from my first acquaintance with music I have never been able to bear the tiresomeness of *concertos*—they are to me the greatest of punishments. It is surely very silly to exhibit before the public, exercises, the results of which alone ought to be presented to it, and which, however necessary for a performer, it is cruel to inflict upon an audience. It appears to me about as wise, as if your son, instead of writing what you could understand, should send you from school a letter filled with great O's and F's, such as children are taught to make when they learn to write.

Performers on instruments, are people who learn how to pronounce well the words of a language, and to give them their proper quantity, but who forget, as they proceed, the meaning of these words. Were it not for this, a flute-player, instead of stringing together unmeaning difficulties, and making ad. libs. a quarter of an hour long, would take for his subject a lively and melodious air, such as

'Quattro baj e sei morelli,'

of Cimarosa, would spoil, and vary it with as many difficulties as he had a mind: and, after all, would only half tire you. If ever he returned to plain sense, he would draw tears from us, by playing without alteration some melancholy or tender air, or would electrify us with the beautiful waltz of the Queen of Prussia.

As for me, I am quite overdone with

hearing three concertos in the same evening. I stand in need of a powerful diversion, and I have made a resolution not to go to bed till I have given you the remaining history of the youth of Haydn.*

Less precocious than Mozart, who, at thirteen years, produced an applauded opera, Haydn, at the same age, composed a mass, which honest *Reüter* very properly ridiculed. This sentence surprised the young man, but full of good sense at that early period, he was aware of its justice: he was sensible that it was necessary to learn counterpoint, and the rules of melody,† but from whom was he to learn them? *Reüter* did not teach counterpoint ‡ to the children of the choir,

---

* The Philharmonic Society of London appears to be of the same opinion, on this subject, with the author, one of its regulations being that no *concerto* shall be played at its meetings, its object being to exhibit the art, and not the feats of dextrous musicians. Performances of this kind resemble those on the tight-rope, and excite no feeling but that of surprise.

† We presume the author here means harmony.

‡ That is, the art of composition.

and never gave more than two lessons in it to Haydn. Mozart had an excellent master in his father, who was an esteemed performer on the violin. It was otherwise with poor Joseph, a friendless chorister in Vienna, who could only obtain lessons by paying for them, and who had not a halfpenny. His father, notwithstanding his two trades, was so poor, that when Joseph had been robbed of his clothes, on his communicating the misfortune to his family, his father making an effort, sent him six florins* to refit his wardrobe.

None of the masters in Vienna would give lessons *gratis*, to a boy of the choir who had no patronage; and it is to this misfortune, perhaps, that Haydn owes his originality. All the poets have imitated Homer, who imitated no one: in this alone he has not been followed; and it is perhaps owing to this, more especially, that he is the great poet whom the world admires. For my own part, I wish, my friend, that all the 'courses of literature' were at the bottom of the ocean: they teach people

---

About eleven shillings.

of small abilities to produce works without faults, and nature makes them produce them without beauties. We are afterwards obliged to wade through these dull essays: our love for the arts is diminished thereby; whilst the want of instruction will, assuredly, never stop the course of a man, whom nature has formed to be great. Look at Shakespeare, at Cervantes; it is likewise the history of Haydn. A master might have prevented him from falling into some of the faults which he committed in the sequel, when he wrote for the church, and the theatre; but he would certainly have been less original. He alone is the man of genius, who finds such delightful enjoyment in his art, that he pursues it in spite of obstacles. The torrent which is destined to become a mighty river, will overthrow the dykes by which its course may be restrained.

Like Jean Jacques Rousseau, he bought, at a second-hand shop, some theoretical books, among others the Treatise by *Fux*, and he set about studying it with a perseverance, which the horrible obscurity of the rules could not overcome. Labouring alone, without a master, he made an infinite number of little discoveries, which were afterwards of use to him. Without either money, or fire, shivering with cold in his garret, and oppressed with sleep as he pursued his studies to a late hour of the night, by the side of a harpsichord out of repair, and falling to pieces in all parts, he was still happy. The days and years flew on rapid wing, and he has often said, that he never enjoyed such felicity at any other period of his life. Haydn's ruling passion was rather the love of music than the love of glory: and even in his desire of glory, not a shadow of ambition was to be found. In composing music, he sought rather his own gratification, than to furnish himself with the means of acquiring celebrity.

Haydn did not learn recitative of *Porpora,* as you have been told; the inferiority of his recitatives to those of the inventor of this kind of music, is a sufficient proof of this; but he learned from him the true Italian style of singing, and the art of accompanying on the piano-forte, which is not so easy a thing as is commonly supposed. He succeeded in obtaining these lessons in the following way.

A noble Venetian, named *Corner*, at that time resided at Vienna as ambassador from the republic. He had a mistress passionately fond of music, who had harboured old Porpora * in the hotel of the embassy. Haydn found means to get introduced into the family, purely on account of his love of music.† He was approved of; and his excellency took him, with his mistress and Porpora, to the baths of Manensdorff, which were the fashionable resort at that time.

Our young man, who cared for nobody but the old Neapolitan, employed all sorts of devices to get into his good graces, and to obtain his harmonic favours. Every day he rose early, beat the old man's coat, cleaned his shoes, and disposed, in the best order,

---

Born at Naples in 1685. I subjoin the epochas of some great artists, of whom I shall often speak.
Pergolese, born 1704, died 1733.
Cimerosa, — 1754, — 1801.
Mozart, — 1756, — 1792.
† En sa qualité de *melomane*.

the antique perriwig for the old fellow, who was sour beyond all that can be imagined. He obtained at first nothing but the courteous salutation of "fool," or "blockhead," when he entered his room in a morning. But the bear seeing himself served gratuitously, and observing, at the same time, the rare qualities of his voluntary lackey, suffered himself occasionally to soften, and gave him some good advice. Haydn was favoured with it more especially, whenever he had to accompany the fair *Wilhelmina*, in singing some of the airs of Porpora, which were filled with basses difficult to understand. Joseph learned in this house to sing in the best Italian taste. The ambassador, astonished at the progress of this poor young man, gave him, when he returned to the city, a monthly pension of six sequins,* and admitted him to the table of his secretaries. This generosity rendered Haydn independent. He was able to purchase a black suit. Thus attired, he went, at day-

---

* About £3 sterling.

break, to take the part of first violin at the church of the Fathers of the order of Mercy; from thence he repaired to the chapel of count *Haugwitz*, where he played the organ: at a later hour, he sung the tenor part at St. Stephen's. Lastly, after having been on foot the whole day, he passed a part of the night at the harpsichord. Thus forming himself by the precepts of all the musical men whom he could scrape an acquaintance, seizing every opportunity of hearing music that was reputed good, and having no fixed master, he began to form his own conceptions of what was fine in music, and prepared himself, without being aware, to form, one day, a style entirely his own.

LETTER V.

Baden, August 28, 1808.

My Friend,

The ravages of time extended their influence to the little fortune of Haydn. His voice broke; and, at the age of nineteen, he quitted the class of *Soprani* at St. Stephen's; or, to speak more correctly, and not to fall all at once into the style of panegyric, he was expelled from it. Being a little mischievous, like all lively young people, he one day took it into his head to cut off the skirt of one of his comrade's gowns, a crime which was deemed unpardonable. He had sung at St. Stephen's eleven years; and, on the day of his expulsion, his only fortune consisted in his rising talent, a poor resource when it is unknown. He, nevertheless, had an admirer. Obliged to seek for a lodging, chance threw in his way a peruke-maker, named *Keller,* who had often admired, at the cathedral, the beauty of his voice; and who, in consequence, offered him an asylum. Keller received him as a son, sharing with him his humble fare, and charging his wife with the care of his clothing.

Haydn, freed from all worldly cares, and established in the obscure dwelling of the peruke-maker, was able to pursue his studies without interruption, and to make rapid progress. His residence here had, however, a fatal influence on his future life; the Germans are possessed with the mania of marriage. To a gentle, affectionate, and timid people, domestic pleasures are of the first necessity. Keller had two daughters; his wife and he soon began to think of marrying one of them to the young musician, and spoke to him on the subject. Absorbed in his own meditations, and thinking nothing about love, he made no objection to the match. He kept his word, in the sequel, with that honour which was the basis of his character, and this union was any thing rather than happy.

His first productions were some short sonatas for the piano-forte, which he sold at a low price to his female pupils, for he had met with a few. He also wrote *minuets, allemands,* and *walzes,* for the *Ridotto.* He composed, for his amusement, a serenata for three instruments, which he performed on fine summer evenings, with two of his friends, in different parts of Vienna. The theatre of Carinthia* was at that time directed by *Bernardone Curtz,* a celebrated buffoon, who amused the public with his puns. Bernardone drew crowds to his theatre by his originality, and by good opera-buffas. He had, moreover, a handsome wife; and this was an additional reason for our nocturnal adventurers to go and perform their serenade under the harlequin's windows. *Curtz* was so struck with the originality of the music, that he came down into the street, to ask who had composed it. " I did," replied Haydn, boldly.—" How! you; at your age?"—" One must make a beginning sometime."—" Gad this is droll; come up-stairs." Haydn followed the harlequin, was introduced to the handsome wife,

---

The most frequented of the three theatres of Vienna.

and re-descended with the poem of an opera, entitled, " *The Devil on Two Sticks.*" The music, composed in a few days, had the happiest success, and was paid for with twenty-four sequins.* But a nobleman, who probably was not handsome, perceived that he was ridiculed, under the name of *the Devil on two Sticks*, and caused the piece to be prohibited.

Haydn often says, that he had more trouble in finding out a mode of representing the motion of the waves in a tempest of this opera, than he afterwards had, in writing fugues with a double subject. *Curtz*, who had spirit, and taste, was difficult to please; but there was also another obstacle. Neither of the two authors had ever seen either sea or storm. How can a man describe what he knows nothing about? If this happy art could be discovered, many of our great politicians would talk better about virtue. *Curtz,* all agitation, paced up and down the room,

---

* Twelve pounds.

where the composer was seated at the pianoforte. " Imagine," said he, " a mountain rising, and then a valley sinking; and then another mountain, and then another valley; the mountains and the valleys follow one after the other, with rapidity; and at every moment, alps and abysses succeed each other."

This fine description was of no avail. In vain did harlequin add the thunder and lightning. " Come, describe for me all these horrors," he repeated incessantly, " but, particularly, represent distinctly these mountains and valleys."

Haydn drew his fingers rapidly over the key-board, ran through the semi-tones, tried abundance of *sevenths*, passed from the lowest notes of the bass to the highest of the treble. *Curtz* was still dissatisfied. At last, the young man, out of all patience, extended his hands to the two ends of the harpsichord, and bringing them rapidly together, exclaimed, " The devil take the tempest!" " That's it, that's it," cried the harlequin, springing upon his neck, and almost stifling him. Haydn added, that when he crossed the Straits of

Dover, in bad weather, many years afterwards, he laughed during the whole of the passage, on thinking of the storm in *The Devil on Two Sticks.*

" But how," said I to him, " is it possible, by sounds, to describe a tempest, and that *distinctly* too?" As this great man is indulgence itself, I added, " that by imitating the peculiar tones of a man in terror, or despair, an author of genius may communicate to an auditor the sensations which the sight of a storm would cause in him ; but," said I, " music can no more represent a tempest, than say, ' Mr. Haydn lives near the barrier of Schönbrunn.' " You may be right," replied he, " but recollect, nevertheless, that words, and especially scenery, guide the imagination of the spectator."

Haydn was in his nineteenth year, when he composed this tempest. You know, that that musical prodigy, Mozart, wrote his first opera at Milan, at the age of thirteen, in competition with *Hasse*, who, after having heard the rehearsal, said publicly, " This boy will throw us all into the shade." Haydn was not so successful; his talent was not for the theatre: and though he has produced operas which no master would be ashamed to avow, he has, nevertheless, remained far behind the *Clemenza di Tito,* and *Don Juan.*

A year after the production of *the Devil on two Sticks,* Haydn entered on his proper career; he presented himself in the lists with six *trios.* The peculiarity of the style, and the novelty of the thing, gave them immediately the greatest celebrity; but the grave German musicians warmly attacked the dangerous innovations * with which they were filled. This nation, which has always had its *faible* in science, still composed its chamber music in all the rigour of *fugued counterpoint.*†

---

* Dangerous innovations! The language of ignorance and imbecility in every age.   T.

† It should be known, that nothing is more ridiculous or pedantic, than the rules of the most seductive of arts. Music stands in need of a *Lavoisier.* I entreat to be excused from explaining the strange words which I am sometimes obliged to use: there is Rousseau's Musical Dictionary to refer to. For instance, after a great deal of

The musical academy, established at Vienna by the great contrapuntist who sat on the throne, I mean, the Emperor Charles VI. still maintained itself in all its vigour. This grave monarch, who, it is said, was never seen to smile,* was one of the most violent amateurs of his time; and the composers in us,† who

---

trouble to make out what *counterpoint* is, we find, that if music were treated with a little method, twenty lines would be sufficient to convey an idea of its meaning. The various substances of nature, from the stone which paves the streets of Paris, to the water of Cologne, are certainly more numerous than the different circumstances which can be remarked in two or three sounds, sung one after the other, or at the same time; yet, the youngest student of the Polytechnic School, after twenty of Fourcroy's lessons, had all these substances classed in his head. This was owing to the rational system which, till 1804, was pursued in that school: the atmosphere of good sense, which was respired there, rejected every thing false or obscure.

Instances of solemn stupidity on a throne, are not wanting in our day: and the 'Great Embroiderer' may dispute the palm with the 'Great Contrapuntist.' T.

† " Composers in us." A common expression in France, to denote a pedant; a man full of book learning, but destitute of natural genius and feeling. It is an allusion to *Les Femmes Savantes*, of Moliere, in which several characters of this sort are introduced, under the names of Vadius, Rasius, and other names, ending in *us*. T.

surrounded him, could not endure any thing that was of a pleasing, rather than of a learned cast. The charming little thoughts of the young musician, the warmth of his style, the liberties which he sometimes allowed himself, called forth against him all the invectives* of the musical monastery. They reproached him with errors of counterpoint, heretical modulations, movements too daring. Happily all this disturbance did no harm to the rising genius : one thing, only, could have injured him—the silence of contempt; and the *debut* of Haydn was attended with circumstances directly opposite.

You must know, my friend, that before Haydn, no man had conceived the idea of an orchestra, composed of eighteen kinds of instruments. He is the inventor of *prestissimo,* the very idea of which made the old squaretoes of Vienna shudder. In music, as in every thing else, we have little conception of what the world was a hundred years back :

---

* Les *Pacômes.*

the *allegro,* for instance, was only an *andantino.*

In instrumental music, Haydn has revolutionized the details, as well as the masses. It is he who has obliged the wind instruments to execute *pianissimo.**

---

* To assert that we owe the introduction of *prestissimo,* and *pianissimo* (for an invention it can scarcely be called), to Haydn, is saying little. Our author's skill was much more shewn, by the variety of notes, of different lengths, which he introduced into his inimitable *adagios.* Before his time, few movements were constructed with notes of more than four degrees duration, the shortest being to the longest as 1 to 8; but we have now whole bars, where 32 notes are played in the time of 1 in the other parts.

We may also mention the extension of the scale into the heights of *altissimo,* as another improvement, which has had a wonderful effect upon melody, and by increasing the number of harmonic combinations, has enlarged the boundaries of thorough bass. For we are by no means of opinion with the doctors of the old school, that all chords are to be found in the septave, but are advocates for the new theory, which acknowledges the chords of the 9th, 11th, and 13th. Indeed, we think it not improbable that our harmonic nomenclature may be extended even to the chord of the 35th, which would be an admixture of all the tones and semitones of the scale.

It was at twenty that he produced his first quartett in B♭ $\frac{6}{4}$ time, which all the musical amateurs immediately learned by heart. I do not know for what reason Haydn, about this time, left the house of his friend Keller; but it is certain, that his reputation, though rising under the most brilliant auspices, had not yet raised him above poverty. He went to reside with a *M. Martinez,* who offered him board and lodging, on condition that he would give lessons on the piano-forte, and in singing, to his two daughters. It was then, that the same house, situated near the church of St. Michael, contained in two rooms, one over the other, in the third and fourth stories, the first poet of the age, and the first symphonist of the world.

In the time of Lulli, shifting upon the violin was unknown; and whenever the note C upon the first string occurred, it was looked upon with great terror, and in order to put the performers upon their guard, it was the practice of the leader to cry out " GARE L'UT," *mind the C.* The difficulty was then got over, by an exertion of the little finger!! G.

Metastasio, also, lodged with M. Martinez, but, as poet to the Emperor Charles VI., he lived in easy circumstances, while poor Haydn passed the winter days in bed for want of fuel. The society of the Roman poet was, nevertheless, a great advantage to him. A gentle and deep sensibility had given Metastasio a correct taste in all the arts. He was passionately fond of music, and understood it well; and this singularly harmonious soul appreciated the talents of the young German. Metastasio, dining every day with Haydn, gave him some general rules respecting the fine arts; and, in the course of his instructions, taught him Italian.

This struggle against want, the early companion of almost all artists who have arrived at distinction, lasted, with respect to Haydn, for six long years. If some rich nobleman had brought him out at that time, and sent him to travel, for two years, in Italy, with a pension of one hundred louis, nothing, perhaps, would have been wanting to his talent; but, less fortunate than Metastasio, he had not his *Gravina.** At length, he obtained a situation in a family; and, in 1758, left the house of Martinez, to enter the service of the count Mortzin.

This nobleman gave musical parties in the evenings, and had an orchestra of his own. Chance brought the old prince Antony Esterhazy, an ardent amateur, to one of these concerts, which happened to commence with a symphony of Haydn, (that in A. $\frac{3}{4}$ time.) The prince was so charmed with this piece, that he immediately entreated the count Mortzin to give up Haydn to him, whom he declared his intention of appointing second leader to his own orchestra. Mortzin consented. Unfor-

---

* The abbé Gian Vincenzo Gravina, was born near Cosenza, in Calabria, in 1664. He was the most distinguished civilian of his time, and wrote some profound works on the Roman jurisprudence; but, his generous patronage of Metastasio, says Tiraboschi, is alone sufficient for his eulogium.

He died at Rome, in the arms of his grateful pupil, in 1718.   T.

tunately the author, who was unwell, was not present at the concert that day; and as the intentions of princes, when they are not immediately executed, are subject to many delays, several months elapsed before Haydn, who was very desirous of entering into the service of the first nobleman in Europe, heard any more of it.

Friedberg, a composer attached to prince Antony, and who admired the rising talents of our young man, sought an opportunity of recalling him to the recollection of his highness. He formed the plan of setting him to compose a symphony, to be performed at *Eisenstädt*, where the prince resided, on his birth-day. Haydn executed it, and it is worthy of him. The day of the ceremony being arrived, the prince, seated on his throne, and surrounded by his court, attended at the usual concert. Haydn's symphony was began. Scarcely had the performers got to the middle of the first *allegro*, than the prince interrupted them, and asked who was the author of that fine composition? "Haydn," replied Friedberg, and he made the poor young man, all trembling, come forwards. " What!" exclaimed he, " is it this Moor's music?" (Haydn's complexion, it must be confessed, gave some room for this sarcasm) " Well, Moor, from henceforth you remain in my service. What is your name?"— " Joseph Haydn."—" Surely I remember that name; you are already engaged to me; how is it that I have not seen you before?" Haydn, confused by the majesty which surrounded the prince, made no reply. The prince continued, " Go, and dress yourself like a professor; do not let me see you any more in this trim, you cut a pitiful figure. Get a new coat, a wig and buckles, a collar, and red heels to your shoes; but I particularly desire that they may be of a good height, in order that your stature may correspond to your intelligence, you understand me; go your way, and every thing will be given you."

Haydn kissed the prince's hand, and retired to a corner of the orchestra, a little grieved, added he, at being obliged to lay aside his natural hair, and youthful elegance.

The next morning he appeared at his highness's levee, imprisoned in the grave costume, which had been enjoined on him. He had the title of second professor of music, but his new comrades called him, simply, *the Moor.*

Prince Antony dying a year afterwards, his title descended to prince Nicholas, if possible, a still more passionate admirer of the musical art. Haydn was obliged to compose a great number of pieces for the *Baryton*, a very complex instrument, now fallen into disuse, and the tone of which, between the tenor and bass, is very agreeable. It was the prince's favourite instrument, which he played upon every day; and every day he expected to find a fresh piece on his desk. The greatest part of what Haydn composed for the Baryton, perished in a conflagration; what remains is of no use. He often said, that the necessity he was under of composing for this singular instrument, contributed much to his improvement.

Before entering on the consideration of the other works of Haydn, it is proper to say a few words respecting an event, which, for a long time, disturbed the tranquillity of his life. He did not forget, as soon as he had the means of subsistence, the promise he had formerly made to his friend Keller the peruke-maker; he married his daughter Ann. He found he had got a prude, who, besides her troublesome virtue, had a mania for priests and monks. Our poor composer's house was continually filled with them. The disturbance of a noisy conversation, prevented him from pursuing his studies; and, further, in order to escape curtain lectures from his wife, he was under the necessity of supplying the convents of each of these good Fathers, gratis, with masses and motets.

To be teazed into troublesome jobs, by perpetual bickering, is, a situation, of all others, the most irksome to men, whose productions depend on the suggestions of their own minds. Poor Haydn sought consolation in the society of mademoiselle Boselli, a lovely singer attached to the service of his prince, and this step did not tend to augment his tranquillity at home. At length he separated from his wife, to whom he behaved, as far as regards pecuniary matters, with perfect honour.*

You see from this account, my friend, that Haydn's youth was on the whole tranquil, and unmarked by any great aberrations. It exhibits a man of sense proceeding steadily to his object. Adieu.

---

* However the circumstances here related may be admitted in palliation of Haydn's conduct in this instance, the laxity of manners, which so generally prevails among musical men, is, with stricter moralists, a serious objection against the art itself, and unquestionably operates to degrade its professors in the estimation of the public.

T,

LETTER VI.

Valley of St. Helen, Oct. 2, 1808.

My dear Friend,

I proceed to the conclusion of my history. Haydn, now received into the Esterhazy family, placed at the head of a grand orchestra, and attached to the service of a patron immensely rich, found himself in that happy union of circumstances, too rare for our pleasures, which gives opportunity to genius to display all its powers. From this moment his life was uniform, and fully employed. He rose early in the morning, dressed himself very neatly, and placed himself at a small table by the side of his piano-forte, where the hour of dinner usually found him still seated. In the evening, he went to the rehearsals, or to the opera, which was performed, in the prince's palace, four times every week. Sometimes, but not often, he devoted a morning to hunting. The little time which he had to spare, on common days, was divided between his friends and mademoiselle Boselli. Such was the course of his life, for more than thirty years. This accounts for the astonishing number of his works. They may be arranged in three classes;—instrumental music, church music, and operas.

In symphony, he is the first of the first; in sacred music, he opened a new path, liable, it is true, to criticism, but by which he has placed himself on a level with the greatest geniuses. In the third, that is, theatrical music, he was only respectable, and this, for many reasons; of which one of the best is, that in this department he was only an imitator.

Since you assure me that my prating does not tire you, I shall speak in regular order of these three kinds of music.

Haydn's instrumental music consists of chamber symphonies, for a greater or less number of instruments, and of symphonies for a full orchestra, which, on account of the great number of instruments necessary, can only be performed, with convenience, in a theatre.

The first of these divisions, comprehends the duets, trios, quartetts, sestetts, octetts, and divertimentos; the sonatas for the pianoforte, the *fantasie*, variations, and *capricci*. In the second are contained the symphonies for the grand orchestra, the concertos for different instruments, the serenades and the marches.

Of all this music, the quartetts, and the symphonies for the grand orchestra, are most esteemed. Haydn has written eighty-two quartetts, and one hundred and eighty symphonies. The first nineteen quartetts, are considered by amateurs merely as divertimentos. The originality and loftiness of his style is not yet fully developed in them. But, in return, each one of the quartetts, from that marked No. 20 to No. 82, would, alone, have been sufficient to establish the reputation of its author.

You know that quartetts are executed by

four instruments, a first violin, a second violin, an alto, and a violoncello. An intelligent woman said, that when she heard a quartett of Haydn's, she fancied herself present at the conversation of four agreeable persons. She thought that the first violin had the air of an eloquent man of genius, of middle age, who supported a conversation, the subject of which he had suggested. In the second violin, she recognized a friend of the first, who sought by all possible means to display him to advantage, seldom thought of himself, and kept up the conversation, rather by assenting to what was said by the others, than by advancing any ideas of his own. The alto, was a grave, learned, and sententious man. He supported the discourse of the first violin by laconic maxims, striking for their truth. The bass, was a worthy old lady, rather inclined to chatter, who said nothing of much consequence, and yet was always desiring to put in a word. But she gave an additional grace to the conversation, and while she was talking, the other interlocutors had time to breathe. It was, however, evident, that she had a secret inclination for the alto, which she preferred to the other instruments.*

---

* This is a very happy illustration of some of the quartetts of Haydn, though it will by no means convey a correct idea of all of them. As this species of composition affords the greatest scope for genius, we shall pursue the idea in quoting an example from the quartetts of Beethoven, in order to mark the characteristic difference of the two authors.

In Beethoven, the bass part is more important. It is not the chattering old lady of Haydn, but assumes another tone, and produces a series of new and sublime sensations. We may instance, in the first quartett dedicated to Count Rasoumoffsky, in F major. In this composition, there is more mind than can be found in a hundred pages of any other author; and, it may be referred to, as a specimen of what may be called the *ethics* of the art. The subject is opened by a dignified movement in the bass, and, though in *allegro* time, with a gravity of manner, and in a tone of authority, much beyond the style of ordinary conversation. It reminds us of a moral discourse, in which much excellent precept, and occasional admonition are conveyed. The accompaniment of the second violin and tenor, represent the effect of this impressive harangue upon the feelings of the by-standers, and, in this point of view, the art exhibits a power of gratification, which is denied to poetry and painting. The theme is wholly argumentative, and seldom deviates from its logical course to appeal to the passions.

Haydn, in the course of fifty years labour, has produced five hundred and twenty-seven instrumental compositions: and has never copied himself but when he intended to do so. For instance, the air of the husbandman, in the oratorio of The Four Seasons, is an *andante* from one of his symphonies, of which he has made a fine counter-tenor air, but which, it must be allowed, flags a little towards the end.

You perceive, my friend, that the greater part of the observations which I should here make, require a piano-forte, and not a pen. At the distance of four hundred leagues from

---

The precepts uttered by the bass, are reiterated with such clearness and eloquence, by the first violin, that we experience a satisfaction similar to that which we feel upon the perception of truth. At times, this well-digested strain is interrupted by short, responsive notes, indicative of clamour and obstinacy, but which, by great art, are made to yield to one another, in a succession of such happy coincidences, that all the softness of agreement and cordial assent is produced. From this point, the movement warms into an affectionate joy, untinctured by merriment or gaiety, which flows in a stream of pure and sober delight to the end. G.

you, and our beloved France, it is of the poetical part only, of Haydn's style, that I can speak.

The *allegros* of his symphonies, which are in general full of life and spirit, carry you out of yourself. They generally commence with a short, easy, and intelligible *theme*. Gradually, and by a procedure full of genius, this theme, repeated by the different instruments, acquires a character of mingled heroism and gaiety. These solemn tints, are like the dark shades of Rembrandt and Guerchino, which produce such effects on the illuminated parts of their pictures.

The author seems to conduct you into the midst of abysses; but, a continued sensation of pleasure, allures you to follow him in his singular course. The character I have just described, appears to me to belong in common to the *prestos* and *rondos*.

There is more variety in the *andantes*, and *adagios:* the lofty style is there displayed in all its majesty.

The phrases, or musical ideas, are finely and nobly developed. Each member is clear and distinct, and the whole stands boldly forward. It is the style of Buffon, when he abounds in ideas. There is more energy, than softness, required to execute properly the *adagios* of Haydn. They have rather the proportions of a Juno, than of a Venus. More grave, than delicate, they breathe a tranquil dignity, full of the power, and, sometimes, with a little of the heaviness, of the Germans.

In the *andantes*, this dignity is occasionally subdued by a moderated gaiety, but still it always predominates. Sometimes, in the *andantes* and *adagios*, the author suffers himself to be suddenly carried away by the copiousness and power of his ideas. This sportiveness, this excess of vigour, animates, enlivens, carries along with it the whole composition, but does not exclude passion and sentiment.

Some of the *andantes* and *allegros* of Haydn appear to have no subject. One is tempted to think the performers have begun at the middle of their parts; but in a short time the true amateur perceives, by his sensations, that the composer has had an object, and a plan.

His *minuets* are the pure emanations of genius. So rich are they in harmony, in ideas, in accumulated beauties, that they would suffice with an ordinary man for a sonata. It was in reference to this, that Mozart used to say of our comic operas, that any man in good health might make one, every day before breakfast. The second parts of Haydn's *minuets* are in general comic, and are delightful for their originality.

The general character of the instrumental music of our author is that of romantic imagination. In vain would you seek in it the correctness of Racine; it is rather the style of Ariosto, or of Shakespeare. For this reason I cannot account for the reputation of Haydn in France.

His genius ranges in every direction with the rapidity of the eagle. The astonishing, and the alluring, succeed each other alternately, and are painted with the most brilliant tints. It is this variety of colouring, it is the absence of every thing tedious, which has probably obtained for him so rapid and extensive a success. Scarcely had he composed his symphonies, before they were performed in America, and the Indies. The magic of his style seems to me to consist in a predominating character of liberty and joy. This joy of Haydn, is a perfectly natural, pure, and continual exaltation; it reigns in the *allegros;* it is perceptible even in the grave parts, and pervades the *andantes* in a sensible degree.

In those compositions, where it is evident from the rythm, the tone, and the general character, that the author intends to inspire melancholy, this obstinate joy, being unable to shew itself openly, is transformed into energy and strength. Observe, this sombre gravity is not pain, it is joy constrained to disguise itself; which might be called the concentrated joy of a savage; but never sadness, dejection, or melancholy. Haydn has never been really melancholy more than two or three times; in a verse of his *Stabat Mater*, and in two of the *adagios* of the *Seven Words*.

This is the reason why he has never excelled in dramatic music. Without melancholy, there can be no impassioned music; and, for this cause, the French people, lively, vain, and light, expressing with quickness all their sentiments, sometimes oppressed with ennui, but never melancholic, will never have any music.

Now we are upon the subject, and that I see you already beginning to scowl, I will tell you the whole of my mind. I shall purposely make use of the most common and intelligible images; and I invite all my brother manufacturers of paradoxes, to follow the same plan.

LETTER VII.

Vienna, October 3, 1808.

I ONCE entered Italy by the Simplon, in company with a gentleman who had never made this tour; and, as we passed within a quarter of a league of the Borromean isles, I was glad to have an opportunity of shewing them to him. We took a boat, and traversed the gardens of this magnificent, and, at the same time, interesting, place. We afterwards returned to the little inn of the *Isola bella*, where we found three covers set on the table, and a young Milanese, whose exterior announcèd an easy fortune, after a few compliments, came and sat down by the side of us. He made very pertinent replies to the questions which I addressed to him. While he was engaged in cutting up a partridge, my friend drew a letter from his pocket, and pretending to read it, said to me in English: "Look at that young man: he has, no doubt, committed some crime which haunts his conscience; he takes us for police-officers, or he is some *Werter*, who has selected this celebrated place to put an end to his existence in a sentimental style." " By no means," replied I, " he is one of the most communicative young men we shall meet with, nay, he may even be considered as lively."

All the French who visit Italy, fall into the same error, arising from the melancholic cast of the Italian character. It is a country in which the passions spring with the greatest facility. Men of such a character can scarcely find amusement, except in the fine arts; and it is thus, I think, that Italy has produced both its great artists, and their admirers; who, by their fondness for the former, and by rewarding their labours, have caused them to arise. It is not that the Italian is incapable of gaiety; see him in a party of pleasure in the country, with agreeable women, his spirits are wild; his imagination is of a surprising vivacity.

I have never, in Italy, fallen into those parties of pleasure, which the slightest mortification of vanity renders sometimes so stupid, in the beautiful parks which surround Paris. Some freezing mortal comes and cuts up all our amusement; the master of the house is out of humour, because his cook is not punctual with the dinner. I am piqued, because the viscount V...., abusing the speed of his English horses, has pushed by me in his curricle, in the plains of St. Gratien, and has covered with dust the ladies who were in my handsome new chariot; but I will have my revenge on him, or my coachman shall have his dismissal. None of these ideas ever enter the head of a young Italian, going to receive ladies at his *villa*. Do you remember to have read Shakespeare's Merchant of Venice? If you recollect, where Gratiano says,

"Let me play the fool:
With mirth and laughter let old wrinkles come," &c.

This is Italian gaiety; it is gaiety which announces happiness. With us, it would almost be accounted ill manners; it would be displaying one's own happiness, and would be deemed egotistical. French gaiety must shew the company that it is gay only to please them; it is necessary, in personating extreme joy, to conceal the real joy, which is caused by success.

French gaiety requires a great deal of wit: it is that of Le Sage and of Gil Blas. Italian gaiety is founded in sensibility; so that when nothing particularly pleases him, the Italian is not gay.

Our young man, at the Borromean isles, saw nothing so very delightful in meeting with two well-educated Frenchmen at a public table; he was polite: we expected him to have been amusing.

In Italy, as the actions of men arise more from the mind of the actor, when this mind is of a common sort, an Italian is the most insipid companion in the world. I was one day complaining of this to the worthy baron W....: " What would you have?" said he; " there is the same difference between the men, as there is between the melons of the two countries. In France, buy them without fear on the spot, they are all passable; in Italy, you may open twenty that are good for nothing, but the twenty-first will be divine."

The conduct of the Italians being founded on their feelings, sufficiently accounts for their love of music, which, by inspiring us with a feeling of regret, sooths our melancholy: and shews also, why a lively and sanguine man, as are three-fourths of the French, can love nothing passionately, because he stands in no need of soothing; and because he has habitually no strong feeling of enjoyment.

What do you say to my philosophy? It has the misfortune to be pretty much in conformity with the theory of the French philosophers, which you now hold in contempt, and which derives the fine arts from *ennui;* only that, instead of ennui, I would say *melancholy,* which supposes a tenderness of feeling.

The ennui of Frenchmen, whom matters of sentiment have never rendered either very happy or very miserable, and whose greatest vexations arise from mortifications of vanity, is dissipated by *conversation,* in which vanity, which is their ruling passion, finds every moment an opportunity of shining, either by what is said, or by the manner of saying it. Conversation, with them, is a game, a mine of important events. This French conversation, such as a stranger may hear every day at the *Café de Foi,* and other public places, seems to me like *the armed commerce of two vanities.*

All the difference between the Café de Foi, and the saloon of madame la marquise du Deffant,* is that, at the Café de Foi, which is the resort of the petty proprietors of the lower classes, vanity is founded on the substance of what is said. Each one, in his turn, relates the flattering things which have happened to him: he who is supposed to be listening, waits, with ill-disguised impatience, till his turn is arrived, and then commences his history, without replying to the other in any sort.

The *bon ton,* which there, as well as in the

---

* In 1779.

saloon, is derived from the same principle, consists, at the Café de Foi, in listening to others, with an appearance of interest, in smiling at the comic parts of their stories; and when speaking of ourselves, in disguising a little the anxious and uneasy air of self-interest. Would you see this self-interest displayed in all the rudeness of nature, enter for a moment the exchange of a commercial town of the south; observe a courtier making a bargain with a merchant. This ill-concealed self-interest gives to some of the pairs of talkers, at the Café de Foi, the appearance of two enemies, brought together by force, to discuss their interests.

In more wealthy and polished society, it is not from the subject of the history, but from the mode of relating it, that the speaker expects a harvest of gratification to his vanity: he accordingly selects a topic as indifferent to himself as possible.

Volney relates, that the French colonists in the United States are little satisfied with their isolated situation, and are saying con tinually, " 'Tis a desolate country, one can find nobody to speak to;" on the contrary, the German and English colonists find no inconvenience in passing whole days in silence.*

I am of opinion, that this delightful conversation, the sovereign remedy for French ennui, does not sufficiently excite the feelings, to soothe Italian melancholy.

It was in consequence of habits resulting from this mode of seeking happiness, that prince N . . . ., who was pointed out to me at Rome, as one of the gayest men of fashion in Italy, was continually giving us music at the house of his mistress, the countess S . . . .

---

* " To *visit*, and *chat*, are, with the French, a habit of such imperious necessity, that, on the whole frontier of Louisiana, or of Canada, one cannot find a single settler out of the reach, and scarcely out of the sight, of another. In many places, when I enquired the distance of the farthest settlement, I received for answer, " It is in the desart, amongst the bears, a league from any habitation, *where there is not a creature to speak to."*

VOLNEY, *Tableau des Etats Unis.*

He had, at his disposal, an income of two or three millions;* his rank, his fortune, his dissipated habits, you would suppose, would have made him a buck of the old school;† but though his military uniform was covered with decorations, he felt only as an artist.

With us, a man who is going to a rendez-vous, or to see whether the brevet, which is to appoint him to an important place, be signed, has his attention sufficiently at liberty to feel jealous of a fashionable cabriolet.

Nature has made the Frenchman vain, and lively, rather than gay. France produces the best grenadiers in the world, for carrying redoubts by the bayonet, and the most amusing people.

Italy possesses no *Collé*,‡ nor any thing

 Of francs.   T.
 † Literally, " a would-be young man." *Un ci-devant jeune homme.*   T.
 ‡ Collé. A writer of *Vaudevilles*, contemporary with Piron.   T.

which approaches the delightful gaiety of *La verité dans le vin.*

Its inhabitants are impassioned, melancholic, tender; it produces Raphaels, Pergoleses, and counts Ugolino.*

---

* Dante. See numerous characters of this description in Sismondi's excellent history of the Italian Republics,

LETTER VIII.

Salzburg, April 5, 1808.

AT length, my dear friend, you have received my letters. The war, which surrounds me here on all sides, gave me some anxiety respecting them. My walks in the woods are disturbed by the sound of arms: at this moment, I distinctly hear the cannon firing, at the distance of a league and a half from hence, in the direction of Munich. Nevertheless, after some melancholy reflections on the circumstances which have deprived me of my company of grenadiers, and which, for twenty years past, have banished me from my country, I have seated myself upon the trunk of a large fallen oak. I find myself under the shade of a beautiful lime-tree; I see around me nothing but a delightful verdure, beautifully set off by the deep blue of the heavens; I take my little portfolio, and my pencil, and after a long silence, proceed with my account of our friend Haydn.

Do you know that I am almost ready to charge you with being schismatic. You seem to prefer him to the divine masters of the Ausonian lyre. Ah! my friend, the Pergoleses and Cimarosas have excelled in that department of our favourite art, which is at once the noblest, and the most affecting. You say that one reason why you prefer Haydn, is, that one may hear him at London, or at Paris, as well as at Vienna, while, for want of voices, France will never enjoy the *Olimpiade* of the divine Pergolese. In this respect, I am of your opinion. The rough organization of the English, and of our dear countrymen, may allow of their being good performers on instruments, but prevents them from ever excelling in singing. Here, on the contrary, in traversing the faubourg Leopoldstadt, I have just heard a very sweet voice singing, in a very pleasing style, the air

Nach dem tode jeh bin ich dein,
Even after death, I still am thine.

As for what concerns myself, I clearly see your malicious criticism through all your compliments. You still reproach me with that inconsistency, which was formerly the constant theme of your lectures. You say that I pretend to write to you about Haydn, and I forget only one thing,—that is, fairly to enter upon the style of this great master, and, as an inhabitant of Germany, to explain to you, as one of the unlearned, *how* it pleases, and *why* it pleases. In the first place, you are not one of the unlearned: you are passionately fond of music : and in the fine arts, this attachment is sufficient. You say that you can scarcely read an air. Are you not ashamed of this miserable objection? Do you take for an artist the antiquated mechanic, who, for twenty years, has given lessons on the piano, as his equal in genius, has made clothes at the neighbouring taylors? Do you consider as an art, a mere *trade*, in which, as in others, success is obtained by a little address, and a great deal of patience?

Do yourself more justice. If your love for

music continue, a year's travelling in Italy will render you more learned than your *savans* of Paris.

There is one thing which I should scarcely have supposed, namely, that by studying the fine arts, one may learn to feel them. A friend of mine could find nothing to admire in the whole Museum of Paris, except the expression of Raphael's St. Cecilia, and the Transfiguration; all the rest were without interest to him, and he preferred the skreen-paintings which are exhibited every two years, to the smoky master-pieces of the ancient schools; in short, painting was almost entirely closed to him, as a source of pleasure. It happened, that, to oblige a friend, he read a history of painting, for the purpose of correcting the style. By chance he went to the Museum, and the pictures recalled to his recollection what he had just been reading about them. He began, imperceptibly, to confirm or annul the criticisms upon them, which he had seen in the manuscript, and soon learned to distinguish the manner of the different schools. Gradually, and without any formed intention, he went three or four times a week to the Museum, which is now his favourite place of resort. He finds a thousand subjects of reflection, in a picture which was before without meaning to him, and the beauty of Guido, which he formerly disregarded, now enchants him.

I am convinced it is the same with music; and that if a person were to learn five or six airs of the *Matrimonio segreto*, he would soon feel the beauty of all the others. The only precaution necessary, is, to confine oneself, for a month or two, to Cimarosa alone. My friend was careful, each week, to inspect only the pictures of one master, or at least of one school.

But, my friend, the task you impose on me, with respect to the symphonies of Haydn, is difficult, not through the want of ideas, but from the difficulty of transmitting them four hundred leagues, and of describing them in words.—Since you will have it so, guard yourself against ennui, as well as you know how, for I will give you an account of what is here thought of the style of Haydn.

During the early part of our acquaintance, I frequently questioned him on the subject. It is very natural to ask a man who performs miracles "How do you do them?" but I always found him shy of entering upon the subject. I thought it would be best to resort to artifice, and, accordingly, with the effrontery of a journalist, and inexhaustible force of lungs, I took upon me to utter certain dark opinions respecting Handel, Mozart, and other great masters, of whom I ask pardon. Haydn, who was gentle and good-humoured, smiled, and suffered me to talk; but, sometimes, after having made me drink a little of his Tokay, he would correct me by a few sensible observations, which came warm from his heart, and displayed his theory. These I hastened to commit to paper, as soon as I had left him. It was by thus acting the part of an agent of *M. de Sartine*,* that I, at length, arrived at an acquaintance with the opinions of this master.

---

* M. de Sartine was Intendant of the Police under Louis XVI.   T.

Who would think it? this great man, under whose authority our miserable pedants of musicians, without genius, would fain shelter themselves, repeated incessantly: " Let " your *air* be good, and your composition, " whatever it be, will be so likewise, and " will assuredly please.

" It is the soul of music," continued he, " it is the life, the spirit, the essence of a " composition. Without this, Tartini may " find out the most singular and learned " chords, but nothing is heard but a la-" boured sound; which, though it may not " offend the ear, leaves the head empty, and " the heart cold."

One day, when I disputed with more nonsense than usual, these oracles of art, Haydn went and fetched a little blotted journal, which he had kept during his residence in London. He there shewed me a hymn, which he heard sung at St. Paul's, in unison, by four thousand children. — " This " simple and natural air," added he, " gave " me the greatest pleasure I ever received " from the performance of music."

Now this air, which produced such an effect on a man who had heard the finest instrumental music in the world, is nothing but*

That you may not accuse me of leaping over difficulties, shall I attempt to give you a definition of singing? Go and hear madame Barilli sing in the *Nemici generosi*, which I see announced in the *Journal des Debats*.

<blockquote>Piaceri dell' anima
Contenti soavi.</blockquote>

Hear her say, in the *Matrimonio segreto*, when she is laughing at her sister, who is quite proud of having married a count,

<blockquote>Signora Contessina.</blockquote>

---

* This chant, for it is not a hymn, was written by Mr. Jones, organist of St. Paul's; but, in passing through the mind of Haydn, it has acquired an elegance, not to be found in the original, by the alteration of two notes in the twelfth bar.   G.

Hear Paolino Crivelli sing, in addressing the count, who falls in love with his mistress,

<blockquote>Deh! Signore!</blockquote>

This is singing.*

Would you, by a method equally easy, learn what is not singing? Go to the Feydeau;† only observe, that they do not play either Gretry, or Della Maria, or the Melomanie; listen to the first air that may be sung, and you will understand, better than by a thousand definitions, what is music without melody.

There is, perhaps, more love of music in twenty of those idle beggars at Naples, called *Lazzaroni*, who sing in the evening along the shore of Chiaja, than in all the elegant crowd who assemble, on a Sunday, at the Conservatoire de la rue Bergere. What rea-

---

* See the note to the Letter on the present state of music in Italy, at the conclusion. We have there endeavoured to describe the qualities requisite in a good singer, and the mode by which they may be acquired, and improved.   G.

† One of the theatres of Paris.   T.

son is there to be angry at this? How long have we been so proud of qualities purely physical? Normandy has no orange-groves, and yet it is a fine country. Happy is he who has estates in Normandy, and permission to reside upon them!—But to return to our subject.

How is it possible to define, in a proper manner, what cannot be taught by any rule? I have before me five or six definitions which I had noted in my memorandum-book: and, truly, if any thing could make me lose the clear idea which I have of singing, it would be the reading of these definitions. They are well arranged words, but convey nothing clearly intelligible. For instance: What is pain? We have all, alas! had sufficient experience to *feel* the reply to this question; and yet any explanation that we should attempt, would only obscure the subject. I hope, therefore, to escape your reproaches, when I decline giving a definition of singing. It may be said to be, what any sensible, though untutored, amateur, will retain on coming away from an opera. Who that has been to hear the Figaro of Mozart, does not come away singing, perhaps as much out of tune as possible,

> Non piu andrai, farfallone amoroso,
> Delle donne turbando il riposo, &c.

The masters will say to you : Choose airs at once easy, clear, and elegant, and which, without being far-fetched, are not too common-place. You will avoid the last defect, and a disagreeable monotony, by introducing discords. They produce, at first, rather an unpleasant sensation ; the ear is impatient to hear them resolved, and experiences a very sensible pleasure, when at length they are so.

Discords awaken the attention. They are like stimulants administered to a lethargic person : the momentary uneasiness which they produce, is transformed into lively pleasure, when we at length arrive at the chord, which the ear has all along expected and desired. The tribute of our praise is due to *Monteverde*, who discovered this mine of beauties, and to *Scarlatti*, who explored it.

Mozart, that genius of pleasing melancholy, so full of ideas, and of so splendid a taste, the author of the air,

> Non so più cosa son
> Cosa faccio,

has sometimes been too free in his modulations.

He has occasionally spoiled some beautiful airs, the first bars of which, are precisely the sighs of a tender heart. By tormenting them a little, towards the conclusion, he often renders them obscure to the ear, though in the score, they are clear to the eye: and sometimes, in his accompaniments, he introduces airs of too different a character from that of the personages to whom they are attributed. But what would not one forgive, in consideration of the air played by the orchestra, towards the middle of the song,

> Vedrò, mentr 'io sospiro,
> Felice un servo mio?   (Figaro.)

an air truly divine, which every man who

feels the pains of love, involuntarily recalls to mind.*

Discords in music, are like *chiaro scuro* in painting; they must be employed with discretion. Look at the Transfiguration, and the Communion of St. Jerome, which are placed opposite to each other in the Museum at Paris. There is a little deficiency of *chiaro scuro* in the Transfiguration: Dominichino, on the contrary, has made better use of it.— Here you must stop, or you fall into the sect of the *Tenebrosi*, who, in the sixteenth cen-

---

* I do not scruple to take my illustrations from music which I have heard at Paris, since my return to France, and subsequently to the date of these letters. It is not permitted to every one to imitate a great writer, who, desirous of giving his friends an exact idea of the desert country which it is necessary to cross before arriving at Rome, says to him, "You have read every thing that has been written of this country, but I know not whether any traveller has given a very correct idea of it . . . . . Represent to yourself something like the desolation of Tyre and Babylon, of which the Scriptures speak." *Genie du Christianisme*, t. 3. p. 367. At Paris, to quote most of the master-pieces of Pergolese, Galuppi, Sacchini, &c. would be a little like talking about the plains of Babylon.

tury, were the ruin of painting in Italy. Professional men will tell you, that Mozart has particularly been too free in the use of the *diminished* and *superfluous* intervals.

Some years after Haydn's establishment at Eisenstädt, when he had formed his style, he sought food for his imagination, by diligently collecting those ancient, and original airs, which are to be found among the people of every country.

The Ukraine, Hungary, Scotland, Germany, Sicily, Spain, Russia, were laid under contribution by him.

An idea may be formed of the originality of these melodies, from the Tirolese air, which the officers who served in the Austrian campaign of 1809, brought back with them to France.

" Wenn ich war in mein . . . .," &c.

At Naples, every year, a short time before Christmas, arrive a number of strolling musicians, furnished with a guitar and a violin, which they do not rest on the shoulder in playing, but hold it as we do the bass. With these they accompany their wild songs, as different from the music of all the rest of Europe, as can be imagined. There is, however, a certain agreeableness about these singular airs, which prevents the ear from being offended by them.

You may form some idea of them, at Paris, from the romance which Crivelli sings, in such delightful style, in the *Nina* of Paesiello. This master has employed himself in collecting ancient airs, supposed to be of Grecian origin, and which are still sung by the half-savage peasants of the extremity of Italy. It is from one of these airs, arranged, that he has made this simple and beautiful romance.

What can be more different than the Spanish *Bolero,* and Henry the Fourth's air, *Charmante Gabrielle?* Add to these, a Scotch air, and a Persian romance, such as are sung at Constantinople, and you will see of what variety music is capable. Haydn knew all these by heart; and they were a continual store for his imagination.

In the same way as Lionardo da Vinci

sketched in a little book, which he always carried with him, the singular faces he met with, Haydn also carefully noted down the passages, and ideas, which came into his head.

When he was in good spirits, and happy, he hastened to his little table, and wrote subjects for airs and minuets. Did he feel himself disposed to tenderness and melancholy, he noted down themes for *andantes* and *adagios;* and, afterwards, in composing, when he wanted a passage of such a character, he had recourse to his magazine.

In general, however, Haydn did not set himself to write a symphony, except he felt himself in a good disposition for it. It has been said, that fine thoughts come from the heart; and the truth of this remark is the more observable, in proportion as the subject, on which an author is employed, is removed from the precision of the mathematical sciences. Tartini, before composing, read one of the soft sonnets of Petrarch. The bilious Alfieri, who, in painting tyrants, has exhibited all the stern bitterness which preys upon them, was fond of listening to music before he sat down to his work. Haydn, like Buffon, thought it necessary to have his hair put in the same nice order, as if he were going out, and dressed himself with a degree of magnificence. Frederic II. had sent him a diamond ring; and Haydn confessed that, often, when he sat down to his piano, if he had forgotten to put on his ring, he could not summon a single idea. The paper on which he composed, must be the finest and whitest possible, and he wrote with so much neatness and care, that the best copyist could not have surpassed him, in the regularity and clearness of his characters. It is true, that his notes had such little heads, and slender tails, that he used, very properly, to call them his *flies legs.*

After these mechanical precautions, Haydn commenced his work, by noting down his principal idea, his *theme,* and choosing the keys through which he wished to make it pass. His exquisite feeling gave him a perfect knowledge of the greater, or less degree of effect, which one chord produces, in succeeding another; and he afterwards imagined a little romance, which might furnish him with musical sentiments and colours.*

---

* Haydn has produced some of his most striking effects by the sudden change of key. Every practitioner in the art must have noticed the various *complexions*, so to speak, by which they are characterized. By *Key*, we mean any system of notes which regards a certain tone as its base or centre, to which all the adjacent harmonies gravitate, or tend. In the 15th century, music was generally written in the key of F, and its relative D minor.—This order of sounds was first adopted, probably on account of its being the most agreeable to the ear. And as some of the grandest sounds of the natural world,—the rushing of the storm, the murmurs of the brook, and the roar of the sea, are to be referred to this harmony, it may be denominated *the key of Nature*. As science improved, other notes were taken as the centres of systems, by which other keys were formed, and we have now not less then 24 keys, both major, and minor.

We shall endeavour to characterize some of them.

F (its relative.) — This key is rich, mild, sober and contemplative.

D Minor. — Possesses the same qualities, but of a heavier and darker cast: more doleful, solemn, and grand.

C — Bold, vigorous, and commanding: suited to the expression of war and enterprize.

A Minor. — Plaintive, but not feeble.

Sometimes he supposed, that one of his friends, the father of a numerous family, ill provided with the goods of fortune, was embarking for America, in hope of improving his circumstances.

G — Gay and sprightly. Being the medium key, it is adapted to the greatest range of subjects.

E Minor. — Persuasive, soft, and tender.

D — Ample, grand, and noble. Having more fire than C, it is suited to the loftiest purposes. In choral music, it is the highest key, the treble having its cadence note on the 4th line.

B Minor. — Bewailing, but in too high a tone to excite commiseration.

A. — Golden, warm, and sunny.

F sharp Minor. — Mournfully grand.

E n sharps. — Bright and pellucid: adapted to brilliant subjects. In this key Haydn has written his most elegant thoughts. *Handel* mistook its properties when he used it in the chorus, " *The many rend the skies with loud applause.*" Though higher than D, it is less loud, as it stretches the voice beyond its natural powers.

B n sharps. — Keen and piercing. Seldom used.

The first events of the voyage, formed the symphony. It began with the departure. A favourable breeze gently agitated the waves.

B flat — The least interesting of any. It has not sufficient fire to render it majestic, or grand, and is too dull for song.

G Minor. — Meek and pensive. Replete with melancholy.

E flat Major. — Full, and mellow: sombre, soft, and beautiful.
It is a key in which all musicians delight. Though less decided in its character than some of the others, the regularity of its beauty renders it a universal favourite.

C Minor. — Complaining: having something of the whining cant of B minor.

A flat Major. — The most lovely of the tribe.
Unassuming, gentle, soft, delicate, and tender, having none of the pertness of A in sharps. Every author has been sensible of the charm of this key, and has reserved it for the expression of his most refined sentiments.

F Minor. — Religious, penitential, and gloomy.

D flat Major. — Awfully dark. In this remote key, Haydn and Beethoven have written their sublimest thoughts. They never enter it but for tragic purposes.

It is sufficient to have hinted at these effects. To account for them, is difficult; but every musician is sensible of their existence.   G.

The ship sailed smoothly out of the port; while, on the shore, the family of the voyager followed him with tearful eyes, and his friends made signals of farewell. The vessel had a prosperous voyage, and reached at length an unknown land. A savage music, dances, and barbarous cries, were heard towards the middle of the symphony. The fortunate navigator made advantageous exchanges with the natives of the country, loaded his vessel with rich merchandise, and at length set sail again for Europe, with a prosperous wind. Here the first part of the symphony returned. But, soon, the sea begins to be rough, the sky grows dark, and a dreadful storm confounds together all the chords, and accelerates the time. Every thing is in disorder on board the vessel. The cries of the sailors, the roaring of the waves, the whistling of the wind, carry the melody of the chromatic scale to the highest degree of the pathetic. Diminished and superfluous chords, modulations, succeeding by semi-tones, describe the terror of the mariners.

But, gradually, the sea becomes calm,

favourable breezes swell the sails, and they reach the port. The happy father casts anchor in the midst of the congratulations of his friends, and the joyful cries of his children, and of their mother, whom he at length embraces safe on shore. Every thing, at the end of the symphony, is happiness and joy.

I cannot recollect, to which of the symphonies this little romance served as a clue. I know that he mentioned it to me, as well as to professor *Pichl*, but I have totally forgotten it.

For the subject of another symphony, Haydn had imagined a sort of dialogue between Jesus Christ, and an obstinate sinner, and, afterwards, followed the parable of the Prodigal Son.

From these little romances, were taken the names by which our composer sometimes designated his symphonies. Without the knowledge of this circumstance, one is at a loss to understand the meaning of the titles. " The Fair Circassian," " Roxalana," " The Hermit," " The enamoured School-master," " The Persian," " The Poltroon," " The

Queen," "Laudohn;" all which names indicate the little romance which guided the composer. I wish the names of Haydn's symphonies had been retained, instead of numbers. A number has no meaning; a title, such as, "The Shipwreck," "The Wedding," guides, in some degree, the imagination of the auditor, which cannot be awakened too soon.

It is said, that no man had such a knowledge of the various effects and relations of colours, the contrasts which they were capable of forming, &c. as Titian. Haydn, likewise, possessed an incredible acquaintance with each of the instruments which composed his orchestra. As soon as his imagination supplied him with a passage, a chord, a single note, he immediately saw by what instrument it should be executed, in order to produce the most sonorous and agreeable effect.*

---

* The manner in which Haydn has employed the wind instruments, opens a field for experiment in the musical art, which may not be exhausted for ages. He was the first who discovered that each instrument has a peculiar faculty, and who appointed to each its proper office. He

If any doubt arose, during the composition of a symphony, his situation at Eisenstadt enabled him easily to resolve it. He rang his

has not only drawn from the several instruments their peculiar language, but has grouped them into classes, for purposes entirely new. Turn to the trio in the Creation, " *On thee each living soul awaits.*" The symphony opens with a flute, two clarionets, two bassoons, and two horns, mingling in a melody, so full and delicious, as to produce that *sated* effect which the words demand.

> " O Lord, on thee they beg their meat;
> Thou openest thy hand,
> And *sated* all they are."

The violas, violoncellos, and double basses, follow in a separate band, and gradually sink into the depths of the darkest melody, to express,

> " *But as to them thy face is hid.*"

This strain is awfully sublime. At the words, " *With sudden terror they are struck,*" we feel a paralytic sensation, never before produced by the power of sound. It is a palsied and shivering effect, which is brought about by a singular junction of time, and accent.

> " Thou takest their breath away;
> " They vanish into dust;"

is so forcible and commanding, that we begin to doubt,

bell, in the way agreed on, to announce a rehearsal; the performers repaired to the rehearsing-room. He made them execute the passage which he had in his mind, in two or three different ways; and having made his choice, he dismissed them, and returned to resume his composition.

Do you recollect, my dear Louis, the scene of Orestes, in Gluck's Iphigenia in Tauris? The astonishing effect of the passages, executed by the agitated violas, would have been lost, if these passages had been assigned to any other instrument.

We often find singular modulations in Haydn, but he was sensible that what is extravagant, diverts the attention of the au-

---

whether it is the sound of strings that we have heard. At the passage,

"*Life with vigour fresh returns,*"

all contrariety is banished, and the different bands coalesce with a smoothness which produce "*new force and new delight.*" All these novelties result from that knowledge of the characteristic powers of the several instruments which Haydn was the first to discover. G.

ditor from what is beautiful; and he never hazards any singular change, without having imperceptibly prepared for it by the preceding chords. Accordingly, when it occurs, we do not find it either unsuitable, or unnatural. He said, that he had taken the idea of several of these transitions from the works of old *Bach*. You know, that Bach himself brought them from Rome.

Haydn readily acknowledged the general obligations he was under to Emmanuel Bach: who, before the birth of Mozart, was considered the first *pianist* in the world; but he also declared, that he owed nothing to the Milanese San Martini, who, he said, was only a dabbler.*

---

* The piano-forte was scarcely known in the time of Bach; and, from the style of his compositions, it is evident that they were the *product* of the harpsichord, an instrument of very limited powers; the boldest effects of which were produced by sprinkling the chords in *Arpeggio*, which occasioned a disagreeable jingling. The early sonatas of Haydn, also, bear marks of the influence of this instrument, and possess nothing of the expression of his later works. The invention of the piano-forte has formed an

I very well remember, however, that when I was at Milan, thirty years ago, at a musical entertainment, which was given to the celebrated *Mislivicek,* when some old symphonies of San Martini were performed, the Bohemian professor suddenly exclaimed, " I have discovered the father of Haydn's style."

This was, doubtless, saying too much; but these two authors had received from nature very similar minds; and it has been proved, that Haydn had great opportunities of studying the works of the Milanese professor. As for the resemblance, take notice of the movement of the second violin, and the viola in Haydn's first quartett in B♭ major, at the commencement of the second part of the

---

era in the art. It has been the means of developing the sublimest ideas of the composer, and the delicacy of its touch has enabled him to give the lightest shades, as well as the boldest strokes of musical expression. It is the only instrument that will represent the effects of a full orchestra, and since its mechanism has been improved, Beethoven has displayed its powers in a way not contemplated even by Haydn himself. G.

first movement. It is altogether in the manner of San Martini.

This San Martini, a man all fire and originality, was also, though residing at a distance, in the service of Prince Nicholas Esterhazy. A banker of Milan, named Castelli, was ordered by the prince to pay San Martini eight sequins (4*l.*) for every piece of music which he should send him. The composer was bound to supply, at least two per month, and had the liberty of sending to the banker as many as he chose. But, in the decline of life, old age rendered him indolent, and I well remember hearing the banker complain to him of the remonstrances he received from Vienna, on account of the unfrequency of his remittances. San Martini replied, grumbling, "I'll write some, I'll write some, but the harpsichord kills me."

Notwithstanding his indolence, the library of the Palfy family alone, contains more than a thousand pieces of this author. Haydn, therefore, had every facility for knowing and studying him, if he ever had the intention.

Haydn, in attending to sounds, had early

observed, to use his own words—"what was good—what was better—what was bad?" I will give you an instance of his simple way of replying, which had a very embarrassing effect. When asked the reason why he had written a particular chord, why he had assigned a passage to one instrument, rather than to another, he seldom made any answer than, " I did it, because it was best so."

This rare man, thrown upon himself in his youth by the avarice of the masters, had acquired his knowledge from himself; he had observed what had passed in himself, and endeavoured to re-produce what he experienced in his own feelings. A common artist merely quotes the rule, or the example, which he has followed; all this he has very clearly in his head.

Haydn had laid down a singular rule, of which I can inform you nothing, except that he would never say in what it consisted. You are too well acquainted with the arts to render it necessary for me to remind you, that the ancient Greek sculptors had certain invariable rules of beauty, called *canons*.

These rules are lost, and their existence is buried in profound obscurity. It appears as if Haydn had discovered something similar in music. When the composer *Weigl* entreated him to communicate these rules to him, he could obtain no other reply than, "Try to find them out."

We are told, likewise, that the charming *Sarti* occasionally composed on arithmetical principles. He even boasted that he could teach this science in a few lessons; but his whole arcanum consisted in getting money from some rich amateurs, who were simple enough to suppose that it was possible to speak a language without understanding it. How can we make use of the language of sounds, without having previously studied the meaning of each of them.

As for Haydn, whose heart was the temple of honour, all those who were acquainted with him, know that he had a secret, which he would not disclose.* He has given to

---

* It is probable that this secret consisted in his knowledge of the intimate dependance of melody upon har-

the public nothing of this sort, except a philharmonic game, in which you obtain numbers, at hazard, by throwing dice. The passages, to which these numbers correspond, being put together, even by a person who has not the least knowledge of counterpoint, form regular minuets.

Haydn had another very original principle. When his object was not to express any particular affection, or to paint any particular images, all subjects were alike to him. "The whole art consists," said he, " in taking up a subject, and pursuing it." Often, when a friend entered, as he was about to commence a piece, he would say with a smile, " Give me a subject." Give a subject to Haydn! who would have the courage to do so?— " Come, never mind," he would say, "give me any thing you can think of;" and you were obliged to obey.

Many of his astonishing quartetts exhibit

---

mony; a principle not generally recognized, but which we have endeavoured to develope in the note at the commencement of Letter XVI. G.

marks of this piece of dexterity. They commence with the most insignificant idea, but, by degrees, this idea assumes a character; it strengthens, increases, extends itself, and the dwarf becomes a giant before our wondering eyes.

LETTER IX.

Salzburg, May 4, 1809.

My Friend,

In 1741, that genius of music, Jomelli, was sent for to Bologna to compose an opera. The day after his arrival, he went to see the celebrated Father Martini, without making himself known, and begged to be received into the number of his pupils. Father Martini gave him a subject for a *fugue;* and finding that he executed it in a superior manner, " Who are you?" said he; " are you making game of me? it is I who need to learn of you."—" I am Jomelli, the professor who is to write the opera to be performed here next autumn, and I am come to ask you to teach me the great art of never being embarrassed by my own ideas."

We, who have nothing to do with music but to enjoy it, are not aware of the difficulty of arranging a beautiful air so as to please an auditor, without transgressing certain rules, of which, it must be allowed, a full fourth, at least, are purely arbitrary. It continually happens, when we are writing, that we have good ideas, but find extreme difficulty in disclosing them, and in giving a suitable turn to the expression. This difficult art, which Jomelli entreated Father Martini to teach him, Haydn discovered of himself. In his youth, he frequently put down on paper a certain number of notes, taken at random, marked the time of each, and obliged himself to make something of them, taking them as fundamentals. The same is related of *Sarti*. At Naples, the abbé Speranza obliged his pupils to take an *aria* of Metastasio's, and to write, in succession, to the same words, thirty different airs. It was by this method that he trained the celebrated Zingarelli, who still enjoys his glory at Rome, and who was able to compose his best works in eight days, and sometimes even in a still shorter period. I myself can bear testimony, that in forty hours, divided into ten days work, he produced his inimitable

Romeo and Juliet. He wrote his opera of Alcina, the first of his celebrated productions, at Milan, in a week. He is superior to all the mechanical difficulties of his art.

One of Haydn's remarkable qualities, the first of those which are not bestowed by nature, is the possession of a *style*. A musical composition is a discourse, expressed by sounds, instead of words. In his discourses, Haydn possesses, in a supreme degree, the art of not only increasing the effect of the principal idea, by accessory ideas, but also of expressing both, in the manner best suited to the cast of the subject : which a little resembles what, in literature, are termed proprieties of style. Thus, the stately style of Buffon admits not of those lively, original, and familiar turns of expression, which are so pleasing in Montesquieu.*

---

* The style of Beethoven is so completely different from that of Haydn, that so far from thinking, as our author observes, at the conclusion of Letter 2, that he has copied from the latter, we should rather refer to him as an instance of the varieties of musical style.

Turn, for example, to his symphony in C major, the

The *theme* of a symphony, is the proposition which the author undertakes to establish, or, to speak more properly, which he endeavours to make you feel. As the orator, after having proposed his subject, developes it, brings forward his proofs, repeats what he is desirous of demonstrating, strengthens it by additional testimonies, and, at length, concludes: so Haydn endeavours to impress

---

first note of which, strikes the auditor by the new way in which its harmony is compounded. It begins with a discord, which imparts a bewailing, and dark effect to the wind instruments, and which rouses the imagination, and leaves the ear unguarded, for sudden and striking impressions. Out of the first movement, starts an unexpected theme, which, ignis fatuus-like, leads us over a dark and mysterious waste, occasionally illumined by a few scattered rays of light, till it conducts us to an *andante*, of inimitable clearness, beauty, and grace, the effect of which, is like bursting into open day, enlivened with all the freshness of spring.

The symphonies of Haydn may be compared to little operas, formed upon natural occurrences, all within the verge of probability. Those of Beethoven, are romances of the wildest invention, exhibiting a supernatural agency, which powerfully affects the feelings and imagination. G.

upon the auditor the theme of his symphonies.

It is necessary to bear in mind this theme, that it may not escape from us. Common composers are satisfied with a servile repetition of it, in making it pass from one key to another; Haydn, on the contrary, every time he resumes it, gives it an air of novelty; sometimes invests it with a certain rudeness, at others, embellishes it with delicacy, and always gives the surprised auditor the pleasure of recognizing it under an agreeable disguise. I am sure that you, who have been struck with the symphonies of Haydn, if you have followed the progress of this *pathos*, have his admirable *andantes* actually present to your thoughts.

In the midst of this torrent of ideas, Haydn knows how to avoid ever transgressing the bounds of nature; he is never eccentric: every thing with him is in the most proper place.

The symphonies of Haydn, like the harangues of Cicero, form a vast magazine, in which all the resources of the art are to be found. With a piano-forte, I could make you distinguish, in one way or other, twelve or fifteen musical figures, as different from one another, as the antithesis and metonymy * in rhetoric: but, at present, I will only point out to you the *suspensions*.

I speak of those unexpected pauses of the whole orchestra, when Haydn, arrived, in the cadence of the musical period, at the note which resolves and concludes the phrase, suddenly stops, at a moment when the instruments seem the most animated, and silences them all.

You think that the first sound that you will hear, as soon as they resume, will be this final note, that which concludes the phrase, and which you have, so to speak, already heard in imagination. By no means. Haydn generally then passes to the *fifth* by a short and graceful transition, which he had already indicated. After having put you off

---

* Grands mots que Pradon prend pour termes de chimie.
BOILEAU.

for a moment, by this sportive trait, he returns to the principal key, and then gives you fully, and to your entire satisfaction, the cadence which he at first seemed to withhold, only in order to render it more agreeable afterwards.

He makes good use of one great advantage which instrumental music has over vocal. Instruments are capable of describing the most rapid and energetic movements, while the voice is unable to reach the expression of the passions, when they require any rapidity in the utterance of the words.

Time is as necessary to the composer, as canvas-room to the painter. They are the *infirmities* of these fine arts. Observe the duet
Sortite, sortite,
between Susanna and Cherubino, at the moment when he is going to jump out of the window. There is an accompaniment, but the words are pronounced too rapidly to be pleasant. In the duet
Svenami,

in the third act of the Horatii, is it not quite out of character, that Camilla, furiously disputing with the stern Horatius, speaks so slowly? I think the duet good, but the slow movement of the words, in so animated a situation, destroys the pleasure. I would even undertake to write Italian words, in which Camilla and Horatius should be two lovers deploring the misfortune of not having seen each other for a few days. I would adapt them to the air of the duet *Svenami*, and I believe that the music would just as well describe the very tolerable distress of my lovers, as the furious patriotism, and despair, of Grassini and Crivelli. If Cimarosa has failed in expressing these words, who can hope to do it? For my own part, I am of opinion that we are arrived, in this respect, at one of the boundaries of the musical art.

A person, who was in the habit of attending the opera, said to one of my friends, "What a great man this Gluck is! his songs are not very agreeable, it is true, but, what expression! Hear Orpheus, singing,

J'ai perdu mon Euridice,
Rien n'egale mon malheur. *

My friend, who has a good voice, answered him by singing the same air:

J'ai trouvé mon Euridice
Rien n'égale mon *bonheur*. †

I desire you will make the experiment with the part before you. If you want an instance of pain, recollect,

Ah! rimembranza amara!

at the beginning of Don Juan. Observe, that the movement is necessarily slow, and that perhaps Mozart himself, would not have succeeded in representing impetuous despair. The despair, for instance, of the passionate lover, when he receives the terrible letter, which consists in these words: "*Well then, No!*" This situation is well expressed in Cimarosa's air.

'Senti indigna! io ti volea sposar,
E ti trovo innamorata.

---

* " I have lost my Eurydice,
Nothing can equal my *distress*."
† " I have found my Eurydice,
Nothing can equal my *felicity*."

Here, again, the unhappy lover is ready to weep,—his reason wavers,—but he is not furious. Music can no more represent fury, than a painter can depict two different periods of the same action. The true movement of vocal music is that of the Matins. Recollect that of Ser Marc Antonio. Hasse, Vinci, Faustina, and Mingoti, were well aware of this, but we have forgotten it.

Still less can music describe all the objects of nature. Instruments possess the power of rapidity of movement, but, for want of words, they can describe nothing with precision. Of fifty sensible people, who hear with pleasure the same symphony, it is probable that no two will be affected by the same image.

I have often thought, that the effect of the symphonies of Haydn and Mozart would be much increased, if they were to be played in the orchestra of a theatre; and if, during the performance, well-painted scenes, analogous to the principal thought of the different passages, were to be exhibited in succession on the stage. A beautiful scene, representing a peaceful sea, and a clear expanse of sky, would heighten the effect, as it appears to me, of an *andante* intended to represent a pleasing tranquillity.

In Germany they have a custom of personating well-known pictures. A whole party will put on Dutch dresses, divide themselves into groups, and, motionless, imitate to uncommon perfection, a picture of Teniers, or Ostade.

Such pictures, on the stage, would be an excellent commentary on the symphonies of Haydn, and would fix them for ever in the memory. I cannot possibly forget the chaotic symphony which opens the Creation, after having seen, in the ballet of Prometheus, Viganò's charming actresses represent, as they follow the movements of the symphony, the astonishment of the daughters of the earth, when their senses are first awakened to the charms of the fine arts. It is in vain to dispute; music, which is the least definite of the fine arts, is not of itself sufficiently descriptive.

In acquiring one of the qualities which are

requisite to describe the rapidity of motion, for instance, it loses the words and touching intonations of the human voice. Does it retain the voice, it then loses the necessary rapidity. *

---

* With the musician, the human voice is regarded as an instrument; but, of all instruments, it has the most powerful effect upon our mind and feelings.

Although it is too limited in compass to produce the sublimer strokes of musical expression, yet, in the softer gradations of the art, its influence is pre-eminently felt. Under the guidance of art, it is combined with speech to form a distinct branch of music, called vocal. This department is exclusively its own, as at present mechanism has not advanced far enough to produce the same combination upon the instruments.

To assist in explaining the nature of this curious, and delicate organ, it may be said that every person has two distinct voices, the *singing*, and the *speaking* voice, between the operations of which there is little or no analogy.

In singing, the sounds are formed in the *Larynx*, which is situated immediately above the windpipe; and the notes of the musical scale are produced by the combined action of the muscles upon certain membranes in the interior of the *larynx*, which form an aperture called the *rima glottidis*.

In the higher notes of the scale, this aperture is propor-

How is it possible to represent a meadow, enamelled with flowers, by sounds different from those which would express the prosperous wind which swells the sails of Paris, when he carries off the beauteous Helen?

Paesiello and *Sarti* share with Haydn the great merit of knowing how to distribute well

---

tionally contracted, and in the deeper intonations, the membranes are relaxed, and the aperture enlarged. In speaking, the *glottis* acts unconsciously, and the tones *coruscate* through all the intervals of the key of the persons' voice. They play with incredible quickness between the key note, through its 3rd, to the 5th above, and, in forcible expressions, will flash from the lower octave to that of the double octave.

The office of the glottis in singing, is the same with that of the *Reed* in musical instruments, and the muscles are made to act upon it with such precision and agility, that it surpasses the most expressive instruments, in rapidity and neatness of execution. The desideratum of the art, is to use both these voices at once, and so to blend one with the other, as that neither shall be injured. This is a rare faculty, which has perhaps not yet been attained in our language. When we listen to vocal music in a language we do not understand, we can then readily perceive the effort which is made to bring these voices together, and it then becomes apparent, how liable words are to injure the beautiful sounds, which feeling and sentiment induce. G.

the different parts of a work: and it is by means of this judicious internal economy, that *Paesiello* composes not merely an air, but a whole opera, with two or three delightful passages. He disguises them, recalls them to the memory, collects them together, and gives them a more imposing air. Gradually, he gains upon the hearts of his auditors, makes them feel the sweetness of his least notes; and thus produces that music of his, so full of graces, and so easy of comprehension. Observe the *Molinara,* which you are so fond of. Compare the accompaniments of the *Pirro,* for instance, with those of the *Ginevra* of Mayer; or, if you would place a dandelion by the side of a rose, think of the accompaniments in the Alcestis of Gluck.

Some little time is necessary to enable us to understand a musical passage, so as to feel it, and thoroughly to enter into it. The most beautiful idea possible, produces only a transient sensation, if the composer does not dwell on it. If he passes too soon to another thought, the gracefulness vanishes. Haydn is admirable in this part also, which is so essential in symphonies, where there is no explanation by words, and which are not interrupted by any recitative or period of silence. Turn to the *adagio* of the quartett, No. 45; but all his works are full of similar examples. As soon as the subject begins to be exhausted, he introduces an agreeable digression, and the pleasure is reproduced, under different and interesting forms. He is sensible that in a symphony, as in a poem, the episodes ought to adorn the subject,—not to cause it to be forgotten. In this respect, he is unique.

Observe, in the *Four Seasons*, the ballet of the peasants, which gradually becomes a fugue full of animation, and forms a charming digression.

The judicious disposition of the different parts of a symphony, produces in the auditor a certain satisfaction, mingled with a pleasing tranquillity, a sensation, as it appears to me, similar to that produced upon the eye by the harmony of colours in a well-painted picture. Look at the St. Jerome of Correggio; the spectator does not enquire into the cause of his feelings, but involuntarily turns his steps to it; which he returns to the Holy Sepulchre of Caravaggio * only in consequence of a determination to do so. In music, how many Caravaggios have we for one Correggio? but a picture may possess great merit, without giving a sensible pleasure to the eye: such are some of the works of the Carracci, who have inclined too much to the *sombre*, whereas, no music, which does not immediately please the ear, can be called music. The science of sounds is so indefinite, that one can be sure of nothing with respect to them, except the actual pleasure which they give.

It is by means of very profound combinations, that Haydn divides the musical thought, or air, among the different instruments of the orchestra. Each has its part, and the part which suits it. I wish, my friend, that in the

---

* This difference would be still more evident, if I could instance in the St. George of the Dresden gallery. The beauty of the Mary, the divine expression of the Magdalen, in the St. Jerome of Paris, do not leave time to observe how finely this picture is painted.

interval between this letter and my next, you could go to your Conversatoire of Paris, where you say the symphonies of our composer are so well performed.

Try, when you hear them, if you can recognise the truth of my reveries; if not, shew me no mercy, for either I have expressed myself ill, or my notions will be as real as those of the good lady, who fancied she saw in the spots of the moon, happy lovers, bending towards each other.

Some writers of operas have also endeavoured to divide the exposition of their ideas between the orchestra, and the voice of the actor. They have forgotten that the human voice has this peculiar quality, that, as soon as it is heard, it draws the whole attention to it. We all unfortunately experience, as age comes on, that in proportion as our sensibility is diminished, and our knowledge increased, we become more attentive to the instruments. But, to the majority of those who are capable of feeling music, the more clearly and distinctly the air is given, the greater the pleasure. The only exceptions known of to this remark, are certain pieces of Mozart. But he is the La Fontaine of music; and as those who have sought to imitate the naïveté of the first poet in the French language, have produced nothing but silliness, so those composers who attempt to follow Mozart, fall into the most impertinent singularities. The sweetness of the melodies of this great man, gives a relish to all his chords, makes every thing pass. The German composers, whom I hear every day, renounce, with good reason, all pretensions to grace, though in a department where it is indispensible; they are always aiming at the terrible. The overture of the lightest comic opera resembles a battle or a burial. They say that the overture of the *Frascatana* is not powerful enough in the harmony.

They are like a painter who is ignorant of the art of shading, who knows nothing of the soft, and the tender, and who tries, with all his might, to draw female portraits. He says to his pupils, in an oracular tone: " Beware of imitating that unfortunate Correggio, that tiresome Paul Veronese, be hard and rough, like me."

"Un jour les Grenovilles se levèrent,
Et dirent aux Coucous, Illustres compagnons."
VOLTAIRE.

---

* " One day the frogs arose,
And said to the cuckoos, Illustrious comrades."

LETTER X.

Salzburg, May 6, 1809.

I HAVE often heard Haydn asked, which of his works he preferred: he replied, *The Seven Words.* I will first give you an explanation of the title. About fifty years since, there was celebrated at Madrid and Cadiz, a service, called the *entierro;* that is, *the funeral* of the Redeemer. The gravity and religious feeling of the Spanish people, invested this ceremony with extraordinary pomp. A preacher explained, in succession, each of the seven words pronounced by Jesus from the cross; and the intervals left between each exposition, for the indulgence of the compunction of the faithful, were to be filled up by a music worthy of the greatness of the subject. The directors of this sacred spectacle, caused an advertisement to be circulated throughout Europe, in which they offered a considerable reward to any composer who should supply seven grand symphonies, expressive of the sentiments which each of the seven words of the Saviour ought to inspire. Haydn alone made the attempt; he sent those symphonies, in which,

> Spiega con tal pietate il suo concetto,
> E il suon con tal dolcezza v' accompagna,
> Che al crudo inferno intenerisce il petto.
> DANTE.

But of what use is it to praise them? It is necessary to hear them with the feelings of a christian,—to weep, believe, and shudder. Michael Haydn, the brother of our composer afterwards added words, and an air, to this sublime instrumental music. Without changing it in any respect, he rendered it an accompaniment; an immense labour, which would have daunted a Monteverde, or a

---

* His prayer is expressed in such touching accents, sounds which accompany it are so soft, that the obdi of hell is melted by them.

Palestrina. This additional air is for four voices.*

Some of the symphonies of Haydn were written for the holidays of the church.† Through all the sorrow which they express, I fancy I can perceive the characteristic vivacity of Haydn, and here and there, movements of anger, by which the author, perhaps, in-

---

* From the preface to the original edition in score, published at Leipsic, by Messrs. Breitkopf and Hartel, it would appear that Haydn himself executed this work. He expresses himself as follows : " Die Musik war ursprünglich ohne Text, und in dieser Gestalt ist sie auch gedruckt worden. Erst späterhin wurde ich veranlasst, den Text unterzulegen, so dass also das Oratorium : ' Die sieben Worte des Heylandes am Kreuze,' jezt zum Erstenmale bey Herrn Breitkopf und Härtel, in Leipzig, als ein vollstandiges, und was die Vokalmusik betrifft, ganz neues Werk erscheint." Wien, im März, 1801. *Joseph Haydn.*

" The music was originally without words, and in this form it has been printed. It is but lately that I had an opportunity of adding these ; so that, consequently, the oratorio of ' The Seven Words of the Saviour on the Cross,' appears now, for the first time, as a complete, and, as far as regards the vocal music, an entirely new work." Vienna, March, 1801. *Joseph Haydn.*   T.

† They are in G major, D major, and C minor.

tended to represent the Jews crucifying their Saviour.

The abstract, my dear Louis, of what I have often experienced, on hearing Haydn's symphonies, when I have endeavoured to trace how they came to please me, is this. I first distinguished their general qualities, or the style which was common to all of them, and afterwards sought for the resemblances which this style might have to that of well-known masters. The precepts given by Bach are found to be occasionally adopted. Something is taken from Fux, and Porpora, with respect to the management, and display, of the different instruments; and in the ideal part, the author has developed some beautiful germs of ideas contained in the works of the Milanese San Martini, and Jomelli.

But these slight traces of imitation are far from depriving him of the merit of possessing an original style, worthy of effecting the revolution which it has actually produced in instrumental music. In the same way, it is not impossible that the lovely Correggio may have taken some ideas from the sublime chiaro-scuro which forms the charm of the Leda, the St. Jerome, and the *Madonna alla Scodella,* in the pictures of Fra Bartolomeo, and Lionardo da Vinci. Nevertheless, he is justly considered as the inventor of a branch of the art, which has made the moderns acquainted with a second source of ideal beauty. As the Apollo exemplifies the beauty of form and contour; so the 'Night' of Dresden, by its shades, and semi tints, awakens in the mind, lost in a pleasing reverie, that sensation of delight, which elevates and carries it out of itself, and which has been called the sublime.

LETTER XI.

Salzburg, May 11, 1809.

MY FRIEND,

NOTWITHSTANDING a cast of physiognomy rather morose, and a short way of expressing himself, which seemed to indicate an ill-tempered man, the character of Haydn was gay, open, and humorous. This vivacity, it is true, was easily repressed by the presence of strangers, or persons of superior rank. In Germany, nothing is suffered to level the distinctions of society: it is the land of ceremony. At Paris, the *cordons bleus* went to see d'Alembert in his garret; in Austria, Haydn never associated with any but the musicians, his colleagues; society, as well as himself, were doubtless losers by this circumstance. His gaiety, and the copiousness of his ideas, well fitted him for the display of the comic in instrumental music, a genus almost new, and in which he would have made great progress;

but to succeed in which, as in every thing that relates to comedy, it is indispensible that the author be in the habit of the most elegant society. Haydn was not introduced to the great world till the decline of life, during his visits to London.

His genius naturally inclined him to use his instruments so as to produce laughter. At the rehearsals, he frequently gave short pieces of this kind of music, in which at present we have but little, to the performers his companions. You will, therefore, excuse me for imparting to you my little store of comic erudition.

The most ancient musical pleasantry with which I am acquainted, is, that of Merula,* one of the most profound contrapuntists of an age when the air had not yet penetrated the music. He composed a fugue representing some schoolboys reciting before their master the Latin pronoun *qui, quæ, quod,* which they had not well learned. The con-

---

* Merula. He flourished about 1630.

fusion, the perplexity, the barbarisms of the scholars, mingled with the exclamations of their enraged master, who exercises the ferule among them, had the happiest effect.

That musical Pindar, the Venetian Benedetto Marcello, so grave and sublime in his sacred compositions, is the author of the well-known piece called the *Capriccio*, in which he ridicules the *castrati*, whom he cordially detested.

Two tenors and two counter-tenors begin by singing together these three verses:

> No, che lassù nei cori almi e beati,
>   Non intrano castrati,
>   Perche scritto è in geral loco·. . . .

The *soprano* here interrupts them, in *solo*, and asks,

> Dite: che è scritto mai?

The tenors and counter-tenors reply in a very low key,

> Arbor che non fra frutto
>   Arda nel fuoco.

On which, the *soprano* cries out at the other extremity of the scale,

> Ahi! ahi!

The effect of this expressive piece is incredible. The extreme distances which the author has placed between the shrill tones of the unfortunate *soprano*, and the deep voices of the tenors, produces the most ridiculous melody in the world.

The nasal uniformity of the Capuchins, who are even expressly forbidden to sing, or to deviate from the key, has furnished Jomelli with a subject for pleasantry.

The elegant *Galuppi*, so well known by his comic operas, and his sacred music, has not thought it beneath him to set to music the singing of a synagogue, and a quarrel between some fruit-women in the market of Venice.

At Vienna, the methodical turn of the people has set apart a particular day for pleasantries of this sort. About the middle of the eighteenth century, the eve of the festival of St. Cecilia was devoted to music in every family, and custom required that the gravest professors should, on that day, present their friends with comic compositions. An Augustine father, of the beautiful convent of St. Florian, in Austria, took a singular text for the subject of his pleasantries: he composed a mass which, without occasioning scandal, has long had the privilege of making the sides both of the singers and auditors ache with laughter.

You are acquainted with the humourous canons of Father Martini of Bologna, that of the Tipplers, that of the Bells, and that of the Old Nuns.

The celebrated Clementi, the rival of Mozart in his compositions for the piano, has published at London, that land of caricatures, a collection of musical caricatures, in which he has mimicked the most celebrated composers for the piano. Whoever has the slightest acquaintance with the manner of Mozart, Haydn, Koseluch, Sterkel, &c. and hears these little sonatas, composed of a prelude and a cadence, immediately guesses the master that is ridiculed: his style is recognised, and especially the little affectations and errors, to which he is most subject.

In the time of Charles VI., the celebrated Porpora lived at Vienna, poor and unemployed. His music did not please the imperial connoisseur, as being too full of *trills* and *mordenti.* Hasse wrote an oratorio for the emperor, who asked him for a second. He entreated his majesty to permit Porpora to execute it. The emperor at first refused, saying that he did not like that capering style; but, touched with Hasse's generosity, he at length complied with his request. Porpora, having received a hint from his friend, did not introduce a single *trill* in the whole oratorio. The emperor, surprised, continually repeated, during the rehearsal; " 'Tis quite a different man; here are no trills!" But when they came to the fugue, which concluded the sacred composition, he observed that the theme commenced with four *trilled* notes. Now you know that in fugues, the subject passes from one part to another, but does not change. When the emperor, who was privileged never to laugh, heard in the full height of the fugue this deluge of trills, which seemed like the music of some enraged paralytics, he could no longer maintain his gravity, and laughed, perhaps for the first time in his life. In France, the land of pleasantry, this might have appeared misplaced; but at Vienna, it was the commencement of Porpora's fortune.

Of all Haydn's comic pieces, there remains but one; that well known symphony, during which all the instruments disappear, one after the other, so that at the conclusion, the first violin is left playing by itself. This singular piece has given rise to three anecdotes, all of which are attested at Vienna by eye-witnesses. Judge how I am embarrassed in making a selection. Some persons say that Haydn, perceiving that his innovations were ill received by the prince's performers, determined to play a joke upon them.

He caused his symphony to be performed, without a previous rehearsal, before his highness, who was in the secret. The embarrassment of the performers, who all thought they had made a mistake, and especially the confusion of the first violin, when at the end he found he was playing by himself, diverted the court of Eisenstädt.

Others assert, that the prince, having determined to dismiss all his band, except Haydn, the latter imagined this ingenious way of representing the general departure, and the dejection of spirits consequent upon it. Each performer left the concert-room as soon as his part was ended. I spare you the third story.*

At another time, Haydn, desirous of diverting the prince's company, went and bought at a fair near Eisenstädt, a whole basket-full of whistles, little fiddles, cuckoos, wooden

---

* The biographer has not mentioned another pleasantry which Haydn has introduced into a Sinfonia, called " *La Distratta.*" Before commencing the last movement, the violins are directed to lower the fourth string, G, down to F. The instruments being thus prepared, the movement commences with a pert and joking subject, which is soon interrupted by a pause; after which, the first violins begin to sound the open strings, E and A, together, for two bars: and the same of D and A, when they arrive at a passage where the lowered string F is directed to be screwed up gradually through four bars, so as to bring it in tune on the fifth bar. You are surprised at the caprice of the performers, who stop one after another, to tune their violins in the middle of the piece, and it is not till after twelve bars have been employed in this ludicrous way, that you are relieved from your embarrassment, and the subject is suffered to proceed. G.

trumpets, and other such instruments as delight children. He was at the pains of studying their compass, and character, and composed a most amusing symphony with these instruments only, some of which even executed *solos* the cuckoo is the general bass of the piece.

Many years afterwards, when Haydn was in England, he perceived that the English, who were very fond of his instrumental compositions, when the movement was lively and *allegro,* generally fell asleep during the *andantes* or *adagios,* in spite of all the beauties he could accumulate. He therefore wrote an andante, full of sweetness, and of the most tranquil movement ; all the instruments seemed gradually to die away ; but, in the middle of the softest *pianissimo,* striking up all at once, and reinforced by a stroke on the kettle-drum, they made the slumbering audience start.

L

LETTER XII.

Salzburg, May 17, 1809.

MY DEAR FRIEND,

WE have, for a sufficient length of time, followed Haydn in a career where he was unquestionably superior; let us now see what he was in vocal music. We possess compositions of his in the three following genera, viz. Masses, Operas, and Oratorios.

We can do little more than conjecture what Haydn was in theatrical music.

The operas which he composed for prince Esterhazy, perished in the conflagration of the archives of Eisenstädt, which, together with Haydn's house, were burned to the ground. He thus lost most of his compositions in this department. The only ones preserved, are the *Armida, La vera Costanza,* and the *Speziale,* which were, perhaps, the least valuable.

When Jomelli went to Padua, to write an opera, he perceived that the vocal performers, both male and female, were utterly destitute of merit, and were, moreover, not at all desirous of displaying any.—" Wretches," said he to them, " I'll make the *orchestra* sing; the opera shall rise to the clouds, and you shall go to the devil."

The band of Prince Esterhazy, though not altogether so bad as that of Padua, was not very capital; besides, Haydn, attached to his country by a thousand ties, did not leave it till the decline of his life, and never wrote for public theatres.

These considerations are preparatory, my dear Louis, to the confession which I am about to make, relative to the dramatic music of our author.

He had found instrumental music in its infancy: vocal music, on the contrary, was at the height of its glory when he appeared. Pergolese, Leo, Scarlatti, Guglielmi, Piccini, and twenty others, had carried it to a degree of perfection, which has never since been reached, or at least surpassed, except by Cimarosa and Mozart. Haydn did not rise to the beauty of the melodies of these celebrated men. It must be allowed, that in this genus he has been surpassed by his contemporaries Sacchini, Cimarosa, Zingarelli, Mozart, &c. and even by his successors, Tarchi, Nazolini, Fioravanti, Farinelli, &c.

You, who are fond of seeking in the mental constitution of artists the causes of the qualities observable in their works, will perhaps agree with me in the idea I have formed of Haydn. It will not be disputed that he had a vast and vigorous imagination, endowed, in a supreme degree, with a creative power; but, perhaps, he did not possess an equal share of sensibility: and yet, unless an author have the misfortune to be afflicted with this, he cannot describe love, he cannot write vocal, or dramatic music. That natural hilarity and joyfulness of character, which I have before alluded to, never allowed a certain tender sentiment of melancholy to approach this tranquil and happy spirit. Now, in order to compose, as well as to hear, dramatic music, a man should be able to say with Jessica,

"I'm never merry when I hear sweet music."
MERCHANT OF VENICE, act 5. scene 1.

A certain degree of tenderness and melancholy is also necessary to find pleasure in the *Cantatrici villane*,* or in the *Nemici generosi*.† The reason of this is evident: if you are in a gay humour, your imagination does not wish to be diverted from the images which occupy it.

Another reason is, that in order to command the feelings of his auditors, it is necessary that Haydn's imagination should be perfectly at liberty; as soon as it is fettered by words, it loses its character: written scenes appear to recall it too often to matters of sentiment; Haydn, therefore, will always hold the first place among landscape painters: he will be the Claude Lorraine of music, but he will

---

* A chef-d'œuvre of Fioravanti, highly esteemed at Paris.

† A highly comic opera of the admirable Cimarosa.

never occupy in the theatre, that is, in music wholly sentimental, the place of Raphael.*

---

* The canzonets, which Haydn wrote during his residence in this country, are but little known on the continent, and must surely have been absent from the author's recollection when he wrote the above remarks. In our opinion, they completely refute any idea of Haydn's inability to excel in the vocal, or sentimental, departments of music.

The first of them,

"My mother bids me bind my hair,"

may be considered as a perfect exhibition of the line of beauty in music. The intervals through which the melody passes are so minute, so soft, and delicate, that all the ideas of grace and loveliness are awakened in the mind, and we admire the genius which could so accompany this beautiful song without injuring its simplicity.

The next, on Absence,

"The season comes when first we met,"

presents a picture, in which all the sombre hues of evening are blended with a masterly hand. In the former were displayed the enlivening tints of the morning, but here nothing sparkles:—a fixed melancholy pervades the piece. In the last couplet, we feel the imterrogatory powers of

You will say, that he who actually possesses this place was the gayest of men. Doubtless, Cimarosa was gay in the world: what can a man do better? but I should be sorry, for the sake of my theory, if love or

music, and our dejection is for a time relieved; but we soon return to the gloom and despondency in which we were before involved.

The Canzonet on Fidelity,

" While hollow burst the rushing winds,"

exhibits a faithful attachment under an excess of misery. The first strokes of the symphony awaken in us a sentiment of terror; and the boldness of the accompaniment raises ideas correspondent with the grand natural imagery to which it refers. In the midst of this tempest of the feelings, some soft rays occasionally intervene to cheer us with hope; but the harmony, in rapid transitions, hurries us back again into its darkest recesses. In the two last lines, the clouds of despair break and vanish, and the inspiring melody of the major key suddenly bursts upon us in a flood of radiant harmony.

Such, in short, is our idea of these elegant compositions, that we would challenge any author, in any language, to produce their equal in simple gracefulness, and exquisite sensibility. G.

revenge had never made a fool of him. Did not one of the most agreeable of his successors, a short time since, pass a whole night, in the month of January, in the most disagreeable place possible, in expectation that a lively female singer would fulfil the promise she had made him?

I would lay a wager, that Cimarosa's gaiety did not consist in epigrams and repartees, like that of Gentil Bernard.*

You see, my friend, that my devotion to my saint does not carry me too far. I place the writers of symphonies in the class of landscape, and the composers of operas in that of historical painters. Twice or thrice only, has Haydn risen to this grand genus; and then he was Michael Angelo, and Lionardo da Vinci.

---

* Pierre Joseph Bernard, born in 1710; died 1779. The politeness of his manners, and the smartness of his repartees, obtained for him the epithet, ' *Gentil*,' by which he is here designated. His poetry chiefly consists of anacreontic, and epigrammatic pieces.   T.

Let us console ourselves; we shall see his talent re-appear, when we come to speak of his sacred music and his oratorios. In the latter more especially, which afford a better opportunity for the display of the Pindaric than of the dramatic genius, he was again sublime, and augmented the glory he had acquired as a symphonist.

I perceive that, through a desire of being impartial, I am, perhaps, doing injustice to our friend. Have you ever heard his Ariadne in Naxos? All my calumnies shall be referred to their proper places.*

---

* What we have seen of his Ariadne in Naxos, is far from lessening our estimation of his talent for the opera. He who composed the air, "*Teseo, mio ben,*" and imparted such tenderness to sounds, must have been capable of excelling in every department of the art. The recitatives are not a tissue of common-place resolutions, which tire the ear, and relax the attention; but are enlivened and interspersed with the most finished strains of melody. The pleasure we derived in perusing this *morceau*, convinces us, that the musical world has reason to lament the conflagration at Eisenstädt, which destroyed his dramatic writings. G.

I am of opinion, that music differs from painting, and from the other fine arts, in this: that in the former, the physical pleasure, received by the sense of hearing, is more powerful and essential than the intellectual enjoyment. This physical pleasure is the basis of music; and, I am inclined to think, that the ear is still more gratified than the heart, in hearing Madame Barilli sing,

> Voi che sapete
> Che cosa è amore.

A fine chord enchants the ear, a false note tortures it: yet, neither of these say any thing intelligible to the mind; nothing that we could *write down* if required. It only gives it either pain or pleasure. It appears, that of all the organs of sense, the ear is most easily affected by agreeable or unpleasant impressions. The smell, and the touch, are also very susceptible of pleasure or pain. The eye is the least sensible of all, and has very little perception of physical pleasure. Show a beautiful picture to a boor, he will experience no great delight, because the gratification arising from the sight of a fine picture, is almost entirely intellectual. He will certainly prefer a gaudy sign-painting to the " Christ calling St. Matthew," of Louis Caracci. Let him, on the other hand, hear a fine air well sung, he will, perhaps, manifest some signs of pleasure; while an ill-sung air will give him some pain. Go to the Museum, on a Sunday, you will find the passage, at a certain part of the gallery, blocked up by the crowd collected before a picture: and every Sunday the same. You would suppose it is a master-piece:—by no means; 'tis a daub of the German school, representing the last Judgement. The populace are fond of seeing the grimaces of the damned. Follow the same people to the spectacle, exhibited gratis in the evening, you will see them applauding, with transport, the airs sung by Madame Branchu; though, in the morning, the pictures of Paul Veronese were without meaning to them.

Hence I conclude, that if, in music, the physical pleasure, which is the principal thing, be sacrificed to any other object, what we hear is no longer music; it is a noise which offends our ears, under pretence of moving our hearts; and this, I think, is the reason why I could never hear any of Gluck's operas through with pleasure. Adieu.

LETTER XIII.

Salzburg, May 18, 1809.

MELODY, that is to say, that agreeable succession of analogous sounds which pleasantly affects the ear, without ever offending it; the melody, for instance, of the air,

Signora Contessina,*

---

* I speak so often of the *Matrimonio segreto*, which is Cimarosa's master-piece, and which I consider as well known at Paris, that I have been advised to give a short abstract of the piece, for those amateurs who reside elsewhere.

Geronimo, a rich merchant of Venice, who was rather deaf, had two daughters, Caroline and Elisette. The lovely Caroline had recently consented to marry, secretly, Paolino, her father's head clerk; *(a)* but the old man

---

(a) The piece opens with two duets, full of tenderness, which explain the plot, and excite an immediate interest in the lovers. *Cara, cara,* is the commencement of the first duet, and the words, *Io ti lascio perche uniti,* of the second.

sung by madame Barilli in the *Matrimonio segreto,* is the principal means by which this physical pleasure is produced. The har-

was aiming at nobility, and they were greatly embarrassed how to make known their marriage to him. Paolino, who sought every opportunity of cultivating his good graces, had arranged a match for Elisette, the eldest daughter, with the count Robinson. Geronimo is delighted with the prospect of being allied to a title, and of seeing his daughter a countess. *(b)* The count arrives, and is presented to the family. *(c)* The charms of Caroline make him change his intention; *(d)* he informs Paolino, Caroline's lover, that he is going to demand her in marriage, instead of Elisette, and that in order to bring the old mer-

(b) He sings the fine counter-tenor air, *Le orecchie spalancate,* in which the truest ridicule, and the most affecting sentiment, are singularly united. We laugh at Geronimo, but we love him; and every odious feeling is removed from the mind of the spectator through all the remainder of the piece.

(c) He sings, as he enters, the air, *Senza far cerimonie.*

(d) Il cor m'ha ingannato. Afterwards follows a fine quartett, describing the most profound passion, without any mixture of melancholy. This is one of those pieces which best mark the difference of the routes followed by Cimarosa and Mozart. Imagine the latter treating the subject of this quartett.

mony comes afterwards. It is the air which is the charm of music, said Haydn, incessantly. It is also that which it is most diffi-

chant to consent to the exchange, a matter of little consequence in a mere match of convenience, he will be satisfied with a portion of 50,000 crowns, instead of 100,000 as agreed on. *(e)* Elisette, who is highly offended at the count's coldness, surprises him, kissing the hand of Caroline, and reports his conduct to Fidalma, the old merchant's sister, *(f)* who, for her part, thinks that her great fortune renders herself a very eligible match for Paolino. Geronimo, who is deaf, does not clearly understand the count's proposal, or the complaints of Elisette, *(g)* and falls into a passion, which concludes the first act. *(h)*

The second contains a dispute between the count and Geronimo: it is the famous duet, *Se fiato in corpo avete;* the despair of Caroline, who is threatened with the convent; the proposal of Fidalma to Paolino; *(i)* and the

(e) A touching duet, which Paolino commences with the beautiful address: ***Deh Signore!***

(f) Air: *Io voglio susurrar la casa e la città.*

(g) Air: *Voi credete che i sposi faccian come i plebei.*

(h) We never find in Mozart passages of this sort, master-pieces of spirit and gaiety; but, at the same time, such an air as *Dove son i bei momenti*, in the mouth of Caroline, would have described her situation in a manner more affecting.

(i) Air: *Ma con un marito via meglio si stà.*

cult to produce. Patience and study are sufficient for the composition of agreeable accords, but the invention of a fine air is a

---

jealousy of Caroline, who sings a noble air, which has been suppressed at Paris, and which is the *air à pretention* of the piece:

> *Pria che spunti in ciel l'aurora.*
> Before the dawn in heaven appear.

She forgives Paolino, who informs her of the measures which he has taken for their secret departure.

The count and Elisette meet, in going to the saloon for torches, as they are about to retire to their apartments for the night. The count declares, that he cannot marry her. *(k)* About midnight, the trembling Caroline appears with her lover. As they cross the saloon, to make their escape, they hear a noise still in the house; and Paolino returns, with his wife, to her chamber. Elisette, whom jealousy prevents from sleeping, hears some persons talking in the chamber, thinks that it is the count, and calls her father, *(l)* and her aunt, who had already retired to rest. They knock at the door of Caroline's room: she comes out with her lover. Every thing is discovered; and

---

(k) Very beautiful air of Farinelli: *Signorina, io non v'amo.*

(l) Air: *Il conte sta chiuso con mia zerellina.*

work of genius. I have often thought, that if there were a musical academy in France, the examination of the candidates might be easily arranged. They need only be requested to send ten lines of music, no more. Mozart would write,

<blockquote>" Voi che sapete."   FIGARO.</blockquote>

Cimarosa,

<blockquote>" Da che il caso è disperato."   MATRIMONIO.</blockquote>

Paesiello,

<blockquote>" Quelli là."   LA MOLINARA.</blockquote>

But what would Mr. . . . ., and Mr. . . . ., and Mr. . . . ., write?

---

at the entreaty of the count, who addresses the father in the fine air,

> *Ascoltate un uom del mondo:*
> Listen to a man of the world:

and who, in order to obtain Caroline's pardon, consents to marry Elisette, the lovers are forgiven.

This piece was originally written by the celebrated Garrick. In the English play, the character of the sister is atrocious, and the whole drama dark and gloomy. The Italian piece, on the contrary, is a sportive little comedy, in which the music is very happily introduced.

M

The truth is, a fine air needs neither ornaments nor accessories in order to please. Would you know whether it be really fine? Strip it of its accompaniments. We may say of a beautiful melody, what Aristenætes said of his mistress:

Induitur formosa est; exuitur ipsa forma est:
Beauteous when robed; unrobed, she is beauty's self.

As for the music of Gluck, to which you refer, Cæsar said to a poet, who was reciting some verses to him, "You sing too much to be reading, and read too much to be singing." Occasionally, however, Gluck has found the way to the heart, either in delicate and tender airs, as in the lamentations of the Nymphs of Thessaly over the tomb of Admetus; or in strong and vibrating notes, as in the scene of Orpheus and the Furies.

It is the same with music in a composition, as with love in the heart,—unless it reign sovereign there, unless every thing be sacrificed to it, it is not love.

This granted, how are we to obtain a fine air? By the same means, exactly, as Corneille found his "*Qu'il mourut.*"* Hundreds of *Laharpes* † can make passable tragedies; they rank with the professors of deep harmony, who abound in Germany. Their music is correct, it is learned, it is elaborate; it has only one fault,—it makes us yawn.

---

* A celebrated passage in Corneille's tragedy of "*Horace.*" The subject is the combat between the Horatii, and Curiatii, as related by Livy. In Act iii. Scene 6, Julia, a Roman lady, informs Horatius, the father, that all is lost for Rome; that two of his sons have already fallen, and that the survivor has only saved himself by flight. This stratagem, by which he divided, and, ultimately, overcame his opponents, the old man considers as the effect of cowardice; and, with true Roman spirit, more afflicted by the supposed degeneracy of his remaining son, than by the loss of the two who have gloriously perished, he breaks forth into indignant imprecations on the poltroon who has thus disgraced the family name. Julia intercedes for him, by asking, "What would you have him do, against three?" The father replies, in the words here quoted, "*Qu'il mourut,*" DIE.

Voltaire says of this passage, that there is nothing comparable to it in all antiquity.   T.

† Laharpe was tutor to Alexander, the present emperor of Russia. Our author's opinion of his literary talents, is sufficiently evident; and we believe it is shared by most of his countrymen.   T.

In my opinion, to produce a musical Corneille, requires the fortunate union of an exquisite ear to an impassioned heart. It is necessary that these two kinds of sensation should be so combined, that even in his most gloomy moments, when he thinks his mistress faithless, the young Sacchini should feel pleasure from a few notes accidentally hummed by a passenger. Hitherto such minds have been produced only in the regions of Vesuvius. What is the reason of this? I cannot tell you, but look at the list of great musicians.

The German music is spoiled by the frequency of modulation, and the richness of the chords. This nation is fond of learning in every thing, and would unquestionably have a better music, or rather a music more, after the Italian style, if its young men were less attached to science, and rather fonder of pleasure. Take a walk in Göttingen; you will see a number of tall, fair, young men, rather pedantic, rather melancholy, walking with a springing gait, scrupulously exact to their hours of study, led away by their imagination, but scarcely ever by their passions.

The ancient Flemish music was only a tissue of chords, destitute of ideas. They made their music as they made their pictures; a great deal of labour, a great deal of patience, and nothing more.

The amateurs throughout Europe, with the exception of the French, think the melody of a neighbouring nation jerking and irregular; at once, trailing and barbarous; and, above all, wearisome. The melody of the English is too uniform, if, indeed, they can be said to possess any.* It is the

---

* If by national melody, be understood those airs, and song tunes, which partake of the peculiar character of the people amongst whom they are found, it must be allowed that we have none.

It is probable that the first regular airs were introduced into this country, by the Troubadours, or Minstrels, from France. But in the musical records of the sixteenth and seventeenth centuries, we find scarcely any thing that will bear the .name of melody. Even the best regulated strains are constructed with so little reference to harmony, that the intervals seem to follow one another more by chance than design.

same with the Russians; and, strange to say, with the Spaniards. Who could have imagined, that a land so favoured by the sun, the country of the Cid, and of those martial troubadours who were to be found even in the armies of Charles V., should have produced no distinguished musicians? That

---

Our countryman, *Purcel*, was the first who connected melody with language, and laid the basis of English song in the national air of "*Britons, strike home.*"

He was, also, the inventor of the *Catch;* a species of music peculiar to this country.

His compositions of this kind, were written for the amusement of the profligate court of Charles II. Many of them are fine examples of *canon*, and *fugue;* and had they been associated with less exceptionable words, would have been universal favourites.

The *Glee* is of later introduction, and was probably derived from the ancient Madrigal. Though its appellation seems to denote, that mirth and jollity are its peculiar department, it is of a more serious cast than the former; and has been carried, by the taste and genius of Webbe, to a degree of perfection, which excites the admiration of foreigners.

The *Anthem* is another species of music exclusively our own; and, in general, our sacred music is highly respectable, where that department of the service is at all attended to in our churches. G.

brave nation, so capable of great things, whose romances breathe such sensibility and melancholy, possesses no more than two or three distinct airs. It should seem, that the Spaniards are not fond of a multiplicity of ideas in their affections; one or two only, but deep, constant, and indestructible.

There is not sufficient distinctness in the music of the Orientals, it resembles more a prolonged cry, than any sort of air.

In Italy, an opera is composed of an air, and of accompaniments, or instrumental music. The latter is rendered entirely subservient to the former, and is used only to increase the effect of it; though occasionally the description of some striking natural scenery, gives a proper opportunity for the instrumental music to display itself. Instruments, having a more extensive compass than the human voice, and a greater variety of sounds, can represent things which the voice cannot: such, for instance, as a tempest, or a forest disturbed by the nocturnal howlings of savage beasts.

In an opera, the instruments may give,

from time to time, those energetic, distinct, and characteristic touches, which give life to the whole composition. As, for instance, the orchestra passage in the quartetto of the first act of the Matrimonio segreto, which follows the words,

> Cosi un poco il suo orgoglio.

Haydn, accustomed to give himself up to the fire of his imagination, and to wield the orchestra as Hercules did his club, when constrained to follow the ideas of a poet, and to moderate his instrumental luxuriancy, appears like a giant in fetters. The music is well constructed, but there is no longer any warmth, genius, or nature. All his brilliant originality disappears; and, wonderful to say, the man who exalts the importance of melody, on every occasion, and who is continually recurring to this doctrine, forgets it in his own works. In the same manner our fashionable authors extol, in inflated periods, the beautiful simplicity of the writers of the age of Louis XIV.

Haydn himself, in some degree, allows his

mediocrity in this genus. He says, that if he had had an opportunity of passing a few years in Italy, of hearing the delightful voices, and studying the masters of the Neapolitan school, he should have succeeded as well in the opera as he has done in instrumental music. This I am doubtful of: imagination and sensibility are two different things. A man may write the fifth book of the Eneid, describe funereal games with a brilliant and majestic touch, paint the combat of Dares and Entellus, and yet be unable to make Dido die in a natural and affecting manner. The passions cannot be contemplated like the setting sun. At Naples, nature offers a beautiful sun-set twenty times in a month, to a Claude Lorraine; but whence did Raphael take the expression of his *Madonna della seggiola?*—from his own mind.

LETTER XIV.

Salzburg, May 21, 1809.

You are desirous, my dear Louis, that I should write to Naples, to obtain some intelligence respecting the music of that country. Since I refer to it so frequently, you say, I ought to make you acquainted with it. You have heard it said, that the music becomes more original in proportion as we advance towards the south of Italy. You love the delightful Parthenope which inspired Virgil : you envy his lot. Wearied with revolutionary storms, you wish you could say :

> Illo me tempore dulcis alebat
> Parthenope, studiis florentem ignobilis otî.

Lastly, you observe, that as the music which was composed there, during the times of this happy *repose,* was intended to please the Neapolitans, and has so well accomplished its object, it is by a native of the country that it ought to be judged.

What you desire is already done. The following sketch of the music of the Neapolitan school, was given me some years ago by a tall abbé, wedded to his violoncello, and a constant frequenter of the theatre of San Carlo, where I believe he has not missed a single performance for forty years. I am only a translator, and have made no alteration in his opinions, with which I do not entirely agree. You will observe that he does not even mention Cimarosa; the reason of this is, that, in 1803, it was not adviseable to name him at Naples.

Naples, October 10, 1803.

" Esteemed Friend,

" Naples has had four schools[*] of vocal and instrumental music : but only three exist

---

[*] Although more money is expended upon music in England than in any other country in Europe, we have no national establishment for the study of the art. Italy, and Germany, have long had their academies, from which we are under the necessity of importing the talent which distinguishes our musical representations.

at this day, which contain about two hundred and thirty pupils. Each school has a different uniform. The scholars of Santa Maria di Loretto are dressed in white; those of La Pietà in turquoise, or sky blue,

---

France, though a nation of less musical pretension than ourselves, has, in the midst of her revolution, established her *Conservatoire*, a sort of musical university, where every branch of the art has its separate school, and professor, and in which all the science of the present day is displayed.

Were the *sinecure* funds, and *nominal* professors, attached to Gresham College, and to both the universities, employed agreeably to their original destination, an academy of music might be established in this country superior to any similar institution in Europe. A music-hall of sufficient magnitude should be erected, in which the students would be called upon to exhibit, monthly, before the public. To this should be attached a library, where every author in the art should be required to deposit the copy-right of his works, and thus would be preserved from perishing, those early writers, many of whom must otherwise soon be lost.

Such an institution, attached to the sister art in Somerset-House, and directed by the well-known taste and judgment of the Regent, would be an ornament to his reign, and an honour to the country. G.

whence they are sometimes called *Turchini;* those of Sant' Onofrio in puce colour and white. It is from these schools that the greatest musicians of the world have proceeded; which is very natural, for our country is fonder of music than any other. The great composers whom Naples has produced, lived at the beginning of the eighteenth century.

" It is proper that we should distinguish the composers who have occasioned revolutions in music in general, from those who cultivated only one species of it.

" Among the former, we shall place before every other Alessandro Scarlatti, who must be considered as the founder of the modern art of music, since it is to him that we owe the science of counterpoint. He was a native of Messina, and died about 1725.

" Porpora died in poverty about 1770, at the age of ninety. He has written many works for the theatre, which are still regarded as models; and his cantatas are even superior.

" Leo was his pupil, and surpassed his

master. He died in 1745, at the age of forty-two. His manner is inimitable : the air

Misero pargoletto,

in his Demophoon, is a chef-d'œuvre of expression.

" Francesco Durante was born at Grumo, a village near Naples. The glory of rendering counterpoint easy was reserved for him. The cantatas of Scarlatti, arranged as duets, I consider as his finest works.

" At the head of the musicians of the second order, we shall place Vinci, the father of all who have written for the theatre. His merit consists in uniting great expression to a profound knowledge of counterpoint. His best work is the Artaxerxes of Metastasio. He died in 1732, in the flower of his age; poisoned, as it is said, by a relative of a Roman lady, for whom he had an attachment.

" Giambattista Jesi, was born at Pergola, in the March of Ancona, from which circumstance he was called Pergolese. He was brought up in one of the schools of Naples, under Durante, and died in 1733, at the age of twenty-five. He was a true genius. His immortal works are the *Stabat Mater*, the air *Si cerca se dice* in the Olimpiade, and the *Serva maestra* in the buffa genus. Father Martini has remarked, that Pergolese was so superior in this last department, and had such a natural inclination for it, that there are comic subjects even in the *Stabat Mater*. In general, his style is melancholy and expressive.

" Hasse, called *the Saxon*, was a pupil of Scarlatti, and was the most natural composer of his time.

" Jomelli was born at Aversa, and died in 1775. He has displayed a comprehensive genius. The *Miserere*, and the *Benedictus*, are his finest works in the noble and simple style; the Armida, and Iphigenia, the best of his compositions for the theatre. He was too fond of the instruments.

" David Perez, who was born at Naples, and died about 1790, composed a *Credo*, which, in certain solemnities, is still sung in the church of the Fathers of the Oratorio, where people still go to hear it as original. He was one of the latest composers who maintained the rigour of counterpoint. He has laboured with success for the church and the theatre.

" Traetta, the master and companion of Sacchini, in the Conservatorio of Saint Mary of Loretto, pursued the same career as his pupil. He had more art than Sacchini, who is considered as having more genius. The character of Sacchini is ease, full of gaiety. Among his serious compositions are distinguished the recitative *Berenice che fai?* with the air which follows it.

" Bach, born in Germany, was educated at Naples. He is a favourite, on account of the tenderness which breathes in his compositions. The music which he wrote for the duet

Se mai più sarò geloso,

appears to advantage even amongst the airs which the most excellent masters have composed to these words. Bach may be said to have been particularly successful in expressing irony.

" All these professors died about 1780.

" Piccini has rivalled Jomelli in the noble style. Nothing can be superior to his duet

Fra queste ombre meste, o cara!

Perhaps he ought to be accounted the founder of the present buffa theatre.

" Paesiello, Guglielmi, and Anfossi, are the most celebrated of his disciples. But notwithstanding their works, the decline of music at Naples is evident and rapid. Adieu."

Æras of some composers.

Durante,	born	1693,	died 1755.
Leo,	—	1694,	— 1745.
Vinci,	—	1705,	— 1732.
Hasse,	—	1705,	— 1759.
Handel,	—	1684,	— 1759.
Galuppi,	—	1703,	— 1785.
Jomelli,	—	1714,	— 1774.
Porpora,	—	1685,	— 1767.
Benda,	—	1714,	— ....
Piccini,	—	1728,	— 1800.
Sacchini,	—	1735,	— 1786.

Paesiello,	born	1741,	died	....
Guglielmi,	—	1727,	—	1804.
Anfossi,	—	1736,	—	1775.
Sarti,	—	1730,	—	1802.
Zingarelli,	—	1752,	—	....
Traetta,	—	1738,	—	1779.*
Ch. Bach,	—	1735,	—	1782.
Mayer,	about 1760.			
Mosca,	about 1775.			

---

* Traetta, a profound, and melancholic artist, excels in the dark and picturesque effects of harmony. In his *Sophonisba*, that queen throws herself between her husband and her lover, who are seeking to combat each other: "Cruel men," says she to them, "what would you do? if you wish for blood, strike! behold my bosom!" and as they still persist in going out for the purpose, she cries out, "Whither are you going? Ah! no!" At this *ah!* the air is interrupted: the composer, seeing that it was necessary here to depart from the general rules, and not knowing how to express the degree of voice which the actress should give, has written above the note G, between parentheses, *(un urlo Francese) a French scream.*

LETTER XV.

Salzburg, May 25, 1809.

My dear Friend,

In the course of my last journey into Italy, I again visited the cottage at Arqua, and the old chair in which Petrarch sat to write his *Trionfi*. I never go to Venice, without visiting the library which has been established in the church where Cimarosa was interred, in 1801.

You will, therefore, perhaps, take some interest in the details, of little moment in themselves which I have collected respecting the life of our composer.

In giving an account of the employment of one of Haydn's days, after his entrance into the service of prince Esterhazy, we have described the course of his life for thirty years. He composed with perseverance, but with difficulty, which certainly did not arise from any deficiency of ideas: but the delicacy of his taste was very difficult to satisfy. A symphony cost him a month's labour, a mass more than twice as much. His rough copies are full of different passages. In a single symphony, we find ideas noted sufficient for three or four. In like manner, I have seen at Ferrara the sheet of paper on which Ariosto has written, in sixteen different ways, the beautiful octave of the Tempest; and it is only at the bottom of the sheet that we find the version which he has preferred.

Stendon le nubi un tenebroso velo, &c.

Haydn himself was wont to say, he always enjoyed himself most when he was at work.

This will account for the amazing number of works which he has produced. Society, which robs artists who live at Paris of three-fourths of their time, deprived him only of those moments in which it was impossible to pursue his studies.

Gluck, in order to warm his imagination, and to transport himself to Aulis, or Sparta, was accustomed to place himself in the middle of a beautiful meadow. In this situation, with his piano before him, and a bottle of Champagne on each side, he wrote in the open air his two Iphigenias, his Orpheus, and his other works.

Sarti, on the contrary, required a spacious dark room, dimly illumined by the funereal light of a lamp suspended from the ceiling; and it was only in the most silent hours of the night that he could summon musical ideas. In this way he wrote the *Medonte*, the rondo

Mia speranza,

and the finest air known, I mean to say,

La dolce compagna.

Cimarosa was fond of noise; he liked to have his friends about him when he composed. It was while he was amusing himself with them that he projected his *Horatii*, and his *Matrimonio segreto;* that is to say, the finest and most original serious opera, and the first comic opera of the Italian theatre. Frequently, in a single night, he wrote the subjects of eight or ten of these charming airs, which he afterwards finished in the midst of his friends. It was after having spent a fortnight in doing nothing but walk about the environs of Prague, that the air

<blockquote>Pria che spunti in ciel l'aurora</blockquote>

suddenly entered his mind, when he was not thinking on the subject.

Sacchini could not write a passage unless his mistress was at his side; and his cats, whose gracefulness he much admired, were playing about him.

Paesiello composed in bed. It was between the sheets that he planned the Barber of Seville, the *Molinara,* and so many other chefs-d'œuvres of ease and gracefulness.

After reading a passage in some holy father, or Latin classic, Zingarelli will dictate, in less than four hours, a whole act of *Pyrrhus,* or of *Romeo and Juliet.* I remember a brother of Anfossi, of great promise, who died young. He could not write a note unless he was surrounded by roast fowls and smoking sausages.

As for Haydn, solitary and sober as Newton, putting on his finger the ring which the great Frederick had sent him, and which he said was necessary to inspire his imagination, he sat down to his piano, and in a few moments soared among the angelic choirs. Nothing disturbed him at Eisenstädt; he lived wholly for his art, exempt from terrestrial cares.

This uniform and pleasing mode of life, filled up with an agreeable occupation, continued without interruption till the death of prince Nicholas, his patron, in 1789.

A singular effect of this retired life was, that our composer, who never left the small town belonging to his prince, was, for a long time, the only musical man in Europe who was ignorant of the celebrity of Joseph Haydn. The first homage he received was of a singular kind. As if fate had decreed that every thing ridiculous in music should originate at Paris, Haydn received, from a celebrated amateur of that country, a commission to compose a piece of vocal music. At the same time, some select passages of

Lulli and Rameau were sent with the letter as models. One may imagine the effect which these papers would produce, in 1780, on Haydn, formed upon the master-pieces of the Italian school, which, for fifty years, had been at the height of its glory. He returned the precious morsels, replying, with a malicious simplicity, " that he was Haydn, and not Lulli, or Rameau; and that if music, after the manner of those great composers, was desired, it should be demanded from them or their pupils; that, as for himself, he unfortunately could only write music after the manner of Haydn."

He had been talked of for many years, when he was invited, almost at the same time, by the most celebrated directors of the theatres of Naples, Lisbon, Venice, London, Milan, &c. to compose operas for them. But the love of repose, a very natural attachment to his prince, and to his methodical habits of life, retained him in Hungary, and overbalanced the desire he constantly felt of passing the mountains. He would, perhaps, never have left Eisenstädt, if madamoiselle Boselli had not died. Haydn, after her loss, began to feel a void in his days. He had recently refused the invitation of the directors of the *Concert spirituel* * of Paris. After the death of his female friend, he accepted the proposals of a London professor, named Salomon, who had undertaken to give concerts in that city. Salomon thought that a man of genius, drawn from his retirement, purposely for the amateurs of London, would bring his concerts into fashion. He gave twenty concerts in the year, and offered Haydn 100 sequins (50*l*.) for each concert. Haydn, having accepted these terms, set out for London in

---

* The *Concert spirituel* is thus described by Rousseau, in his *Dictionnaire de musique.*

"CONCERT SPIRITUEL. A concert which serves as a *spectacle* at Paris, when the other places of public amusement are shut. It is established in the chateau of the Tuilleries: the performers are very numerous, and the room very handsome. The music consists of motets and symphonies, and the performers occasionally give themselves the pleasure of disfiguring some Italian airs." T.

1790, at the age of fifty-nine. He spent more than a year there. The new music which he composed for these concerts was greatly admired.* The simplicity of his manners, added to certain indications of genius, could not fail to succeed with a generous and reflecting nation. The English would often observe him, as he walked in the street, eye him in silence from head to foot, and go away saying, " That is certainly a great man."

---

* The finest of his instrumental pieces were composed in this country. His mind evidently received a stimulus from the new scenes in which he was placed; and, during his short stay in London, his genius shone with unusual splendour. His great industry and celerity in writing, were amply shone in the numerous pieces he at that time composed, at the head of which we may place the twelve sinfonias, published by Salomon, which are projected upon a more enlarged view of the art than any of his former ones. They are written for an orchestra of not less than twenty distinct instruments, the peculiar faculties of which are skilfully exhibited. These compositions are justly regarded by all the musicians of the present day, as the finest works of imagination which the art possesses, and are esteemed the first models of excellence that have appeared in this new genus of music.   G.

Before Haydn had lost his interest in conversation, he related with pleasure many anecdotes respecting his residence in London. A nobleman, passionately fond of music, according to his own account, came to him one morning, and asked him to give him some lessons in counterpoint, at a guinea a lesson. Haydn, seeing that he had some knowledge of music, accepted his proposal. " When shall we begin?"—" Immediately, if you please," replied the nobleman;" and he took out of his pocket a quartett of Haydn's. " For the first lesson," continued he, " let us examine this quartett, and tell me the reason of certain modulations, and of the general management of the composition, which I cannot altogether approve. since it is contrary to the rules."

Haydn, a little surprised, said, that he was ready to answer his questions. The nobleman began, and from the very first bar found something to remark upon every note. Haydn, with whom invention was a habit, and who was the opposite of a pedant, found himself a good deal embarrassed, and replied continually: " I did so, because it has a good effect; I have placed this passage here, because I think it suitable." The Englishman, in whose opinion these replies were nothing to the purpose, still returned to his proofs, and demonstrated very clearly that his quartett was good for nothing. " But, my Lord, arrange this quartett in your own way; hear it played, and you will then see which of the two is the best."——" How can yours, which is contrary to the rules, be the best?"—— " Because it is the most agreeable."—My Lord still returned to the subject; Haydn replied, as well as he was able, but at last, out of patience, " I see, my lord," said he, " that it is you who are so good as to give lessons to me, and I am obliged to confess, that I do not merit the honour of having such a master." The advocate of the rules went away, and cannot to this day understand how an author who adheres to them should fail of producing a *Matrimonio segreto.*

A gentleman of the navy came to him one morning: " Mr. Haydn, I presume?"—" Yes, Sir."—" Are you willing to compose me a march for the troops I have on board? I will give you thirty guineas; but I must have it done to-day, because I sail to-morrow for Calcutta." Haydn agreed to do it. As soon as the captain was gone, he opened his piano-forte, and in a quarter of an hour the march was ready.

Feeling some scruples at gaining so easily what appeared to him a very considerable sum, he returned home early in the evening, and wrote two other marches, intending first to give the captain his choice of them, and afterwards to make him a present of all three, as a return for his liberality.

Early the next morning came the captain.—" Well, where's my march?"—" Here it is."—" Will you just play it on the piano?"— Haydn played it. The captain, without saying a word, counted the thirty guineas on the piano, took the march, and walked away. Haydn ran after him to stop him: "I have written two others, which are better: hear them, and then make your choice."—" I like the first very well, and that is sufficient."—

But hear them." — The captain marched

down stairs, and would hear nothing. Haydn pursued him, crying after him: " I make you a present of them."—The captain, quickening his pace, replied, " I won't have them."—" But, at least hear them." —" The devil should not make me hear them."—

Haydn, piqued, immediately hastened to the Exchange, enquired what ship was on the point of sailing for the Indies, and the name of the commander. He then rolled up the two marches, inclosed a polite note, and sent the parcel on board to the captain. The obstinate fellow, suspecting that the musician was in pursuit of him, would not even open the note, and sent back the whole. Haydn tore the marches into a thousand pieces, and never forgot the captain so long as he lived.

He used to relate, with much pleasure, a dispute which he had with a music-seller in London. Amusing himself one morning, after the English fashion, in shopping, he enquired of a music-seller if he had any select and beautiful music? " Certainly," replied the shopman, " I have just printed some sublime music of Haydn's."—" Oh," returned Haydn, "I'll have nothing to do with that." —" How, Sir, you will have nothing to do with Haydn's music! and pray what fault have you to find with it?"—" Oh, plenty; but it is useless talking about it, since it does not suit me: show me some other." The music-seller, who was a warm Haydnist, replied, " No, Sir, I have music, it is true, but not for such as you;" and turned his back upon him. As Haydn was going away, smiling, a gentleman of his acquaintance entered, and accosted him by name. The music-seller, still out of humour, turned round at the name, and said to the person who had just entered the shop : " Haydn!—aye, here's a fellow who says he does not like that great man's music." The Englishman laughed; an explanation took place, and the music-seller was made acquainted with the man who found fault with Haydn's music.

During his residence in London, our author enjoyed two great gratifications. One was, in hearing Handel's music; the other, in going to the ancient concert. This last is a society established for the purpose of preserving music, which, in the fashionable world, is called ancient. They give concerts, at which are performed the master-pieces of Pergolese, Leo, Durante, Marcello, Scarlatti,—in a word, of that constellation of distinguished men, who appeared, almost at the same time, about the year 1730.*

---

* It is certainly unwise to neglect the productions of genius, to whatever period they may belong. Yet, as music, like every other branch of art, and knowledge, is progressive, it cannot surely be expedient, constantly to refer to the works of our forefathers, as the only models of excellence.

The Philharmonic Society is established exclusively for the study of *modern* instrumental music, and whoever has had an opportunity of listening to its orchestra, composed of the first masters in the country, can hardly fail to recognise the superiority of later times in this department.

To do perfect justice to the works of the great modern composers, it is requisite that they should be executed by men, similar in musical taste, and genius, to themselves. So different do they appear in the hands of this distinguished society, from the style in which they are usually exhibited, that the effect resembles the pure effulgence produced in the recent experiments of Sir Humphrey Davy, when compared with the 'dusky beam' of ordinary brightness. G.

Haydn remarked to me, with surprise, that many of these compositions, which had transported him to the skies, when he studied them in his youth, appeared much less beautiful to him forty years afterwards. " It had the same melancholy effect upon me," said he, " as the sight of an ancient mistress." Was this merely the usual effect of advanced age, or did these sublime pieces give our composer less pleasure from having lost the charm of novelty?

Haydn undertook a second journey to London, in 1794. Gallini, the manager of the King's theatre, in the Haymarket, had engaged him to compose an opera, which he intended to get up with the greatest magnificence. The subject was the descent of Orpheus to hell. Haydn began to work, but Gallini found difficulty in obtaining permission to open his theatre. The composer, who was hankering after home, had not patience to wait till permission could be obtained. He left London, with eleven parts of his Orpheus, which, as I am informed, are his best productions in theatrical music, and returned to Austria, never more to leave it.*

He often saw, in London, the celebrated Mrs. Billington, whom he enthusiastically admired. He found her one day, sitting to Reynolds, the only English painter who has succeeded in portraits. He had just taken that of Mrs. Billington, in the character of St. Cecilia, listening to the celestial music, as she is usually drawn. Mrs. Billington shewed the picture to Haydn. " It is like," said he, " but there is a strange mistake."— " What is that," asked Reynolds, hastily ?— " You have painted her listening to the angels; you ought to have represented the angels listening to her." Mrs. Billington sprung up, and threw her arms round his

---

* The songs of Eurydice in this unfinished opera, full of tenderness and beauty, are powerfully contrasted with the nervous and formidable strains of the Furies, and the piece, in general, exhibits marks of genius sufficient to convince us that Haydn would have distinguished himself in the drama, equally with symphony, had he been led to employ himself upon that department.   G.

neck. It was for her that he composed his *Ariadne abbandonata,* which rivals that of Benda.

One of the English princes commissioned Reynolds to take Haydn's portrait. Flattered by the honour, he went to the painter's house, and sat to him, but soon grew tired. Reynolds, careful of his reputation, would not paint a man of acknowledged genius, with a stupid countenance, and deferred the sitting to another day. The same weariness and want of expression occurring at the next attempt, Reynolds went to the prince, and informed him of the circumstance. The prince contrived a stratagem; he sent to the painter's house a pretty German girl, in the service of the queen his mother. Haydn took his seat for the third time, and as soon as the conversation began to flag, a curtain fell, and the fair German, elegantly attired in white, and crowned with roses, addressed him in his native tongue: "O, great man, how happy am I to have an opportunity of seeing thee, and of being in thy presence!" Haydn, delighted, overwhelms the lovely enchantress with questions; his countenance recovered its animation, and Reynolds seized it with rapidity.

George III., who liked no music but Handel's, was not insensible to that of Haydn. He and the queen gave a flattering reception to the German professor; and the University of Oxford sent him a doctor's diploma, a dignity which had been conferred on only four persons since the year 1400, and which Handel himself had not obtained.

Custom requiring that Haydn should send to the university a specimen of musical learning, he addressed to it a sheet of music so composed, that, whether it was read backwards or forwards, beginning at the top, the bottom, or the middle of the page, in short, in every possible way, it always presented an air, and a correct accompaniment.*

He left London, delighted with Handel's music, and carrying with him a few hundred guineas, which seemed to him a treasure.

On his return through Germany, he gave

---

* We have given this musical curiosity at the conclusion. G.

a few concerts; and, for the first time, his little fortune received an augmentation. His appointments in the Esterhazy family, were of small amount; but the condescension with which he was treated by the members of that august house, was of more value to a man whose works are the productions of his feelings, than any pecuniary advantages. He had always a cover at the prince's table; and when his highness gave a uniform to his orchestra, Haydn received the dress, usually worn by persons coming to Eisenstädt to pay their court to the prince. It is by a course of attentions such as these, that the great families of Austria gain the affections of all by whom they are surrounded; it is by this moderation that they render tolerable, and even agreeable, privileges and manners which put them almost on an equality with crowned heads. German pride is ridiculous only in the printed accounts of their public ceremonies; the air of kindness which accompanies the reality, gives a pleasing colour to every thing.

Haydn took with him, from London, 15,000

florins.* Some years afterwards, the sale of the score of the *Creation,* and the *Four Seasons,* brought him an additional sum of 2,000 sequins,† with which he purchased the small house and garden in the fauxbourg Gumpendorff, on the road to Schönbrunn, where he resides. Such is the state of his fortune.

I was with him at his new house, when he received a flattering letter from the French Institute, to inform him that he had been nominated foreign associate. Haydn suddenly melted into tears when he read it, and never referred without emotion to this letter, which is, in reality, distinguished by that dignified and graceful turn of expression, in which the French succeed with a felicity superior to every other nation.‡

---

* About 1,400*l.*
† About 1,000*l.*
‡ The late R. B. Sheridan was put in nomination at the same time to fill this honorary station, but the choice of the Institute fell on the Father of Harmony. G.

LETTER XVI.

Salzburg, May 28, 1809.

COME, my friend,—the same Haydn who, in instrumental music, was sublime, in the opera, only respectable, now invites you to follow him to the sanctuary, where,

> La gloria di colui che tutto muove,

inspired him, at times, with hymns worthy of their divine object.

Nothing has been more justly admired, and at the same time more warmly censured, than his masses; but in order to form a correct estimate of their beauties, their faults, and the causes which occasioned them, the most expeditious method will be to see what was the state of sacred music about the year 1760.

Every one knows that music formed a part of the sacred worship, both of the Jews and the Gentiles, and it is to this circumstance that we owe those irregular, but lofty and beautiful, melodies which the Gregorian and Ambrosian chants have preserved to us. The learned assert, with sufficient probability, that these airs, the vestiges of which still remain, are the same as were employed in Greece, in the worship of Jupiter and Apollo.*

---

* Music has probably shared the fate of the other arts, and the arrangement of it on scientific principles, or what is called Harmony, may be said, with more propriety, to have been revived, than invented, by the moderns.

Dr. Burney has, indeed, cited twenty authorities to prove that the Greeks were acquainted with melody only, and that they were ignorant of all admixtures of sound, except the unison, and the octave. But it might as well be argued, because no specimens of their painting have reached us, that they were ignorant of all admixture of colours.

Indeed, the distinction that has been made between Harmony and Melody seems to us altogether unfounded.

Harmony is a thing inherent in nature. Every sound given out by a sonorous body, is as much composed of three ingredients, as every ray of light is of the three prismatic colours. If we listen to St. Paul's bell, we shall hear it distinctly utter the following tones,

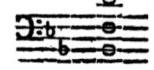

Guido Aretino is considered as having discovered the first ideas of counterpoint, in 1032; and it was soon afterwards introduced

---

which are a combination of the fifth, and tenth, with the key note. The unison of these three tones forms what is termed concord, and every sound in nature is similarly compounded. It is from observing these effects, that the musical scale has been formed; which may be called the prism of the art, by means of which, all combinations of sound may be separated into their constituent parts.

By the musical scale, is here meant those intervals, or distances, according to which sounds are arranged, as marked by the twelve semi-tones. Each of these is capable of further·division, almost to infinity. It is possible to time 100 strings, or more, in regular ascent of pitch between C, and C sharp, so as to be clearly distinguished by the ear. When all these gradations of sound are mingled together, we hear only a confused noise. When they are made to follow each other at harmonic distances, melody is produced.

Melody, then, may be defined to be *a succession of sounds at harmonic distances.*

It is only one of the accidents, or forms, of harmony, and its excellence and beauty will always depend on the order of chords through which it is made to pass, or, in other words, on the correctness of the harmony by which it is generated.

Upon this theory, it seems impossible to refuse to the

into sacred music; but till the time of **Palestrina**, that is to say, till about the year 1570, this music was nothing but a tissue of harmonious sounds, almost destitute of perceptible melody. In the fifteenth, and the earlier part of the following century, the professors, in order to render their masses more agreeable, composed them upon the air of some popular song. It is thus that more than a hundred masses were composed upon the air of the well-known ballad of " *The armed Man.*"

The studied singularity of the middle age, led other masters to write their sacred music according to the cast of dice: each number thus obtained, had musical passages, which

---

Greeks all knowledge of the scientific part of music. The Athenian ear, so delicate with respect to the measure of their poetry, and the accent of their language, could surely receive little gratification from the rude, and barbarous strains which are found among nations of savages. Nor is it possible to suppose that such music could have inspired the imagination of their poets with the wonders they have ascribed to it, or have been thought worthy of the peculiar protection of one of their favorite deities. G.

corresponded to it. At length, Palestrina* appeared. This immortal genius, to whom we owe the modern melody, shook off the fetters of barbarism; he introduced into his compositions an air, grave indeed, but continued and perceptible, and his music is still performed in St. Peter's, at Rome.

About the middle of the sixteenth century, the composers had taken such a fancy to *fugues* and *canons*, and collected these figures in such a singular manner, in their works for the church, that during the greater part of that period this pious music was extremely ridiculous. This abuse, after a length of time, excited the complaints of the devout; and it was often proposed to banish music from the churches. In short, Marcellus II., who occupied the papal chair, in 1555, was on the point of issuing the decree of suppression, when Palestrina entreated his holiness to hear a mass which he had composed. The pope having

---

* Palestrina was born in 1529, nine years after the death of Raphael, and died in 1594.

consented, the young musician caused to be performed before him a mass for six voices, which appeared so beautiful, and so full of dignity, that the pontiff, instead of putting his project in execution, ordered Palestrina to compose some works of the same kind for his chapel. The mass in question is still extant, and is known by the name of pope Marcello's mass.

We should distinguish between those musicians, who are great by their natural genius, and those who have produced great works. Palestrina and Scarlatti occasioned the art to make astonishing progress. They had, perhaps, as much genius as Cimarosa, though his compositions are so much more pleasing than theirs. What would not Mantegna, whose works excite laughter in three-fourths of the spectators at the Museum, have produced, if, instead of contributing to the education of Correggio, he had been born at Parma, ten years after that distinguished man. What, above all, would not the great Lionardo da Vinci, that favourite of nature, created for the perception of beauty, have accomplished, had he been permitted to behold the pictures of Guido.

An artist in painting, or music, at the present day easily surpasses Giotto or Palestrina; but what point would these real artists have reached, had they possessed the same advantages with our contemporary workman? The Coriolanus of La Harpe, if published in the time of Malherbe, would have obtained for its author a renown almost equal to that of Racine. A man born with any degree of talent, is naturally carried by the age in which he lives, to the point of perfection, which that age has reached. The education which he has himself received, the degree of information possessed by the spectators who applaud him;—every thing conducts him thus far; but if he goes farther, he becomes superior to his age, and evinces the character of genius. He then labours for posterity, but at the same time his works are not so likely to please the taste of his contemporaries.*

---

* Beethoven is a striking illustration of this remark. His genius seems to anticipate a future age. In one compre-

We have seen, that towards the end of the sixteenth century, the church music nearly resembled that of the theatre. Soon after-

hensive view, he surveys all that science has hitherto produced; but regards it only as the basis of that superstructure which harmony is capable of raising. He measures the talents and resources of every preceding artist, and, as it were, collects into a focus their scattered rays. He discovers that Haydn and Mozart alone have followed nature, yet he explores the hidden treasures of harmony with a vigour superior to either. In sacred music, he is pre-eminently great. The dark tone of his mind, is in unison with that solemn style which the services of the church require; and the gigantic harmony which he wields, enables him to excite by sounds, a terror hitherto unknown.

In the Mount of Olives, this sublimity is fully displayed. The movement which describes the march of the Roman soldiers, when they go out in search of Jesus, is remarkable for novelty and effect, " *He came towards this mountain, He'll not escape our search.*" It partakes of the solemnity of a march, yet possesses a character of activity and enterprise. The mutations of the harmony, are constantly turning the course of the melody into every direction. No place or corner seems unexplored.

The last chorus may be quoted as a specimen of the true sublime. The sinfonia which introduces it, when performed in a spacious church, is a continued clash of wards an instrumental accompaniment was given to the sacred airs.

At length, about 1740, and not till then, Durante * conceived the idea of marking the sense of the words, and sought for agreeable melodies, which might give additional effect to the sentiments they expressed. The revolution produced by this very natural idea was general, on the other side of the Alps; but the German musicians, faithful to ancient customs, still retained in sacred song something of the rudeness and tiresomeness of the middle ages. In Italy, on the contrary, sentiment prevailing over propriety, the music of the church and the theatre soon became the same. A *Gloria in excelsis,* was nothing but

---

sounds, so tremendous, as to awaken the sentiment of danger in the highest degree. During the solemn enunciation of the words " *Hallelujah to the Father, and the Son of God,*" a succession of vivid and appalling shocks of sound proceeds from the accompaniment, the effect of which is truly electrical. G.

* Durante, a pupil of Scarlatti, was born at Naples, in 1693, and died in 1755, the same year with Montesquieu.

a lively air, in which a happy lover might very well express his felicity, and a *Miserere*, a plaintive strain full of tender languor.

Airs, duets, recitatives, and even sportive rondos, were introduced into the prayers. Benedict XIV. hoped to remove the scandal by proscribing wind instruments; he retained only the organ; the unsuitableness, however, was not in the instruments, but in the music.

Haydn, who was early sensible of the dryness of the ancient sacred music, of the profanity of the ornaments which the modern Italians have introduced into the sanctuary, and the inexpressive and monotonous character of the German music, saw that by following his own ideas of propriety, he should create a manner entirely new. He therefore adopted little or nothing from the music of the theatre: he preserved, by the solidity of the harmony, a part of the dark and lofty style of the ancient school; he supported, with all the richness of his orchestra, airs, solemn, tender, and dignified, yet full of brilliancy; and, from time to time, adorned with flowers and graces this sublime mode of celebrating the divine perfections, and acknowledging his benefits.

The only person who preceded him in this genus was San Martini, the Milan composer, of whom I have already spoken.

On hearing a mass of Haydn's performed in one of the immense gothic cathedrals, so frequent in Germany, where a solemn twilight scarcely penetrates through the coloured windows, you feel, at first, agitated, and afterwards elevated, by that mingled character of seriousness, antiquity, imagination, and piety, which distinguishes them.

In 1799, I was confined at Vienna by a fever. The bells announced a mass at a church not far from my room: my ennui got the better of my prudence, and I rose and went to console myself with a little music. I inquired as I entered, and found it was the festival of St. Ann, and that they were going to perform a mass of Haydn's in B$\flat$ major, which I had never heard. Scarcely had it begun before I felt myself affected. I broke out into a perspiration, my head-ache went away: I left the church with a cheerfulness to which I had been long a stranger, and the fever never returned.

I am of opinion that many of the complaints of our nervous ladies might be cured by my remedy, but not by that ineffectual music which they go to hear at a concert, after having put on a charming bonnet. Women, never in their lives, nor do we ourselves, while young, give a full attention to music, except when we hear it in the dark. When at liberty from the business of appearing charming—when we have no longer our part to act, we can give ourselves up to the music; but in France we take precisely the contrary dispositions with us to the concert. I used to think myself obliged to be more brilliant than usual on such occasions. But if, during a morning walk to Monceaux, while seated in a verdant grove, secluded from every eye, with a book in your hand, your attention should be suddenly arrested by the sound of voices and instruments from a neighbouring habitation, and you should hear distinctly a beautiful air, in vain will you attempt again and again to resume your reading. You will, at length, be entirely carried away; you will fall into a reverie: and when, after an hour or two, you return to your carriage, you will feel yourself relieved from that secret heaviness which often rendered you unhappy without your being able clearly to explain the nature of your uneasiness. You will be softened into tears; you will begin to *regret*, and this is a feeling never experienced by the really miserable; to them, happiness seems no longer possible. The man who feels *regret*, recollects a happiness he once enjoyed, and he will gradually bring himself to hope that he may again attain to it. Good music never mistakes its aim, but goes at once to the heart in search of the chagrin which consumes us.

In all cases of cures effected by music, I am of opinion, to speak like a grave physician, that it is the brain which re-acts powerfully on the rest of the organization. The music must begin by bewildering us, and by making us regard as possible things which we did not dare to hope. One of the most singular instances of this transient insanity, of this forgetfulness of ourselves, our vanity, and the part we are acting, is that of *Senesino*, who was to perform, on a London theatre, the character of a tyrant, in I know not what opera: the celebrated Farinelli sustained that of an oppressed prince; Farinelli, who had been giving concerts in the country, arrived only a few hours before the representation, and the unfortunate hero, and the cruel tyrant, saw one another for the first time, on the stage. When Farinelli came to his first air, in which he supplicates for mercy, he sung it with such sweetness and expression, that the poor tyrant, totally forgetting himself, threw himself upon his neck, and repeatedly embraced him.

One more story. In my early youth, I went with some other young people, equally devoid of care, one day, during the extreme heats of summer, to seek for coolness and fresh air on one of the lofty mountains which surround the Lago Maggiore in Lombardy. Having reached by day-break the middle of the ascent, we stopped to contemplate the Borromean isles, which were displayed under our feet, in the middle of the lake, when we were surrounded by a large flock of sheep, which were leaving the fold to go to their pasture. One of our party, who was no bad performer on the flute, and who always carried his instrument along with him, took it out of his pocket. " I am going," said he, " to turn Corydon, let us see whether Virgil's sheep will recognize their pastor." He began to play. The sheep and goats, which were following one another towards the mountain, with their heads hanging down, raised them at the first sound of the flute; and all, with a general and hasty movement, turned to the side from whence the agreeable noise proceeded. Gradually they flocked round the musician, and listened with motionless attention. He ceased playing: still the sheep did not stir. The shepherd, with his staff, obliged those nearest to him to move on. They obeyed; but no sooner did the fluter begin again to play, than his innocent auditors again returned to him. The shepherd, out of patience, pelted them with clods of earth, but not one would move. The fluter played with additional skill; the shepherd fell into a passion, whistled, swore, and pelted the poor fleecy amateurs with stones. Such as were hit by them began to march, but the others still refused to stir. At last, the shepherd was obliged to entreat our Orpheus to stop his magic sounds; the sheep then moved off, but continued to stop at a distance as often as our friend resumed the agreeable instrument. The tune he played was nothing more than the favourite air of the opera at that time performing at Milan.

As music was our continual employment, we were delighted with our adventure; we reasoned upon it the whole day, and concluded that physical pleasure is the basis of all music.

Well, but, say you, what is become of Haydn's masses? Right; but what does it signify? I write for amusement, and we have long agreed to lay aside restraint on both sides.

The masses of Haydn, then, are inspired by a sweet sensibility. The ideal part is brilliant, and, in general, dignified; the style is noble, full of fire, and finely developed; the *Amens* and *Hallelujahs* breathe all the reality of joy, and are of a spirit unequalled. Occasionally, when the character of a passage would otherwise be of too gay, and profane a cast, Haydn sobers it by profound and retarding chords, which moderate this worldly joy. His *Agnus Dei* are full of tenderness. Turn more particularly to that in the mass, No. 4; it is celestial music. His fugues are of the first order, and breathe all the fire, dignity, and exaltation of an enraptured mind.*

---

* As these compositions are little known in this country, a more accurate description of them may not, perhaps, be unacceptable to the reader. Of the six masses for a full orchestra, it would be difficult to select any one as superior to the rest. They are constructed upon the most magnificent scale; and require the space of a cathedral fully to develope the lofty sentiments which they contain. The chorusses must, also, be broken by the service, to take off that weight upon the ear, which would be occasioned by an uninterrupted performance of them.

The first mass in B, is of a mild and placid cast: every movement is solemn and beautiful. The "*Gloria in excelsis Deo,*" is wrought with more fire than any of the

He sometimes adopts the artifice which distinguishes the works of Paesiello. He selects from the beginning an agree-

---

others, and is an exception to the general character of the piece. The Hosanna is peculiar for its graceful simplicity.

Mass, No. 2, is in C major, and is more grand and animated.

No. 3, in D minor, is conceived with great sublimity; the trumpets, which are heard in the intervals, give it a majestic air. The *Gloria* is introduced by the major-key in great splendour; and the soft flowing stream of melody which proceeds from the violins, prepares us for the words, "*et in terra pax.*" In the *Credo*, a close canon of two choirs, accompanied by the orchestra, the author has employed the ancient style, which in his hands becomes doubly interesting; the beauties of the old school are displayed, without its deformities.

No. 4, in B, contains some beautiful quartettos, and fine fugues.

No. 5, in C, is of a grand cast, and is the only one in which a song is introduced.

No. 6, in B, opens in a most impressive style, interspersed with *solos*, which agreeably relieve the ear. The "*In gloria Dei Patris,*" the "*Et Incarnatus,*" and the "*Benedictus,*" are all excellent; and the last chorus, "*Dona nobis pacem,*" is a combination of beauty and sublimity, that will rarely be surpassed. G.

able passage, which he repeats in the course of the piece; frequently it is only a simple cadence. It is scarcely credible what an effect this simple method of repeating the same passage has, in giving an unity, a religious and affecting colour to the whole. This style, you are aware, borders on monotony; but a good master knows how to avoid it; instance in the *Molinara*, and the *Deux Journeés* of Cherubini. You will observe in the overture to that fine composition, a cadence, which your ear will notice, because there is something entangled and singular in it. It appears again in the trio of the first act, afterwards in an air, and lastly in the finale; and every time it returns, our pleasure in hearing it is increased. The predominating passage is rendered so sensible in the *Frascatana* of Paesiello, that it forms of itself the whole finale. In Haydn's masses this passage is at first scarcely observed, on account of its gracefulness, but at every return, it acquires additional force and beauty.

Let us now hear the advocates on the opposite side, and I assure you that it is not energy that Haydn's opponents want. They accuse him, first, of having destroyed the species of sacred music established and adopted by all the professors. This species, however, no longer existed in Italy, and, in Germany, they had returned to the monotonous and inexpressive noise of the middle ages. If monotony be seriousness, certainly nothing could be more so.

Either write no music for the church, or let it be good. Did any one ever find fault with Raphael for introducing celestial figures in his sacred pieces? Is not the charming St. Michael of Guido, which distracts the attention of the devout, still displayed in St. Peter's at Rome? Why should music, then, be forbidden to please? If you require theological reasons, we have David's example on our side. "If the psalm be mournful," says St. Augustine, "mourn with it; if it celebrate the praises of God, do you also sing the wonders of the Creator."

A *Hallelujah* then ought not to be sung to the air of a *Miserere*. Here the German masters recede a step; they will allow a little variety in the air, but require the accompaniment to be always noisy, austere, and clumsy. Are they in the wrong? I know that a celebrated Hanoverian physician, worthy to be a native of the country of the Frederics, the Catherines, the Mengs, and the Mozarts, once said to me with a smile, "A German of the common class requires a stronger physical effort, more bustle, and more noise to move him than any other creature upon earth. We drink too much beer; you must fairly flay us if you wish to tickle us."

If the object of music in the church, as elsewhere, be to give a greater effect to the sentiments expressed by the words, Haydn has attained the perfection of his art. I defy any Christian, who has heard on Easter-day a *Gloria* of this composer, to leave the church without feeling his heart expand with sacred joy; an effect which Father Martini and the German harmonists, apparently, did not wish to produce; and it must be confessed that in this respect, at least, they have not failed.

If these gentlemen be wrong in the principal accusation they have brought against Haydn, they are right in some inferior points; but Correggio likewise, in his attention to gracefulness, has occasionally fallen into the affectation of it. Look at the divine *Madonna alla scodella* of the Museum: when you are out of humour, you will think the action of the angel, who is tying the ass of Joseph, affected; at another time this angel will appear to you charming. Haydn's faults are sometimes more positive: in a *Dona nobis pacem* of one of his masses, we find, as a principal passage, a pleasantry in *tempo presto*. In one of his *Benedictus*, after many pranks of the orchestra, a thought frequently returns in *tempo allegro*, which may be found in an *aria buffa* of Anfossi. It there produces a good effect, because it is in its proper place.

He has written some fugues in *sextuple* time, which, as soon as the movement becomes quick, are absolutely comic. When the repentant sinner bemoans his faults at the foot of the altar, Haydn often paints the seducing charms of the sin, instead of the penitence of the sinner. He sometimes employs $\frac{3}{4}$ or $\frac{3}{8}$

time, which remind the auditor of the waltz, and the country-dance.

This is offending against the physical principles of music. Cabanis * will tell you that joy accelerates the circulation of the blood, and requires *tempo presto*: that melancholy abates, retards the course of the humours, and inclines us to *tempo largo*: that happiness requires the major key, and melancholy the minor: on this last truth are founded the styles of Mozart and Cimarosa.†

---

* A French medical writer of eminence, still living. T.

† The physical principles of music, or the natural causes of its power over our feelings, have not yet been satisfactorily explained.

The influence of the popular airs of different countries upon their inhabitants, has been sufficiently accounted for by the doctrine of association. But the general question is too extensive to admit of a solution from this principle alone, and must be investigated with reference to the original constitution of nature.

Joy, as our author remarks, always expresses itself in the major key: sadness in the minor; and this effect of the animal spirits on the tones of the voice, is observable also in the brute creation. The cuckoo, at the commencement of spring, sings in the major third, but falls into the

Haydn apologized for these errors, which his judgment could not fail to recognise, by saying, that whenever he thought on God, he

---

minor when her vigour is exhausted by the business of incubation.

If we suppose the state of society to have been progressive, that

"The savage of the human kind
" By *time* was softened into man,"

we may refer to a period, when language was probably little more than the simple utterance of the tones in which the passions universally express themselves.

It is this language of nature which is understood by the new-born infant: and a little observation may satisfy us, that it is still, the most effectual medium of communicating our feelings. How much more powerfully are we affected by the impassioned eloquence of the orator, than by the silent address of the writer. How unintelligible would be the most familiar expressions of common conversation, if pronounced in a tone foreign to the sentiment.

There is, then, independently of words, a language of the passions, consisting of the tones, in which they are universally and instinctively uttered, and which may be regarded as the primitive and natural language of man.

It is in its reference to these original sounds, which we shall call the *instinctive tones of nature*, that the empire of music over the feelings is founded. If we attend to could only conceive of him as a being infinitely great, and infinitely good. He added, that this last quality of the divine nature inspired

---

them, we shall find that they may all be referred to the gradations of the musical scale.

It has been observed, that in the tones of woe, we invariably recognize the minor 3d, and in those of joy, or exultation, the harmony of the major. If four minor 3ds be combined, they form the chord of the extreme flat 7th, which excites in us fear and alarm: because it is a clutter of sounds, indicating rage and ferocity. These tones escape us in the ebullitions of our worst passions, and are heard in the savage murmurs of wild beasts.

When the minor 3d forms the 7th of the relative key, by being compounded with brighter sounds, it loses much of the melancholy which before characterized it, and becomes highly sympathetic. We never fail to utter this tone in moments of the greatest interest, and it may be regarded as the most affecting chord in music.

It is the business, then, of the composer, to supply the modulation by which the passions may be awakened; but much of the effect produced on the auditor, will depend upon the mode in which this modulation is given.

It should, therefore, be the object of the instrumental, as well as the vocal performer, to copy the manner in which the instinctive tones are uttered; and the power of either to move us, will be in proportion to his just conception of the sentiment of his author, and his skill him with such confidence and joy, that he could have written even a *Miserere* in *tempo allegro*.

For my own part, I think these masses rather too much in the German style. I mean, that they are, often, too much loaded with accompaniments, which injure, in some degree, the effect of the air.

They are fourteen in number. Some of them composed during that unfortunate period for the house of Austria, the seven years war, breathe a truly martial ardour; they resemble, in this respect, the sublime odes which the celebrated tragic poet, Collin,* poured forth extempore, on the approach of the French army, in 1809.

---

in giving to that sentiment the tone which nature has assigned to it.

The superiority of modern music arises, in a great degree, from the increased attention which has been paid to the philosophy of the art; and we are confident that effects, still more novel and interesting, will be produced, in proportion as its principles are more closely studied, and more correctly known. G.

* For an account of this poet, see madame de Stael's 'Germany,' part ii. chap. 25. T.

LETTER XVII.

Salzburg, May 30, 1809.

My dear Louis,

It remained for me to speak of our author's greatest work, *The Creation*. It is the epic poem of music. You must know that I have communicated the contents of my letters to a lady of Vienna, who has taken refuge in these mountains, like many others of the first families of that unfortunate city. The secretary of this lady transcribes my letters, and thus spares me what I consider the most disagreeable of all tiresome things—the going twice over the same ideas. I told her I should be obliged to skim over the *Creation*, which I have not heard more than once or twice. " Well," said she, " I will undertake this letter to your Paris friend." As I made a few polite objections : " Do you think me then incapable," said she, " of writing to an agreeable Parisian, who is fond of *you*, and of music?—No, indeed, Sir; the utmost I shall allow you to do, will be to correct some of the verbal errors of my letter; but be careful not to meddle too much with my ideas: that is all I ask of you."

This preamble is, as you see, a piece of treachery towards her. Do not fail, then, to reply to the letter on the *Creation*, and above all things, criticise it without mercy. Say that my style is effeminate, that I am lost in minutiæ, that I see effects which have never existed, but in my own fancy: and take particular care to reply promptly, in order to prevent any idea of collusion between us. Your criticisms will procure us here some charming sallies of vivacity.

LETTER XVIII.

Salzburg, May 31, 1809.

WE are always complaining, my friend, that we have come into the world too late, that we have to admire only what is past, and are contemporary with nothing great in the arts. But, great men are like the summits of the Alps; when you are in the valley of Chamouny, Mont Blanc itself, amidst neighbouring summits covered like it with snow, seems no more than any other lofty mountain; but when, on your return to Lausanne, you see it towering above every thing that surrounds it; when, at a still greater distance, in the plains of France, after every other mountain has disappeared, you still behold in the horison this enormous white mass, you recognise the Colossus of the ancient world. How have you learned in France, vulgar souls as you are, to appreciate the genius of Moliere?—by experience only—by seeing that, after a century and a half, he alone still rises above the horison. We are in the same situation with respect to music, as the Parisians of the time of Louis XIV. were with respect to literature. The constellation of great men is but just set.

None of the academicians have produced a more celebrated work than the *Creation*, which will probably descend to posterity.

I am of opinion that Pergolese's *Stabat Mater*, and one of his interludes, that the *Buona Figluola*, and the *Dido* of Piccini, the *Barber of Seville*, and the *Frascatana* of Paesiello, the *Matrimonio segreto*, and the *Horatii* of Cimarosa, the *Don Juan*, and the *Figaro* of Mozart, the *Miserere* of Jomelli, and a few other works, will bear it faithful company.

You shall hear, my dear friend, what we at Vienna admire in this work. Recollect, that in proportion to the facility with which I could render my ideas intelligible to you, if we were conversing by the side of a pianoforte, will be the difficulty of conveying them by the post from Vienna to Paris;—to that scornful Paris, where they think that what cannot be comprehended at once, and without effort, is not worth taking the trouble to understand. The case is always very plain; when the alternative is, either that he who addresses you is a fool, or that there is some little deficiency on your part, you never hesitate in your decision.

Long before Haydn rose to the Creation, he had composed (in 1774) an oratorio entitled *Tobias*, an indifferent performance, two or three passages of which only, announce the great master. You know that, while in London, Haydn was struck with Handel's music: he learned from the works of the English musician the art of being majestic. One day at Prince Schwartzenberg's, when Handel's *Messiah* was performed, upon expressing my admiration of one of the sublime choruses of that work, Haydn said to me thoughtfully, "This man is the father of us all."

I am convinced that if he had not studied Handel, he would never have written the Creation: his genius was fired by that of this master. It was remarked by every one here, that after his return from London, there was more grandeur in his ideas;* in

---

* Haydn was present at the performance in Westminster Abbey, in 1791, and there heard, for the first time, the effect of an orchestra of more than a thousand performers—viz.

Violins	250	Oboes	40	VOCAL.	
Violas	50	Bassoons	40	Trebles	160
Violoncellos	50	Horns	12	Altos	92
Double Basses	27	Trumpets	14	Tenors	152
		Trombones	12	Basses	159
Drums	8.	Organ	1.	Total	1077.

This vast assemblage attracted persons from the most distant parts of Europe, who returned gratified by the extraordinary effects which they had heard. The union of so many voices and instruments, in one band, forms an epoch in the history of the art. The writer noticed two circumstances worthy of remark. 1. The great softness with which the songs were executed. Although 377 stringed instruments accompanied the single voice, such was the lightness of the effect, that they did not overpower, or incommode it. From the great extent of the surface from which the sounds emanated, they were diffused through the atmosphere, so as completely to fill it. No single instrument was heard, but all were blended together in the softest showers of harmony.

short, he approached, as far as is permitted to human genius, the unattainable object of his songs. Handel is simple; his accompaniments are written in three parts only; but to use a Neapolitan phrase of Gluck's,

---

2. The loud parts, which it was thought would have been too violent for the ear to sustain, fell far short of that breadth of tone in the bass, which was desired. The foundation was too slight for so vast a superstructure; there was not a sufficient mass of sound in the lower part,—nor did it sink deep enough.

The instruments at present known, are inadequate to pour upon the orchestra that volume of sound, which the pieces of the great German composers demand. It is in the lower regions of the scale, that we are most deficient in power. One or two octaves have been added to its height, during the last century, but no one has yet dared the ' unfathomable depths' of harmony. The magnitude of sound desired, might perhaps be obtained by causing large bodies to revolve in the air by means of machinery. The note produced would depend on their form, and the degree of rapidity with which they were whirled. Immense tubes upon the principle of the *trombone* might also be worked by the same means, so as to descend two octaves below that instrument. It is only by means of engines of this kind, that the grand orchestra can be brought to perfection, or the full effect of many awful combinations of the modern art displayed.   G.

there is not a note that does not *draw blood*. Handel was very sparing in his use of wind-instruments, the harmony of which has a sweetness even superior to that of the human voice. Cimarosa has employed flutes only in the first passages of the *Matrimonio segreto ;* Mozart, on the other hand, makes a constant use of them..

The *Oratorio* was originally invented in 1530, by St. Philip Neri, for the purpose of awakening a somewhat profane zeal in Rome, by gratifying the senses with the interest and voluptuousness of the drama.

Before the time of Haydn, it was thought to have obtained perfection in the hands of Marcello, Hasse, and Handel, who have written so many, and such sublime ones. Zingarelli's *Destruction of Jerusalem,* which is performing at Paris, and which pleases you, notwithstanding its unmerited mutilations, is no longer a proper oratorio. A pure work in this department ought, like those of the masters I have just mentioned, to present a mixture of the grave and *fugued* style of church music, with the clearness and expression of that of the theatre. The oratorios of Handel and Marcello have *fugues* in almost every scene; and Weigl has done the same in his great oratorio of the Passion. The Italians of the present day, on the contrary, have brought the oratorio very near to the opera. Haydn intended to follow the former, but his ardent genius could feel no enthusiasm except when employed upon its own productions.

One of Haydn's friends was the Baron *Von Swieten,* the emperor's librarian, a very learned man, even in music, and a tolerable composer. The baron was of opinion that music, which succeeds so well in expressing the passions, might also describe the objects of nature, by awakening in the mind of the auditor the emotions which these objects occasion. Men admire the sun; by exciting, therefore, the highest degree of admiration, we shall recal the idea of the sun. This mode of reasoning may appear rather superficial, but M. Von Swieten firmly believed in it. He pointed out to his friend, that though some scattered passages of the descriptive genus were to be met with in the works of the great masters, yet the harvest of this field remained on the whole untouched. He proposed to him to be the *Delille* * of music, and the invitation was accepted.

Handel might have found in the works of Milton the subject of the oratorio of the Creation; but, I know not why, that great composer did not avail himself of it. *Lydley* extracted a second oratorio from the text of Milton; and when Haydn finally quitted London, Salomon the professor gave him *Lydley's* words. Haydn brought them with him to Vienna, without much intention of making use of them; but M. Von Swieten, to encourage him, not only translated the English text into German, but added choruses, airs, and duets, in order that his friend's talent might have more frequent opportunities of displaying itself.†

---

* Delille, though far inferior to our Thompson, of whom he is often an unsuccessful imitator, is considered as occupying his place in the literature of France. T.

† The original contains so gross an anachronism, that I cannot suppose the passages to be correct, and have,

Haydn was sixty-three years old when he undertook this great work; and was employed two whole years upon it. When urged to bring it to a conclusion, he calmly replied, " I spend much time over it, because I intend it to last a long time."

In the beginning of the year 1798, the oratorio was completed; and, in the following Lent, it was performed, for the first time, in the rooms of the Schwartzenberg palace, at the expense of the *Dilettanti* society, who had requested it from the author.

---

therefore, turned it as above. The French is as follows: " Du vivant de Handel, Milton avait fait pour ce grand compositeur un oratorio intitulé la Creation du Monde, qui, je ne sais pourquoi, ne fut pas mis en musique."

I am equally at a loss to understand who the *Lydley* here spoken of is. In the score now before me, published at Vienna, under Haydn's own direction the English words are evidently translated from the German. In the chorus, " 'The heavens are telling the glory of God," the passage,

Dem kommenden Tage, sagt es der Tag;

has been converted into nonsense by the attempt to follow the German arrangement of the words. T.

Who can describe the applause, the delight, the enthusiasm of this society. I was present; and I can assure you, I never witnessed such a scene. The flower of the literary and musical society of Vienna were assembled in the room, which was well adapted to the purpose, and Haydn himself directed the orchestra. The most profound silence, the most scrupulous attention, a sentiment, I might almost say, of religious respect, were the dispositions which prevailed when the first stroke of the bow was given. The general expectation was not disappointed. A long train of beauties, to that moment unknown, unfolded themselves before us; our minds, overcome with pleasure and admiration, experienced, during two successive hours, what they had rarely felt,—a happy existence, produced by desires, ever lively, ever renewed, and never disappointed.

You talk so much in France of *Delille*, and description, that I shall make no apology for a digression respecting descriptive music. Digression, and description, go hand in hand, and the latter would die of inanition, if stripped of all that did not belong to it.

A strong objection may be raised against descriptive music. Some unlucky wag may say, in the words of Voltaire,

> Mais, entre nous, je crois que vous n'existez pas.

They who believe in the *real presence,* reason as follows: Every one must be sensible that music may imitate nature in two ways; by physical, and by sentimental imitation. You remember in the *Nozze di Figaro,* the *tin, tin,* and the *don, don,* by which Susanna so humourously mimics the sound of Count Almaviva's bell, when he summoned her husband for some long commission, in the duet,

> Se a caso madama
> Ti chiama, &c.

This is physical imitation. In a German opera, a stupid fellow falls asleep on the stage, while his wife, at the window, sings a duet with her lover. The physical imitation of the snoring of the husband, forms a humourous bass to the soft things which the lover is addressing to the wife : here again is an exact imitation of nature.*

This direct imitation amuses for a moment, but soon tires. In the sixteenth century, some of the Italian masters made this species of imitation the basis of a whole opera. In the *Podesta di Coloniola,* the professor Melani has inserted the following air, during which the whole orchestra imitates the animals mentioned in it.

> Talor la granochiella nel pantano
> Per allegrezza canta, quà, quà, rà ;
> Tribbia il grillo, trì, trì, trì ;
> L'agnellino fa bè, bè ;
> L'usignuolo, chiù, chiù, chiù ;
> Ed il gal curi chì, chì.

The learned will tell you that in ancient times Aristophanes employed this kind of imitation on the theatre.† Haydn has used it with great moderation in the *Creation,* and the

---

* That is,—of Nature *a la Française.*   T.

† The verses in the play of 'The Frogs' are known to every school-boy.

βρεκεκεκὶξ, κοὰξ, κοάξ.

BATPAXOI. *Passim.*   T.

Four Seasons. He has given, for instance, most beautifully, the cooing of the doves;* but he resolutely opposed the descriptive baron, who was desirous of hearing also the croaking of the frogs.

In music, the best physical imitation is, perhaps, that which only just indicates its object; which shews it to us through a veil, and abstains from scrupulously representing nature exactly as she is. This kind of imitation is the perfection of the descriptive department. Gluck has given a pleasing instance of it in the air of *The Pilgrim of Mecca*, which resembles the murmur of a brook. Handel has imitated the tranquil fall of the snow, the flakes of which gently descend to the silent earth;† and Marcello has surpassed every rival in his cantata of *Calisto transformed into a bear*.

---

* The beauty of the imitative passage, is nearly lost by the injudicious arrangement of the English words. The literal translation of the original is

'And sweetly—coo the tender turtle-doves.   T.

† We believe no such passage is to be found in his works.   G.

The spectator shudders at the ferocity of the savage accompaniment, which represents the cries of the furious bear, at the moment when Juno transforms the unfortunate nymph into a cruel and pitiless brute.

It is this species of imitation which Haydn has carried to perfection. You are aware, my friend, that all the arts are founded, to a certain degree, on what is not true: an obscure doctrine, notwithstanding its apparent clearness, but from which the most important principles are derived. It is thus that from a dark grotto springs the river which is to water vast provinces. We will one day discuss this subject more at length.

You have more pleasure in seeing a beautiful picture of the garden of the Tuileries, than in beholding the same garden, faithfully reflected, from one of the mirrors of the chateau. Yet the scene displayed in the mirror has far more variety of colouring than the painting, were it the work of Claude Lorrain: the figures have motion; every thing is more true to nature: still you cannot help preferring the picture. A skilful artist never departs from that degree of falsity which is allowed in the art he professes. He is well aware that it is not by imitating nature to such a degree as to produce deception, that the arts give pleasure: he makes a distinction between those accurate daubs called eye-traps, and the St. Cecilia of Raphael.

Imitation should produce the effect which the object imitated would have upon us, did it strike us in those fortunate moments of sensibility and enjoyment which awaken the passions.

So much for the *physical* imitation of nature by music.

The other kind of imitation, which we shall denominate *sentimental*, (if you do not think the term too ridiculous) retraces not things, but the feelings which they inspire. The air,

Deh ! Signore !

sung by Paolino in the *Matrimonio segreto*, does not exac ly describe the distress of a man who sees his mistress carried off by a great lord, but it paints a profound and tender sadness The words particularise this tenderness, draw the outlines of the piece, and the union of the words and the music, for ever inseparable in our hearts when we have once heard them, forms the most lively picture of impassioned feeling ever drawn.

Music of this sort, like the impassioned passages of the *Nouvelle Héloise*, or the *Letters of a Portuguese Nun*, may seem tiresome to many persons:

On peut être honnête homme,

and not relish it. A man may have this little deficiency, and be very remarkable on other accounts. I would lay a wager that Mr. Pitt cared very little for the air,

Fra mille perigli,

sung by madame Barilli in the *Nemici generosi;* and yet, if ever I have a kingdom to govern, Mr. Pitt may be sure of being minister of finance.*

Will you allow me to make a very ridiculous comparison? Will you promise, seriously,

---

* Would to heaven that he had never been ours!—but the date of this letter is 1809. T.

not to laugh? It is a German idea with which I am going to present you. I have been reading in *Othilia,* or *The Elective Affinities* of Göthe, the following

Fragment of a letter of Othilia.

"In the evening, I went to the opera with the captain. It began later than in our little town, and we could not talk without being overheard. We insensibly began to examine the company who surrounded us. I wished to work, and asked the captain for my bag. He gave it me, but entreated me, in a low voice, not to take out my net. I assure you, said he, that to work in an opera-box will appear ridiculous at Munich, at *Lambach* it is all very well. I had already got my purse in one hand, and the little bobbin of gold thread in the other, and was going to begin my work. 'Stay,' said the captain, alarmed, 'I will tell you a story about gold thread bobbins.'— 'Is it a fairy tale?'—' Unfortunately it is not.'

"I was involuntarily comparing the sensibility of each of the spectators who surround us, to your little bobbin of gold thread. The bobbin, which is in the mind of each of those who have taken a ticket, is more or less supplied with gold thread. The enchanter Mozart must seize by his magic sounds the end of this thread; the possessor of the bobbin then begins to feel, and continues to do so as long as the golden thread is winding off his bobbin. But no sooner is it exhausted, no sooner does the musician paint a degree of emotion which the auditor has never experienced, than, crack! away goes the thread, and the interest of the auditor expires. The furniture of the bobbin consists in the recollections of an impassioned heart. Of what use is all the talent of Mozart when exerted on unfurnished bobbins?

"Take *Turcaret** to the *Matrimonio segreto;* however abundant the gold thread on his coat, there is very little on the bobbin, to which we compare his mind: soon will it be exhausted, and Turcaret will be tired of the sighs of Caroline. And very naturally. What

---

Turcaret is the principal character in Le Sage's celebrated comedy of that name, written to satirize the *farmers-general* of France. T.

sympathy can he feel with her recollections? What are the strongest emotions which he has experienced. The vexation of finding himself taken in for a large sum in some bankruptcy; the misfortune of seeing the fine varnish of his chariot scratched by a cart; these are the sorrows which would call forth his sensibility. For the rest, he has had a good dinner, is in good spirits, and would like a country-dance. His wife, on the contrary, who is seated by him, and who has lost an adored lover in the last campaign, comes to the performance without any expectation of pleasure, from mere considerations of propriety. She is pale; her eye fixes on nothing with interest: she takes but little at first, in the situation of Caroline.

"The daughter of Geronimo has her lover with her; he is alive, how can she be unhappy? The music becomes almost intolerable to this suffering heart, which would gladly relinquish its sensibility. The magician has great difficulty in seizing the golden thread; but, at length, she becomes attentive, her eye fixes, and becomes moist. The profound distress expressed in the air

Deh! Signore!

begins to affect her. Her tears are on the point of flowing; she is embarrassed to conceal them from her husband, who is dropping asleep, and who would think all this emotion very silly. The composer will lead this poor afflicted spirit wherever he chooses; many tears will it cost her: long will the golden thread last. Look at the people about you; read in their eyes ..... The performance began."

When music succeeds in pourtraying imagery, as the stillness of a fine summer's night, for instance, we say that it is picturesque. The *Creation* is the most beautiful work of this kind, as *Don Juan,* and the *Matrimonio segreto,* are the finest examples of expressive music.

The Creation commences with an overture representing Chaos. The ear is struck with a dull and indefinite noise, with inarticulate sounds, with notes destitute of any perceptible melody. Some fragments of agreeable passages are next perceived, but still imperfectly formed, and always deprived of cadence. Afterwards follow half-formed images, some grave, others tender : every thing is mingled ; the agreeable and the powerful succeed each other accidentally ; the great borders on the little ; the austere and the cheerful are confounded together. An assemblage the most singular of all the figures of music, of trills, flights, *mordenti,* syncopes, discords, give, it is said, a very good idea of Chaos.*

---

* The writer of these notes gave a short description of the chaos, in a paper which he transmitted to the Monthly Magazine, for March, 1811, which is here quoted, for the purpose of shewing how very similar were the sensations produced upon his mind upon hearing this extraordinary composition.

" Were it necessary to bring farther illustrations of the superior powers of the new music, compared with that of the ancients, we might attempt a description of the Chaos, which opens the work we have been quoting.

" It commences with all the known instruments, displayed in 23 distinct parts. After these are amalgamated in one tremendous note, a slight motion is made percep-

It is my imagination which tells me this. I admire the talent of the artist: I recognise in his performance every thing that I have mentioned; I may admit, that probably it could not be better done: but still I would ask baron Von Swieten, who formed the idea of this symphony: "Is it possible to describe

---

tible in the lower parts of the band, to represent the rude masses of nature in a state of Chaos. Amidst this turbid modulation, the bassoon is the first that makes an effort to rise, and extricate itself from the cumbrous mass. The sort of motion with which it ascends, communicates a like disposition to the surrounding materials, but which is stifled by the falling of the double basses, and the *contra fagotto.*

"In this mingled confusion, the clarionett struggles with more success, and the ethereal flutes escape into air. A disposition verging to order is seen and felt, and every resolution would intimate shape, and adjustment, but not a concord ensues! After the volcanic eruptions of the *clarini* and *tromboni,* some arrangement is promised; a precipitation follows of the discordant sounds, and leaves a misty effect that happily expresses the 'spirit of God moving upon the face of the waters.' At the fiat 'Let there be light!' the instruments are unmuted, and the audience is lost in the refulgence of the harmony." G.

the Chaos by music? Would any one who had not received a previous intimation, recognise the Chaos in this overture?" I will candidly confess one thing, which is, that in a ballet which Viganò caused to be performed at Milan, and in which he has represented Prometheus inspiring with souls human beings not yet raised above the brutes, this chaotic music, illustrated by the dancing of three charming actresses, expressing with perfect nature the first dawn of sentiment in the mind of beauty; I will confess, I say, that this commentary has displayed to me all the merit of this symphony; I now understand and derive much pleasure from it. All the other music of the Prometheus appeared to me insignificant and tiresome in comparison.

After having seen Viganò's ballet, which drew all Italy to it, I said to myself,—in the Chaotic symphony, the *themes* not being resolved, there is no melody; consequently no gratification for the ear; consequently no music. It is as if you should require a painter to represent a perfectly dark night, a total absence of light. Would a piece of canvas in a frame, let it be as black as it would, be a picture?

Music reappears in all her charms in Haydn's oratorio, when the angels begin to relate the great work of the Creation. We soon come to the passage which describes the creation of light,

"*And God said; let there be light! and there was light!*"

It must be confessed that nothing can have a grander effect. Before this fiat of the Creator, the musician has gradually diminished the chords; he introduces the unison, and the piano still growing softer, as the suspended cadence approaches:—at last this cadence bursts forth in the most sonorous manner at the words,

"*And there was light!*"

This burst of the whole orchestra in the resounding key of C, accompanied with all the harmony possible, and prepared by the gradual fading of the sounds, actually produces upon us, at a first representation, the effect of a thousand torches suddenly flashing light into a dark cavern.

The faithful angels afterwards describe, in a fugued passage, the rage of Satan and his accomplices precipitated into an abyss of torments by the hand of him whom they hate. Here Milton has a rival. Haydn employs profusely all that is disagreeable in the *enharmonic* genus; horrible discords, strange modulations, and chords of the diminished seventh. The harshness of the words further increases the horrors of this chorus. We shudder, but the music begins to describe the beauties of the newly-created earth, the celestial freshness of the first verdure which adorned the world, and our minds are at length tranquillized. The air which Haydn has chosen to describe the groves of Paradise might have been, it is true, of a less common character. There wants here, a little of the heavenly melody of the Italian school. But, in the return of the air, Haydn reinforces it with so much skill, the harmony which accompanies it is so noble, that one must have in one's recollection, the airs of Sacchini, to feel that there is any deficiency in this.*

The delightful retreat of Adam and his companion is disturbed by a tempest; the

---

* We confess we are surprised that the author should set up as a model of imitation, a style so puerile as the Italian. The writers of this school have fancied that melody was a distinct, and superior art, and have even endeavoured to disengage it from harmony.

If we look into the compositions of the last century, we cannot but notice the meagerness of the accompaniment. It was a notion with them, that a full chord would overload, and destroy the melody, and we accordingly find all the works of that period, of a light, and flimsy texture, wholly devoid of that strength, and force, which characterize the German school. To the latter we are indebted for all the discoveries in harmony;—for those new admixtures of sound, which have exploded the absurd phraseology of chords by *supposition, retardation, suspension,* and the like.

As for the air here referred to, it is not to be found in the Oratorio. The description of the groves occurs in the last part of the song, " *With verdure clad,*" which he criticises in the following page, and we know of no other. Did such a song exist in the original manuscript? G.

winds are heard to roar; the thunder splits the ear, and resounds at a distance in prolonged rollings; the hail clatters on the leaves; and, lastly, the snow softly descends in large flakes to the silent earth.

Floods of the most brilliant and majestic harmony encompass these descriptions. The songs of the archangel Gabriel, especially, who is the Coryphœus, display, in the midst of the choruses, uncommon energy and beauty.

One of the airs is employed in representing the effects of the waters, from the mighty, roaring billows of the agitated sea, to the little brook which gently murmurs at the bottom of its valley. The little brook is given with uncommon felicity, but it must be confessed, that the very idea of an air intended to describe *the effect of water* has something singular in it, and does not promise any very high gratification.

Correggio may be required to give the picture of a rayless night, or of a sky blazing with radiance in every direction. The idea is absurd; but a Correggio, notwithstanding its absurdity, will find means to introduce a thousand pleasing accessories, and his work will be agreeable.

Some other brilliant points are also distinguished in the Creation: for instance, an air of which Haydn was very fond, and which he had re-cast three times. Its object is to describe the earth putting forth trees, plants, flowers, and odoriferous shrubs of every kind. A tender, gay, and simple air would have been best suited to this purpose: and I must confess I have always thought that, in this favourite air of Haydn's, there was more affectation than grace and ingenuity.

This air is followed by a brilliant fugue, in which the angels praise the Creator, and where Haydn re-appears with all his advantages. The repetition of the subject, which is the essence of the *fugue,* has here the effect of representing the zeal of the angels celebrating, with united voices, their divine Creator.

You next pass to the rising of the

sun, which appears, for the first time, in all the pomp of the most magnificent spectacle, which the eye of man can contemplate.*

It is followed by the rising of the moon, which silently advances through the clouds, and illumines the night with her silver radi-

---

* Perhaps there is nothing in nature, which is capable of being so well represented, by sound, as light. The answer of the blind man, who, on being asked what idea he had of scarlet, replied, that it was like the sound of a trumpet, is less absurd than may at first be apprehended. It should be observed, that the character of different instruments, depends not merely on the acuteness or gravity of their tone, but, also, on the degree of force with which sounds are produced by them. If, as Sir Isaac Newton supposed, the impulse upon the nerves of the eye, produced by colours, is similar in kind, or degree, to that produced upon the ear by sounds, the impression upon the sensorium, or seat of sensation in the brain, will probably be the same, or so nearly so, that the ideas of the respective external objects will be associated in the mind. According to this theory, the different musical instruments may be characterised by correspondent colours, so as to be fancifully classed in the following manner:

ance. It will be observed, that a whole day must be passed over, otherwise the rising of

Wind Instruments.		Stringed Instruments.	
Trombone	Deep Red	Violin	Pink
Trumpet	Scarlet	Viola	Rose
Clarionette	Orange	Violoncello	Red
Oboe	Yellow	Double bass	Deep crimson red
Bassoon (Alto)	Deep Yellow		
Flute	Sky Blue		
Diapason	Deeper Blue		
Double Diapason	Purple		
Horn	Violet		

The sinfonia in the Creation, which represents the rising of the sun, is an exemplification of this theory. In the commencement of this piece, our attention is attracted by a soft streaming note from the violins, which is scarcely discernible, till the rays of sound which issue from the second violin, diverge into the chord of the second, to which is gradually imparted a greater fulness of colour as the violas and violoncellos steal in with expanding harmony.

At the fifth bar, the Oboes begin to shed their yellow lustre, while the flute silvers the mounting rays of the violin. As the notes continue ascending to the highest point of brightness, the orange, the scarlet, and the purple, unite in the increasing splendour; and the glorious orb at length appears refulgent with all the brightest beams of harmony. G.

the sun could not be immediately succeeded by that of the moon; but we are considering a descriptive poem, in which transitions are every thing. The first part concludes with a chorus of angels.

A charming harmonic artifice is observable in the finale of this first part of the Creation. When arrived at the cadence, Haydn does not arrest the orchestra, as is sometimes the case in his symphonies, but falls into modulations ascending by semi tones. The transitions are reinforced by sonorous chords, which seem, at every bar, to announce this cadence, so much desired by the ear, but which is always delayed by some modulation still more unexpected and beautiful. Our astonishment increases with our impatience; and, when the cadence at length arrives, it is saluted with a general burst of applause.

The second part opens with an air majestic in the beginning, afterwards gay, and tender towards the conclusion, describing the creation of the birds. The different characters of this air well represent the audacious eagle, which, just created, seems to spurn the earth, and dart towards the sun, the gaiety of the lark,

> C'est toi, jeune alouette, habitante des airs !
> Tu meurs en preludant a tes tendres concerts,

the amorous doves, and lastly the plaintive nightingale. The accents of the songstress of the Night are imitated as near to nature as possible. A beautiful trio represents the effect produced by the immense whale, as he agitates the waves which are separated by his enormous mass.* A well executed recitative shews us the generous courser, proudly neighing amidst vast meadows: the active and ferocious tyger, rapidly traversing the forests, and gliding

---

* This is not accurate. The trio represents, with inimitable grace, the gently sloping hills, adorned with verdure; the bass solo which describes the vast inhabitants of the sea, follows afterwards.

> " Upheaved from the deep th' immense Leviathan
> Sports on the foaming wave."

The lashing of the tail of this monster, and the dashing of the spray, are admirably given by the sonorous flourishes which start from the double basses. G.

between the trees; the fierce lion roars at a distance, while the gentle sheep, fearless of danger, are peacefully feeding.

An air, full of power and dignity, announces the creation of man. The movement of the harmony, which corresponds with the words

" Behold a man he stands, the King and Lord of all!"

has been well preserved in the German. This language allows of an augmentative figure, which in French is ridiculous, but in German is full of majesty. The text, literally translated, is

" Behold man, the *manly*, the king of nature!"

The epithet added to the word *man*, repels every low and groveling idea, in order to concentrate our attention on the noblest, and most majestic attributes of the exalted, and happy being, whom the Creator has just formed.

The music increases in force and elevation at each of these last words, and makes a superb cadence on "*the king of nature.*" It is impossible not to be struck with it.

The second part of this air, describes the creation of the charming Eve, that beauteous creature, born for love. This termination of the air gives us an idea of Adam s happiness. It is universally esteemed the finest part of the Creation ; and, according to my ideas, the reason is, that Haydn here returns to the empire of the passions, and that his subject was one of the greatest felicities of which the heart of man is susceptible.

The third part of the Creation, is the shortest. It is a beautiful translation of the most pleasing part of Milton's poem. Haydn. paints the transports of the first and most innocent of attachments, the tender converse of the first pair, and their pure and dreadless gratitude towards the infinite goodness which created them, and which seems to have created for them all nature. The most ardent joy breathes in every bar of the *allegro*. There is also apparent in this part, a devotion of a more ordinary kind mingled with terror.

Lastly, a chorus, partly *fugued,* and partly ideal, terminates this astonishing production with the same fire and majesty with which it commenced.*

---

* As our author has only spoken generally, of the third part of this oratorio, we are tempted to continue the description to the end. The air, which represents the Creation of man, is esteemed the chef d'œuvre of the piece. *Cherubini* has copied the subject into his ode on the death of Haydn. The chorus "*Achieved is the glorious work*" is a fugue of great strength, and power, ingeniously accompanied by the orchestra. The sinfonia which opens "*the fair morn*" of creation, is performed by a celestial band of flutes, and horns, aided by the soft *pizzicato* of the stringed instruments. This exquisite harmony ascends to the heavenly vaults with the praises of the blissful pair, and is joined by a choir of angels, chanting "*for ever blessed be his power.*"

The distant effect of the responsive choir gives us an idea of space, and amplitude, which nothing but soft music can produce. It is like that misty atmosphere, which artists, in painting, introduce for the same purpose in their designs. The duetto "*Graceful Consort*" in our opinion, is the most exquisite composition in the work. It is full of tenderness and affection.

The "*dew dropping morn*" is introduced by an inspiring strain from the French horn, which breathes the freshness of that "sweet hour of prime." The chorus commences with the unfortunate word "*sing*" which would be better rendered, "PRAISE *the Lord ye voices all.*"

Haydn had a singular advantage in the composition of the vocal part. He had at his disposal for the soprano, one of the finest female voices then existing, that of mademoiselle *Gherard*.

This music requires to be executed with grace, correctness, and expression. The least ornament would entirely change the character of the style. A *Crivelli* is absolutely necessary; the graces of *Tachinardi* would here be out of place.

The voices, heard amidst this clash of sounds, have a rich and noble effect. The fugue which follows, is strong and masterly. In the alleluia part, the principal voices appear, in *solo*, with singular beauty, and form a fine contrast to the masses of sound, struck out by the orchestra.

The last word of the piece is also unfortunate " His praise shall last for *aye*" and would be better rendered, " *His praise shall last for evermore.*"

The short concussions which terminate this divine Oratorio, leave the mind of the auditor lost in sacred awe at the sublimity of the work which Genius has dared to plan and to execute. G.

LETTER XIX.

Salzburg, June 2, 1809.

My Friend,

I RETURN to our subject. The *Creation* met with rapid success: all the papers of Germany gave an account of the astonishing effect which it had produced at Vienna; and the score, which was printed in a few weeks afterwards, enabled the amateurs throughout Europe to form a judgment of it. The rapid sale which it experienced, added a few hundred louis to the author's little fortune. The publisher had placed German and English words under the music: they were translated into Swedish, French, Spanish, Bohemian, and Italian. The French version is pompously dull, as any one may experience at the Conservatoire de la rue Bergère. The author, however, is not chargeable with the little effect produced by the Creation the first time it was executed at Paris. A few minutes before the performance began at the Opera-house, the infernal machine of the 3d Nivose exploded in the *rue St. Nicaise.*

There are two Italian translations. The first, which is ridiculous, has been printed under the Paris score. The other was superintended by Haydn and the baron Von Swieten, and, though the best, has only been printed under the small score for the piano, published by Artaria. The author, M. Carpani, is a man of talent, and moreover an excellent connoisseur in music. It was executed under the direction of himself and Haydn, at the house of one of those rare men who are wanting to the splendour of France : I mean, the prince Lobkowitz, who employs an illustrious life, and an immense fortune, in enjoying and protecting the arts.

Observe, that it is impossible to judge of this music, which is all harmony, unless that harmony be complete. A dozen singers or instruments collected round a piano-forte, let them be as good as they may, would give but a very imperfect idea of it : whereas a good voice, and a tolerable accompaniment, are sufficient to enable us to enjoy the *Stabat Mater* of Pergolese. This work of Haydn's requires at least twenty-four voices, and sixty instruments. France, Italy, England, Holland, and Russia, have heard it thus performed.

Two things are criticised in the Creation: the vocal part, and the general style of the piece. The songs are certainly above mediocrity, but I am of opinion with the critics, that five or six of *Sacchini's* airs, thrown into this mass of harmony, would have imparted a celestial grace, an ease and a dignity, which we now seek in vain. *Porpora* or *Zingarelli* would perhaps have done the recitatives better.*

---

* Here again we entirely dissent from the author. In our opinion, nothing that the art contains is to be compared, for various and beautiful description, with the recitative in which the Creation of the beasts is related. It begins with the lion:

"*Cheerful roaring stands the tawny lion.*"

In unison with the trombones, is added the *contra-fagotto*, an instrument of terrific power, which is made to fall on a

I must also allow, that a *Marchesi*, a *Pacchiarotti*, a *Tenducci*, an *Aprile*, would despair of executing music of this kind, in which the

---

deep unexpected note, so as to imitate the tremendous roar of the animal. Next,

" *In sudden leaps the flexible tyger appears,*"

whose vigorous alertness is depicted in rapid flights, by the stringed instruments.

" *The nimble stag bears up his branching head,*"

in a *presto*, which succeeds. By the accent here given, the notes are ingeniously made to bound, as it were, in short convulsive steps, which admirably represent the light motions of that graceful animal.

" *The sprightly steed, with flying main, and fiery look,*"

follows next, and affords a further illustration of the power of accent. The music is made to prance; and in a darting flourish, which is affixed to this vigorous passage, the snorting of the noble courser is well conveyed.

As sudden changes in measure, and sound, constitute one of the greatest beauties in music, the author, in this part of the recitative, has introduced a transition which captivates us. To the rude strokes and sudden jirks of the former strains, succeeds a gentle, and placid movement, which depicts the cattle going out " *to feed in meadows green.*" The flute and bassoon begin this pastoral strain, which expresses, by its gentleness, the slow-moving fleecy flocks;

vocal part frequently stops, to give an opportunity for the instruments to unfold the sentiment. At the very commencement, for instance, in the first part of the first tenor air, it is obliged to stop after the words

" Disorder yields,"

to let the instruments come in.

With this exception, Haydn may be defended. I would boldly ask those who criticise him: "What is beauty in singing?" If they are honest, they will reply, that, in music, as in love, it is what we think so, what pleases us. The *Rotondo* of Capri, the *Apollo* of the Belvidere, the *Madonna della Seggiola*, the *Night* of *Correggio*, will be considered as beautiful, wherever man is not savage. While, on the contrary, the works of *Carissimi*, of

---

when, on a sudden, there arises a flutter of tremulous sounds, announcing " *the whirl of a host of insects,*" from which we fall into a slow-moving line of harmony to represent, " *in long dimensions, creeps, with sinuous trace, the worm.*" All these striking imitations are found within the compass of a single recitative.—To what author can we turn for its parallel ? G.

Pergolese, of *Durante,* I do not say in the cold regions of the north, but even in the fine climate which inspired them, are held, indeed, in a sort of traditional esteem, but do not give the same pleasure as formerly. They are still continually talked of, but I see every where preferred, a *rondo* of Andreossi, a scene of Mayer, or the works of some less distinguished composers. I am quite astonished at this revolution, which I have not, indeed, experienced in myself, but which I have seen with my own eyes in Italy. For the rest, it is certainly very natural to think that which pleases us beautiful. What true lover has not been able to say to his mistress,

> *Ma spesso ingiusto al vero,*
> *Condanno ogni altro aspetto;*
> *Tutto mi par difetto*
> *Fuor che la tua beltà.*
> METASTASIO.

Perhaps the reason why the same things are always beautiful in the arts of design is, that in these arts, the intellectual pleasure greatly predominates over the physical. There is more scope for the exercise of our reason.

Every sensible man is aware, for instance, that the figures of Guido are more beautiful than those of Raphael, which in their turn have more expression. In music, on the contrary, where two thirds, at least, of the pleasure is physical, it is the senses which decide. Now the senses may feel pleasure or pain at any given moment, but do not admit of comparison. Every man's experience will shew that the moments in which he has felt the most lively pleasure or pain, leave no very distinct traces in his recollection.

Mortimer returned in a state of anxious solicitude, from a long voyage. He adored Jane; but she had not replied to his letters. On his arrival at London, he went to seek her at her house in the country He arrives: she was walking in the park. He hastens to her with a beating heart: he meets her, she holds out her hand, and receives him with agitation; he sees that he is beloved. As they were walking together in the park, Jane's robe became entangled in a bush of the thorny acacia. In the sequel, Mortimer was happy; but Jane! was faithless. Twenty times have

I maintained that Jane never loved him, but he always mentioned, as a proof of her attachment, the manner in which she received him on his return from the continent. However, he could never give me any particulars; he only starts when he sees an acacia: this is all that he distinctly recollects of the most delightful moment of his life.

Your pleasure increases the first seven or eight times you hear the duet

Piaceri dell' anima, contenti soavi!
CIMAROSA, Nemici Generosi.

But when you have once fully comprehended it, your gratification will diminish at each repetition. If, in music, pleasure be the only thermometer of beauty, this duet will become less admirable, the more you hear it. When you shall have heard it for the thirteenth time, let the actress substitute the duet

Cara, cara!

of the *Matrimonio,* supposing you not to be acquainted with it; this will please you much more because it will be new to you. If you were afterwards asked which of these two duets you thought the most beautiful, and were to reply according to your real sentiments, I imagine you would be not a little embarrassed.

Suppose you had apartments in the palace of Fontainebleau, and that in one of the rooms was placed the St. Cecilia of Raphael. This picture is returned to the Museum, and exchanged for the Rape of Helen by Guido. You admire the charming figures of Hermione and Helen; nevertheless, if you are asked which is the finest of these two pieces, the sublime expression of the St. Cecilia, enchanted with the celestial music, and letting fall the instruments on which she was playing, decides you in its favour, and you award the palm to it. Now, why is this expression sublime? For three or four reasons which I see you ready to state. But this is argument, and an argument that may be written down: whereas it seems to me impossible to write four lines, unless it be in unmeaning, poetical, prose, to prove that the duet *Piaceri dell' anima,* is better or worse than the duet *Cara, cara,* or than that in Figaro, *Crudel perchè finora.*

One cannot feel, at the same moment, the effect of two melodies. The pleasure they may give us does not leave traces in the memory sufficiently strong, to unable us to judge of them at any distance of time.

I see but one exception. A man hears the air,

Fanciulla sventurata.
Nemici Generosi.

at Venice, in the theatre of the Phœnix, sitting by the side of a woman whom he loves to distraction, but who does not return his passion. He afterwards hears again this charming air on his return to France. He starts; with him, ideas of pleasure are for ever associated with these sounds so sweet; but, in this case, this air is like Mortimer's thorny acacia.

The works of great artists, when once they have attained a certain degree of perfection, have equal claims on our admiration: and the preference which we give, sometimes to one, and sometimes to another, depends entirely on our temperament, or the humour we happen to be in. One day it is Dominichino who pleases me, and whom I prefer to Guido: the next, the celestial beauty of the heads of the latter has a superior attraction, and I like the Aurora of the Rospigliosi palace better than the Communion of St. Jerome.

I have frequently heard it remarked in Italy, that in music, beauty consists, in a great degree, in novelty. I am not speaking of the mechanical part of the art. Counterpoint has something mathematical in it; a blockhead, with patience, may become respectably learned in it. This branch has nothing to do with beauty; it has a *regularity* susceptible of demonstration. As for the department of genius, melody, there are no rules for this. No art is so unprovided with precepts for the production of beauty. So much the better for it, and for us.

Genius has pursued its march, but the poor critics have not been able to take account of the path followed by the first geniuses, and to signify to succeeding great men that they were not to depart from it. Cimarosa, when he caused his air,

Pria che spunti in ciel l'aurora

to be performed at Prague, was not told by pedants: "Your air is beautiful because you have adhered to such a rule, established by Pergolese, in such an air; but it would have been still more so, if you had conformed yourself to a certain other rule, from which Galuppi never departed." Did not the painters, of the time of Dominichino, almost persuade him that his Martyrdom of St. Andrew at Rome was not beautiful?

I might here tire you with pretended rules laid down for the construction of beautiful airs; but I am generous, and resist the temptation of inflicting upon you the ennui they have occasioned myself.

The more melody and genius there is in any music, the more liable it is to be affected by the instability of human things; the more harmony it contains, the more secure is it of success. The grave church chants, contemporary with the divine *Serva Maestra* of Pergolese, have not worn out with the same rapidity.

But, I am, perhaps, talking at random on this subject, for I must confess, that this

Serva Maestra, with Italian singing, gives me more pleasure, and especially a more inward pleasure, than all the operas of the very modern Paer put together.

If we are right in our remarks on that part of music which soonest feels the effects of time, Haydn may expect a longer life than any other composer. He has displayed his genius in the harmony, that is to say, in the durable part.

I give you the following quotation from the Spectator, that is, from a very rational writer.

" Recitative music, in every language, should be as different as the tone, or accent, of each language; for, otherwise, what may properly express a passion in one language, will not do it in another. Every one, who has been long in Italy, knows very well that the cadences in their *Recitativo*, are only the accents of their language, made more musical, and tuneful.

" Thus the notes of interrogation, or admiration, in the Italian music, are not unlike the ordinary tones of an English voice, when we are angry: insomuch, that I have often seen our audiences extremely mistaken, as to what has been doing on the stage, and expecting to see the hero knock down his messenger, when he has been asking him a question; or fancying that he quarrels with his friend when he only bids him good-morrow."

SPECTATOR, No. 29.

Music, which acts upon the imagination, has a more intimate relation, than painting for instance, to the peculiar organization of the individual. If it gratifies him, it is by causing his fancy to present to him certain agreeable images. His heart, disposed to tenderness, by the actual pleasure he receives from the sweetness of the sounds, delights in these images, enjoys the felicity they present to him, with an ardour which he would not experience at any other time. Now it is evident that these images must be different, according to the different imaginations which produce them. What can be more opposite than a fat, well-fed German, fresh, and fair, drinking beer, and eating bread and butter all day, and a dark, brown Italian, thin almost to leanness, with sallow complexion, and eye of fire, living on coffee, and other slender and sober diet! How can the same thing be expected to please beings so dissimilar, speaking languages so totally different from each other. They cannot possibly have the same abstract idea of beauty. If the rhetoricians will insist that there is an ideal beauty common to both, the pleasure, produced by what these two persons equally admire, will be necessarily very faint. They will both admire the funeral games of the fifth book of the Eneid: but whenever you desire to excite in them a strong emotion, you must present to them images analogous to their very different natures. How will you bring a poor Prussian student of Königsberg, who is shivering with cold for eleven months of the year, to relish the eclogues of Virgil, and to feel the pleasure of being in the shade of a cool grotto by the side of a bubbling spring?

Viridi projectus in antro.

A comfortable room, well heated by a good

stove, would afford him a much more agreeable image.

We may apply this illustration to all the fine arts. To an honest Fleming, who has never studied design, the forms of Ruben's women are the most beautiful in the world. Let not us who admire slenderness of form above every thing else, and to whom the figures even of Raphael's women appear rather massive, be too ready to laugh at him. If we were to consider the matter closely, it would appear that each individual, and, consequently, each nation, has a separate idea of beauty, which is a combination of every thing that pleases him most in things of the same nature.

The ideal beauty of Paris, is that which most gratifies the majority of the Parisians. In music, for instance, M. Garat pleases them a hundred times more than Madame Catalani, though all, I know not why, would not allow that they were of this opinion. In a matter so indifferent to the welfare of the state as the fine arts, what mischief could this harmless liberty occasion?

We need only open our eyes to perceive, twenty times in a day, that the French nation has changed its habits within the last thirty years. Nothing less resembles what we were in 1780, than a young Frenchman of 1814. We were lively and restless;—these gentlemen are almost English. There is more gravity; more of what is rational, and less of what is agreeable. Our youth, who will be the whole nation twenty years hence, having changed, our poor rhetoricians must reason more beside the mark than usual, if they will have the fine arts to remain the same.

" For my own part, I must confess," said a young colonel to me, " that, since the campaign of Moscow, I do not think Iphigenia in Aulis so fine a tragedy. Achilles appears to me rather too much of a dupe, and I begin to prefer Shakespeare's Macbeth."

But I am rather wandering: it is evident, that I am not a young Frenchman of 1814. Let us return to our point, which is to ascertain, whether, in music, the ideal beauty of a Dane can be the same with that of a Neapolitan.

The nightingale is a favourite in every country; and the reason is, that its song, heard during the fine evenings at the close of spring, which are every where the most delightful moments of the year, is agreeable in itself, and associated with a thousand charming ideas. It signifies not that I am a native of the north; the song of the nightingale always reminds me of my walks home at Rome, after the *conversazioni*, at two o'clock in the morning, during the fine summers' nights. One is deafened, in passing along those solitary streets, by the vibrating notes of the nightingales which are kept in every house. The song of this bird reminds us the more strongly of the fine days of the year, as from not being able to hear it whenever we please, we do not wear out this pleasure by partaking of it at unfavourable periods, when we are not disposed to enjoy it.

Haydn wrote his Creation to German words, which are not capable of Italian melody. How could he, even if he had wished it, have written melodies like those of *Sacchini?*

Born in Germany, knowing his own feelings, and those of his countrymen, he apparently wished to please them in the first place. We may criticise a man when we see him mistake the road to his object; but is it reasonable to quarrel with him on the choice of the object? A great Italian master has produced the only criticism worthy of Haydn and of himself. He has re-cast, from one end to the other, all the music of the Creation, which will not see the light till after his death. This master thinks that Haydn, in symphony, is a man of genius, but, in every thing else, only estimable. For my own part, I am of opinion, that when the two *Creations* shall both have been published, the German one will always be preferred at Vienna, and the Italian at Naples.*

---

* I hope I may be excused a repetition. I have a great desire to quote a letter, the original of which I sent to my friend about the same time with the present. It was written in French, by an amiable canoness of Brunswick, whose loss we have now to deplore.

She thus concluded a letter on Werter, who, it is known, was born at Brunswick, and was the son of the abbé de J..... She was describing exactly, at my request, the kind of taste which Werter had in music.

..... " As of all the arts, music is that which is most capable of giving delicate shades, and whose descriptive powers follow the movements of the soul the farthest, I may make a distinction between sensibility after the manner of Mozart, and sensibility after the manner of Cimarosa.

" Forms like that of Wilhelmina de M . . . . and of the angel in the picture of Parmesano, which I have in my chamber, (the Madonna al longo collo,) seem to me, to announce beings whose strength is overcome by their sensibility—who, in moments of emotion, become *emotion itself.* There is no room for any thing besides ;— courage, a regard for reputation,—every thing is, not merely surmounted, but disregarded. Such a being would the beauteous angel just mentioned be, singing at the feet of an adored godmother

Voi che sapete.

The northern nations seem to me to be the subjects of this music, *which is their queen.*

" When you are better acquainted with Germany, and have met with some of those unfortunate girls who every year die of love in this country—don't laugh, monsieur le François—you will see the sort of power which our music has over us. Look round on a Sunday evening at *Hantzgarten,* or in those English pleasure-grounds where the young people of the cities of the north go to walk on holiday evenings. Look at those pairs of lovers who are taking coffee by the side of their parents, while troops of Bohemian musicians are playing on the horn, their walzes, and their slow and affecting music.

Observe their eyes fix; see them press each other's hands over the little table, under the eye of their mother; for they are, as we say here, *betrothed*. Well; a conscription carries off the lover; his *betrothed* is not absolutely in despair, but she loses her spirits, and sits up all night to read romances. In a little time, her breast is affected,—and she dies without the best physicians being able to find a remedy for this malady. But nothing appears externally. You perhaps saw her, a fortnight before, making tea at her mother's house;— you merely thought her out of spirits. You inquire about her, and receive for answer, ' Poor such a one ?' —' She is dead of grief.' There is nothing extraordinary in such a reply in this country. ' And where is her lover?'—' At the army, but we hear nothing from him.'

"These are the hearts which Handel, Mozart, Bocchirini, and Berda, know how to touch.

"The brown and energetic women which the south of Europe produces, must be fond of the music of Cimarosa. They would poignard themselves for a living lover, but would never die with languishing after a faithless one.

"The female airs of Cimarosa, and of all the Neapolitan masters, indicate power, even in moments the most impassioned. In the *Nemici generosi*, which was performed at Dresden two years ago, our Mozart would have made something divinely tender of

Non son villana, ma son dama.

Cimarosa has made a lively and rapid little air of this declaration, because the situation called for it; but a German woman would not have pronounced these words without tears."

FRAGMENT

OF THE REPLY TO THE PRECEDING LETTER.

Montmorency, June 29, 1809.

I AM charmed with your letter, my dear Edward; our ideas are the same in other words. Do not give yourself any concern. It is not the fault of your great composers, that their charming melodies are not equally agreeable to every one. This arises from the very nature of the delightful art which renders them immortal. In respect of the mode in which they give pleasure, sculpture and music are as opposite as possible.

It is to be observed, that it is always from sculpture that we draw our examples of ideal beauty. Now, in sculpture, there is a general idea of beauty, because there is much less difference in the form of the human body in different countries, than in the constitution which is given by the climate. A handsome young peasant from the neighbourhood of Copenhagen, and a young Neapolitan, equally distinguished for his beauty, differ less in external form, than in their passions and characters. It is, therefore, more easy to establish an universal idea of beauty in the art which imitates these exterior forms, than in those which call into action the various affections of minds so different.

Besides the absolute beauty of the figure, much importance is attached, in the arts of design, to expression. But these arts do not imitate the moral nature of man so closely as poetry, and, consequently, are not liable to displease a Dane, because they are warmly admired by a Neapolitan. In a thousand actions of life, very capable of being exactly represented in romance or comedy, that which appears charming at Naples, will be thought outré and indelicate at Copenhagen; and that which is delicate in Zealand, will be frozen on the banks of the Sebetes. The poet, then, must make his choice, and endeavour to please either the one or the other. Canova, on the contrary, is not embarrassed by such considerations. His Paris and his Helen will be as divine at Copenhagen as at Rome, only every man will enjoy their beauty, and admire their author, in proportion to his own sensibility. Why? Because these charming figures represent only moderate affections, common to the Dane and the Neapolitan. Had they been capable of imitating stronger passions, they would soon have arrived at the point where the sensibility of the native of the south separates from that of the inhabitant of the north. What then must be the embarrassment of the musician, who, of all artists, most closely describes the affections of the human heart; yet who can only describe them, by bringing into action the imagination and the sensibility of each of his auditors, and by incorporating them, so to speak, with his work! How could you possibly expect a native of the north to feel Cimarosa's air, *Come! io vengo per sposarti!* The distracted lover who sings it, must appear to him neither more nor less than a madman escaped from Bedlam. *God save the King*, on the other hand, would, probably, be thought insipid at Naples. Do not then be uneasy about your dear Cimarosa; he may go out of fashion, but the justice of posterity will assuredly place him, for talent, by the side of Raphael. Only the talent of the latter is felt by all the world, or at least by all Europe; whereas, in music, it is natural that each country should have its Raphael. Each of the worlds which revolve over our heads has, in like manner, its sun, which, to the neighbouring worlds, is only a star, more or less brilliant according to its distance. So Handel, that sun of England, is only a star of the first magnitude to the country of the Mozarts and Haydns; and as we approach nearer the equator, he is reduced to a size still smaller, to the happy inhabitant of the shore of Pausilippo.

LETTER XX.

Halein, June 5, 1809.

My dear Louis,

Two years after the Creation, Haydn, animated by success, and encouraged by his friend Von Swieten, composed a new oratorio, *The Four Seasons.* The descriptive baron had taken the text of them from Thompson. There is less sentiment in this work than in the Creation, but the subject admitted of gaiety, the joy of the vintage, profane love; and the Four Seasons would be the finest thing extant, in the department of descriptive music, if the Creation did not exist.

The music of it is more learned, and less sublime, than that of the Creation. It, nevertheless, surpasses its elder sister in one point; that is, the quartetts. Why, in other respects, should we find fault with this music? It is not Italian, say you. Be it so. I allow, that the symphony suits the stubborn organization of the Germans; but this is to our advantage. So, in the other arts, it is not amiss that each country should have a peculiar cast of countenance. The general pleasure is augmented by it. We enjoy the Neapolitan airs of Paesiello, and the German symphonies of Haydn. When shall we see Talma, after having one day performed Andromache, exhibit to us the next, the unhappy Macbeth drawn into guilt by the ambition of his wife? It should be known, that the Macbeth, Hamlet, &c. of M. Ducis, though no doubt very good pieces, have about as much resemblance to the plays of the English poet, as to those of Lope de Vega. It seems to me, that with respect to works of romance, we are precisely at the same point as we were fifty years ago with regard to Italian music. There will be a great outcry; pamphlets, satires, perhaps even blows, will be dealt about at some future time, when the public, at rest from political agitation, shall be competent to judge of literature. But this public, tired at length of the insipid pupils of the great Racine, will be desirous of seeing Hamlet, aud Othello. The comparison fails only in one point; which is, that these pieces will not supersede Phœdra, or Cinna; and that Moliere will still remain without a rival—simply, because he is unique.

The text of the Four Seasons is despicable. As to the music, represent to yourself a gallery of pictures, differing in style, subject, and colouring. This gallery is divided into four apartments, in the middle of each of which, appears a large principal picture.

The subjects of these four pictures are, for the first, the snow, the north winds, the frost, and its horrors.

In the Summer, a storm; in the Autumn, hunting; and in Winter, the village evening.

It immediately occurs, that an inhabitant of a more fortunate climate, would not have introduced snow, and the horrors of winter, into a picture of the spring. According to my taste, it is but a dismal commencement of the work. According to the amateurs, these rude sounds have a wonderful tendency to increase the subsequent pleasure.

With you, my friend, I shall not go through the Four Seasons, step by step.

In representing the summer's sun, Haydn was under the necessity of endeavouring to keep clear of the first sun-rise in the Creation; and this art, which we would fain consider as descriptive, is so vague, so anti-descriptive, that, notwithstanding the incredible pains which the first symphonist of the world has taken, he has fallen into some degree of repetition.

The oppression, the exhaustion of every thing that breathes, and even of the plants, during the intense heat of a summer's day, is perfectly given. This very natural description concludes in a general silence. The clap of thunder, with which the storm commences, breaks this silence. Here, Haydn is in his element; all is fire, tumult, noise, and terror. It is one of Michel-Angelo's pictures. At length, the tempest ceases, the clouds disperse, the sun re-appears, the drops of water, with which the leaves of the trees are charged, glitter in the forest; a charming evening succeeds to the storm, night comes on, and all is silent; except that, from time to time, the stillness is broken by the cry of some nocturnal bird, or the sound of a distant bell,

> Che pare il giorno pianger che si muore:
> "*Which seems to mourn the dying day.*"

The physical imitation is here carried to its height. But this tranquil scene forms, by no means, a striking conclusion of the summer, after the tremendous passage of the tempest.

The chase of the stag, with which the autumn opens, is a happy subject for music. Every one recollects the overture of Henry IV.

The vintage, in which some tipplers are singing in one part, while the young people of the village are engaged in dancing, forms an agreeable picture. The song of the drinking party, is blended with the air of a national dance of Austria, arranged as a fugue. The effect of this spirited passage is very great, especially in this country. It is often played in Hungary, during the vintage. It is the only instance, I think, in which Haydn, when directly imitating nature, has availed himself of the predilections of his countrymen as a means of success.

The critics objected to the Four Seasons, that it contained even fewer airs than the Creation, and said that it was a piece of instrumental music, with a vocal accompaniment. The author was growing old. He is also accused, ridiculously enough in my opinion, of having introduced a little gaiety into a serious subject. And why is it serious? Because it is called an *oratorio*. The title may be ill chosen; but is it not rather a fortunate thing, that a symphony, which produces no very profound emotions, should be occasionally lively? The *chilly* accuse him, with more justice, of having put two winters into one year.

The best critique that has been given of this work, is that which Haydn himself addressed to me, when I went to give him an account of the performance of it in the palace Schwartzenberg. The applause had been universal, and I hastened out to congratulate the author. Scarcely had I opened my lips, when the honest composer stopped me: "I am happy to find that my music pleases the public, but I can receive no compliment on this work from you. I am convinced that you feel yourself that it is not the *Creation:* and the reason is this. In the Creation, the actors are angels; here, they are peasants." This remark is excellent, as relating to a man whose talent was rather for the sublime than the tender.

The words of the Four Seasons, commonplace enough in themselves, were flatly translated into several languages. The music was arranged in quartetts, and quintetts, and was introduced still more than that of the Creation, into amateur concerts. The little melody contained in it, being principally in the orchestra, the air remains almost entire, even when the vocal part is taken away. Further than this, I am probably not a competent judge of the Four Seasons. I never heard it more than once, and then my attention was much diverted.

I was disputing with a Venetian, who sat by me, on the quantity of melody existing in music, towards the middle of the eighteenth century. I remarked that, at that time, there was scarcely any thing that could be called an air, and that the music was doubtless little else than an agreeable noise.

My companion started from his seat at these words, and related to me the adventures of one of his countrymen, the singer Alessandro Stradella, who lived about the year 1650.

He frequented the most distinguished house in Venice, and ladies of the first rank disputed the advantage of taking lessons from him. It was in this way that he became acquainted with Hortensia, a Roman lady, who was beloved by a noble Venetian. Stradella fell in love with her, and had little difficulty in supplanting his rival. He carried off Hortensia to Rome, where they gave it out that they were married. The furious Venetian sent two assassins in search of them, who, after having vainly sought for them in many towns of Italy, at length, discovered the place of their retreat, and arrived at Rome one evening when Stradella was giving an oratorio in the handsome church of St.

John Lateran. The assassins determined to execute their commission when the people came out of the church, and went in to watch one of their victims, and to examine whether Hortensia was among the spectators.

Scarcely had they listened, for a few moments, to the delightful voice of Stradella, than they began to soften. They were seized with remorse, they melted into tears, and their last consideration was how to save the lovers, whose destruction they had sworn. They waited for Stradella at the door of the church, and saw him coming out with Hortensia. They approached, thanked him for the pleasure they had just received, and informed him that he owed his life to the impression which his voice had made upon them. They then explained to him the horrible object of their journey, and advised him to leave Rome immediately, in order to give them an opportunity of making the Venetian believe that they had arrived too late.

Stradella and Hortensia lost no time in profiting by the advice, and repaired to Turin.

The noble Venetian, on receiving the report of his agents, became only the more furious. He went to Rome, for the purpose of concerting his measures with Hortensia's own father. He succeeded in persuading the old man that his dishonour could only be washed away in the blood of his daughter and her ravisher, and the unnatural father set out for Turin, with two assassins, after having procured letters of recommendation to the marquis Villars, who was then the French ambassador at that court.

In the mean time, the duchess regent of Savoy, having heard of the adventure of the two lovers at Rome, was desirous of saving them. She put Hortensia into a convent, and gave Stradella the title of her first musician, as well as apartments in her palace. These precautions appeared to be effectual, and the lovers enjoyed, for some months, a perfect tranquillity, when, one evening, as he was taking the air upon the ramparts of the town, Stradella was attacked by three men, who stabbed him in the breast, and left him for dead. They were the father of Hortensia, and his two companions, who immediately took refuge in the palace of the French ambassador. M. de Villars, unwilling to afford them protection after the commission of a crime so notorious, or to surrender them to justice after having granted them an asylum, gave them an opportunity of escaping a few days afterwards.

Nevertheless, contrary to all expectation, Stradella recovered from his wounds, and the Venetian beheld his projects a second time frustrated; but without abandoning his plans of revenge. Rendered only more wary by his former failures, he sought to take his measures with greater certainty, and contented himself, for the present, with setting spies over Hortensia, and her lover. A year passed in this way. The duchess, more and more interested in their fate, was desirous of marrying them, and rendering their union legitimate. After the ceremony, Hortensia, tired of the confinement of the convent, was desirous of seeing the port of Genoa. Stradella conducted her thither, and the very day after their arrival, they were found poignarded in their bed.

This melancholy adventure is said to have taken place in the year 1670. Stradella was a poet, a composer, and the first singer of his time.

I replied to the compatriot of Stradella, that mere sweetness of sound, though destitute of all melody, gives a very considerable pleasure even to the most savage minds. When Murad IV., after having taken Bagdad by assault, in 1637, ordered a general massacre of the inhabitants, one Persian only dared to raise his voice; he demanded to be conducted to the emperor, as having something of importance to communicate to him before he died.

Having prostrated himself at the feet of Murad, *Scakculi*, such was the Persian's name, cried, with his face to the earth: " Destroy not, O Sultan, with me, an art of more value than thy whole empire: listen to my song, and then thou shalt command my death."

Murad having signified his assent, *Scakculi* drew from under his robe a little harp, and poured forth, extempore, a sort of romance on the ruin of Bagdad. The stern Murad, in spite of the shame which a Turk feels on betraying the least emotion, was melted to tears, and commanded the massacre to be stopped. *Scakculi* followed him to Constantinople, loaded with riches, and introduced there the music of Persia, in which no European has ever been able to distinguish any kind of air whatsoever.

I think I see in Haydn, the Tintoret of music. Like the Venetian painter, he unites to the energy of Michel-Angelo, fire, originality, and fertility of invention. All this is invested with a loveliness of colouring, which renders pleasing even the minutest details. I am, nevertheless, of opinion, that the Tintoret of Eisenstädt, was more profound in his art than the Venetian one; more particularly, he knew how to work slowly.

The mania of comparisons seizes me. I trust you with my collection, on condition that you will not laugh at it too much. I fancy, then, that

Pergolese, and ⎱
Cimarosa . . ⎰ are the Raphaels of music.

Paesiello . . . is . . . . . . Guido
Durante . . . . Lionardo da Vinci
Hasse . . . . Rubens
Handel . . . . Michel Angelo
Galuppi . . . . Bassano.
Jomelli . . . . Lewis Caracci
Gluck . . . . Caravaggio
Piccini . . . . Titian
Sacchini . . . . Correggio
Vinci . . . . Fra Bartolommeo
Anfossi . . . . Albano
Zingarelli . . . . Guerchino
Mayer . . . . Carlo Maratti
Mozart. . . . . Dominichino.*

---

* It is rather remarkable, that the annotator should have compared Mozart to the same painter ; as the following extract from the Monthly Magazine, March, 1811, will shew, " I cannot conclude these observations upon the new music, without paying a tribute to the memory of Mozart. For feeling and expression, this

The least imperfect resemblance, is that of Paesiello and Guido. As for Mozart, Dominichino should have a still stronger cast of melancholy, to resemble him entirely.

The painter had expression, but it was

---

favourite of the muses may be denominated the DOMINICHINO of our art. During the short time that he flourished, he exhibited the most exquisite flights of fancy. His melodies are unrivalled for grace and simplicity; and since his death, it is said that Haydn has affirmed that his compositions were models of the most refined elegance, and that in his old age he was studying the works of his pupil.

" His imagination has infused a sublimity into the opera, that now renders it the highest of all intellectual pleasures. And it is to be lamented that a great nation, like England, has not talent, or ability, sufficient to represent and perform any of the works of this great master.

" We are still doomed to listen to the effeminate strains of Italy, while the gorgeous and terrific *Don Juan*, and the beautiful *Clemenza de Tito* lye unopened, and unknown. But the same apathy and puerility which we have censured in the students of the old school, is found to prevail within the walls of the first theatre in the world; and it is matter of curious moment, that we are now in possession of the very works that are to form the acme of theatrical representation in a succeeding age." G.

confined for the most part to that of innocence, timidity, and respect. Mozart has pourtrayed the most impassioned and delicate tenderness, in the airs,

> *Vedrò mentr'io sospiro*
> of the Count Almaviva;
> *Non so più cosa son, cosa faccio,*
> of Cherubino;
> *Dove son i bei momenti,*
> of the Countess;
> *Andiam, mio bene*
> of Don Juan;

the purest grace in

> *La mia Doralice capace non è*
> in. Cosi fan tutti;

and in

> *Giovanni che fate al amore,*
> of Don Juan.

The air of happiness, and beauty, by which Raphael's figures are distinguished, is clearly to be recognised in the melodies of Cimarosa.

His distressed characters are, in general, drawn with great success; instance in Caroline, in the *Matrimonio segreto*. Those of Mozart, on the contrary, resemble the virgins of Ossian, with fair hair, and blue eyes bedewed with tears. They are not, perhaps, so handsome as these brilliant Italians, but they are more interesting.

Hear the part of the Countess, in the *Nozze di Figaro,* sung by madame Barilli; suppose it played by an impassioned actress, by madame Strina-Sacchi, beautiful as mademoiselle Mars, you will say, with Shakespeare, that she is

Like patience sitting on a monument.

On cheerful days, you will prefer Cimarosa; on melancholy ones, Mozart will have the advantage.

I might lengthen my list by introducing the *mannerist* painters, and placing by the side of their names, those of Gretry, and of almost all the young German and Italian composers. But these ideas are probably so peculiar to the writer, that, to you, they will seem strange.

Baron Von Swieten was desirous of engaging Haydn in a third descriptive oratorio, and would have succeeded; but he was arrested by death. I also stop, after having gone over with you all the compositions of my hero.

Who would have supposed, when I first wrote to you about Haydn, fifteen months ago, that my chattering would have lasted so long?

Your kindness has prevented your being tired with my letters, and they have procured me an agreeable diversion two or three times a-week. Preserve them. If ever I go to Paris, I shall perhaps read them again with pleasure. Adieu.

x

LETTER XXI.

Salzburg, June 8, 1809.

THE musical career of Haydn terminates with the *Four Seasons*. The labour of this work exhausted his declining strength. " I have done," said he to me, a short time after finishing this oratorio, " my head is no longer what it was. Formerly, ideas came to me unsought ; I am now obliged to seek for them, and for this I feel I am not formed."
He wrote, after this, a few quartetts, but could never finish that numbered 84, though he was employed upon it, almost without interruption, for three years. In the latter part of his time he employed himself in putting basses to ancient Scotch airs, for each of which he received two guineas from a London bookseller. He arranged near three hundred of these, but, in 1805, by order of his physician, he discontinued this occupation

also. Life was retiring from him; he was seized with vertigoes as soon as he sat down to the piano-forte.

From this time, he never left his garden at Gumpendorff. He sent to his friends, when he was desirous of reminding them of him, a visiting card of his own composition. The words of it are,

"My strength is gone, I am old and feeble.

The music which accompanies them, stopping in the middle of the period, without arriving at the cadence, well expresses the languishing state of the author,

Hin ist alle mein Kraft. Alt und schwach bin ich.

At present, this great man, or rather what remains of him here, is occupied by two ideas only: the fear of falling ill, and the fear of wanting money. He is continually sipping a few drops of Tokay, and receives, with the greatest pleasure, presents of game, which serve to diminish the expence of his little table.

The visits of his friends rouse him a little, and he sometimes follows an idea pretty well. For instance. In 1805, the Paris papers announced that he was dead; and, as he was honorary member of the Institute, that illustrious body, which has nothing of the German sluggishness about it, caused a mass to be celebrated in honour of him. The idea of this much amused Haydn. He remarked, " If these gentlemen had given me notice, I would have gone myself to beat the time to the fine mass of Mozart's, which they have had performed for me." But, notwithstanding his pleasantry, in his heart, he was very grateful to them.

A short time afterwards, Mozart's widow, and son, gave a concert at the pretty theatre *de la Wieden*, to celebrate Haydn's birth-day. A cantata was performed, which the young Mozart had composed in honour of the immortal rival of his father. The native goodness of German hearts should be known, to form an idea of the effect of this concert. I would engage, that, during the three hours it lasted, not a single pleasantry, of any kind, passed in the room.

That day reminded the public of Vienna of the loss they had already sustained, as well as of that which they were about to experience.

It was agreed to perform the Creation, with the Italian words of Carpani, and one hundred and sixty musicians assembled at the palace of prince Lobkowitz.

They were aided by three fine voices, madame *Frischer*, of Berlin, Messrs. *Weitmüller*, and *Radichi*. There were more than fifteen hundred persons in the room. The poor old man, notwithstanding his weakness, was desirous of seeing, once more, that public for which he had so long laboured. He was carried into the room in an easy chair. The princess *Esterhazy*, and his friend madame de *Kurzbeck*, went to meet him. The flourishes of the orchestra, and still more the agitation of the spectators, announced his arrival. He was placed in the middle of three rows of seats, destined for his friends, and for all that was illustrious in Vienna. *Salieri*, who directed the orchestra, came to receive Haydn's orders before they began. They embraced; *Salieri* left him, flew to his place, and the orchestra commenced amidst the general emotion. It may easily be judged, whether this religious music would appear sublime to an audience, whose hearts were affected by the sight of a great man about to depart out of life. Surrounded by the great, by his friends, by the artists of his profession, and by charming women, of whom every eye was fixed upon him, Haydn bid a glorious adieu to the world, and to life.

The chevalier Capellini, a physician of the first rank, observed, that Haydn's legs were not sufficiently covered. Scarcely had he given an intimation to those who stood around, than the most beautiful shawls left their charming wearers, to assist in warming the beloved old man.

Haydn, whom so much glory, and affection, had caused to shed tears more than once, felt himself faint at the end of the first part. His chair was brought. At the moment of leaving the room, he ordered the chairmen to stop; thanked the public first, by an inclination of his head; then, turning to the orchestra, with a feeling truly German, he raised his hands to heaven, and with eyes filled with tears, pronounced his benediction on the ancient companions of his labours.

LETTER XXII.

Vienna, August 22, 1809.

ON my return to the Austrian capital, I have to inform you, my dear friend, that the larva of Haydn has also quitted us. That great man no longer exists, except in our memory. I have often told you, that he was become extremely weak before he entered his seventy-eighth year. It was the last of his life. No sooner did he approach his piano-forte, than the vertigo returned, and his hands quitted the keys to take up the rosary, that last consolation.

The war broke out between Austria and France. This intelligence roused Haydn, and exhausted the remnant of his strength.

He was continually enquiring for news; he went every moment to his piano, and sang, with the small thread of voice which he yet retained,

" God preserve the emperor!"

The French armies advanced with gigantic strides. At length, on the night of the 10th of May, having reached Schönbrunn, half a league's distance from Haydn's little garden, they fired, the next morning, fifteen hundred cannon-shot, within two yards of his house, upon Vienna, the town which he so much loved. The old man's imagination represented it as given up to fire and sword. Four bombs fell close to his house. His two servants ran to him, full of terror. The old man, rousing himself, got up from his easy chair, and with a dignified air, demanded : " Why this terror? Know that no disaster can come where Haydn is." A convulsive shivering prevented him from proceeding, and he was carried to his bed. On the 26th of May, his strength diminished sensibly. Nevertheless, having caused himself to be carried to his piano, he sung thrice, as loud as he was able,

" God preserve the emperor!"

It was the song of the swan. While at the piano, he fell into a kind of stupor, and, at last, expired on the morning of the 31st, aged seventy-eight years and two months.

Madame de Kurzbeck, at the moment of the occupation of Vienna, had entreated him to allow of his being removed to her house in the interior of the city: he thanked her, but declined leaving his beloved retreat.

Haydn was buried at Gumpendorff, as a private individual. It is said, however, that prince Esterhazy intends to erect a monument to him.

A few weeks after his death, Mozart's *requiem* was performed in honour of him, in the Scotch church. I ventured into the city, to attend this ceremony. I saw there some generals and administrators of the French army, who appeared affected with the loss which the arts had just sustained. I recognized the accents of my native land, and spoke to several of them; and, among others, to an amiable man, who wore that day the uniform of the Institute of France, which I thought very elegant.

A similar respect was paid to the memory of Haydn at Breslau, and at the Conservatoire of Paris, where a hymn of Cherubini's composition was performed. The words are insipid, as usual; but the music is worthy of the great man whom it celebrates.

During all his life, Haydn was very religious. Without assuming the preacher, it may be said, that his talent was increased by his sincere faith in the truths of religion. At the commencement of all his scores, the following words are described,

In nomine Domini,
or, *Soli Deo gloria,*

and at the conclusion of all of them is written,

Laus Deo.

When, in composing, he felt the ardour of his imagination decline, or was stopped by some insurmountable difficulty, he rose from the piano-forte, and began to run over his rosary. He said, that he never found this method fail. " When I was employed upon the Creation," said he, " I felt myself so penetrated with religious feeling, that, before I sat down to the piano-forte, I prayed to God with earnestness, that he would enable me to praise him worthily."

Haydn's heir is a blacksmith, to whom he has left 38,000 florins in paper, deducting 12,000, which he bequeathed to his two faithful servants. His manuscripts were sold by auction, and purchased by prince *Esterhazy*.

Prince *Lichtenstein* was desirous of having our composer's old parrot, of which many wonderful stories were told. When he was younger, it was said, he sung and spoke several languages, and people would have it, that he had been instructed by his master. The astonishment of the blacksmith, when he saw the parrot sold for 1,400 florins, diverted all who were present at the sale. I do not know who purchased his watch. It was given to him by admiral Nelson, who called upon him, when he passed through Vienna, and asked him to make him a present of one of his pens, begging him to accept, in return, the watch he had worn in so many engagements.

Haydn wrote for his epitaph

Veni, scripsi, vixi.

He has left no posterity. Cherubini, Pleyel, Neukomm, and Weigl, may be considered as his disciples.

Haydn had the same weakness as the celebrated Austrian minister, prince Kaunitz; he could not bear to be painted as an old man. In 1800, he was seriously angry with a painter who had represented him as he then was: that is to say, in his seventy-eighth year. " If I was Haydn, when I was forty," said he to him, " why would you transmit to posterity a Haydn of seventy-eight? Neither you nor I gain by the alteration."

Such were the life and death of this celebrated man. *

---

* There are many biographical accounts of Haydn. I think, as is natural, that mine is the most exact. I spare the reader the reasons on which I found this assertion; but if any man of information should dispute the facts I have advanced, I would defend their veracity. As to taste in music, every man has one of his own, or none

Why did all the illustrious French writers in the belle lettres, properly so called, La Fontaine, Corneille, Moliere, Racine, Bossuet, happen to meet about the year 1660?

Why did all the great painters appear about the year 1510? Why has nature been so sparing, since these fortunate æras? Important questions, of which the public adopts

---

at all. For the rest, there is not, perhaps, a single phrase in this account which has not been translated from some foreign work. There is no great room for vanity in a few lines of reflections on the fine arts. We plume ourselves, in the present day, on teaching others what to do. In happier times, a man founded his reputation on what he had done himself: and it must be confessed, that it was a more direct way of proving his acquaintance with his principles.

Optumus quisque facere, quam dicere, sua ab aliis facta laudari, quam ipse aliorum narrare malebat.
SALLUST.

The author has expunged, as far as he was able, the innumerable repetitions of the original letters, which were written to a man, formed to be superior in the fine arts, but who had but just discovered that he was fond of music.

a new solution every ten years, because a satisfactory one has not yet been found.

One thing is certain, that after these periods, we have nothing. Voltaire has a thousand various merits: Montesquieu teaches us the most useful of the sciences, with all the interest possible: Buffon has descanted on nature with magnificence: Rousseau, the greatest of them all in literature, is the first French writer for beautiful prose. But as literati, that is, as men who gave pleasure by means of printed words, how inferior are these great men to La Fontaine, or Corneille, for instance!

It is the same with painting, if you except the fortunate irruption which, a century after Raphael and Correggio, gave to the world Guido, the Caracci, and Dominichino.

Does the same fate await music? Every thing would lead us to suppose so. Cimarosa, Mozart, and Haydn, have just left us, and nothing appears to repair their loss. Do you ask why? This is my answer. The artists of the present day imitate them:— they imitated nobody. Having once acquired a knowledge of the mechanical part of the art, each of them wrote what pleased his own taste. They wrote for themselves, and for those organized like themselves.

Pergolese, and *Sacchini,* wrote from the dictation of the passions. At present, our most distinguished artists are employed on works of amusement. What can be more diverting than the *Cantatrici villane* of Fioravanti? Compare them with the *Matrimonio segreto.* The *Matrimonio* gives extreme pleasure when one is in a certain temper; the *Cantatrici* are always amusing. I would remind you of the exhibition given at the Tuileries, in 1810. Every body preferred the *Cantatrici* to all the other Italian operas; because, to be amused by these lovely inhabitants of Frascati, requires the smallest degree of sensibility which music can do with, and this was precisely the proportion which the audience brought with them. To be formally dressed, and in sight of a court filled with the anxieties of ambition, is certainly a situation, of all others, least favourable to music.

In the arts, and, I think, in all human pursuits which admit of originality, a man is either himself,—or nobody. I infer, therefore, that the musicians who devote themselves to the department of amusement, think that genus the best, and are men without any real warmth of feeling. Now what are the arts, without true feeling in the artist

After the celestial purity of Virgil, the wit of Seneca came into fashion at Rome. We, at Paris, have also our Senecas, who, while they extol the beautiful simplicity of Fenelon, and the age of Louis XIV. depart from it, as far as possible, by a style full of point and affectation. Thus, also, Sacchini, and Cimarosa, are disappearing from the Italian theatres, to make room for composers, who, in their eagerness to distinguish themselves, fall into what is far-fetched, extravagant, and unnatural, and seek rather to astonish than to affect. The difficulty and tiresomeness of the *concerto* is every where introduced, and what is still worse, the continual use of these high-seasoned dishes renders us insensible to the perfumed flavour of the peach.

It is said, at Paris, that those who are desirous of preserving a pure taste in literature, read, as models, only the writers who appeared before the close of the seventeenth century, and the four great authors of the following one. They refer to the books which have been published since, and to those which daily issue from the press, for the facts which they contain,

Historia, quoque modo scripta, placet:

but endeavour to preserve themselves from the contagion of their style.

Perhaps our young musicians ought to do the same. What other method is there of escaping that general *Senecism*, which is corrupting all the arts, and to which Canova is the only living exception, that I know of; for Paesiello has ceased his labours.

CATALOGUE

Of the works which Joseph Haydn, aged seventy-three years, recollected to have composed since the age of eighteen.

    118 Symphonies.

Pieces for the baryton, a favourite instrument of the late prince Nicholas Esterhazy.

    125 Divertimentos for the baryton, viola, and violoncello.
    8 Duets.
    12 Sonatas for the baryton and violoncello.
    6 Serenades.
    5   do.   in 8 parts.
    3   do.   in 5.
    1   do.   in 3.
    1   do.   in 4.
    1   do.   in 6.
    3 Concertos for two violins and a bass.

Total 165 Pieces for the baryton.

Divertimentos for various instruments in 5, 6, 7, 8, *and* 9 *parts.*

5 Pieces in 5 parts.
1 do. in 4.
9 do. in 6.
1 do. in 8.
2 do. in 9.
2 do. (Haydn did not recollect how many instruments.)
2 Marches.
21 Pieces for 2 violins and violoncello.
6 Sonatas for the violin with accompaniment for the viola.
Echo for 4 violins and 2 violoncellos.

Concertos.

3 for the violin.
3 for the violoncello.
2 for the contrabasso.
1 for the horn in D.
2 for two horns.
1 for the clarinet.
1 for the flute.

Masses, Offertories, Te Deum, Salve Regina, Choruses.

1 Mass. *Celeusis.*
2 Masses. *Sunt bona mixta malis.*
2 Masses. *Brevis.*
1 Mass of St. Joseph.
6 Masses for the troops in time of war.
7 Solemn masses.
4 Offertories.
1 Salve Regina, for four voices.
1 Salve, for the organ solo.
1 Chant for the Advent.
1 Response. *Lauda Sion Salvatorem.*
1 Te Deum.
2 Choruses.
1 Stabat Mater for a full orchestra.

82 Quartetts.
1 Concerto for the organ.
3 Ditto for the harpsichord.
1 Divertimento for the harpsichord, violin, two horns, and an alto.
1 do. for two performers.
1 do. for the baryton and two violins.

4 Divertimentos for two violins and an alto.
1 Divertimento, with twenty variations.
15 Sonatas for the piano-forte.
1 Fantasia.
1 Capriccio.
1 Thema, with variation in G.
1 do. with variation in F.
29 Sonatas for the piano-forte, violin, and violoncello.
42 Allemandes, among them some Italian songs and duets.
39 Canons for several voices.

German Operas.

The Devil on Two Sticks.
Philemon and Baucis, for puppets, in 1773.
The Witches Sabbath, do. in 1773.
Genoviefa, do. in 1777.
Dido, do. in 1778.

Italian Operas.

La Cantarina.
Lo Incontro improvvis
Lo Speziale.

La Pescatrice.
Il Mondo della Luna.
La Isola disabitata.
La Infedeltà premiata.
La Vera Costanza.
Orlando Paladino.
Armida,
Acide e Galatea.
La Infedeltà delusa.
Orfeo.

Oratorios.

The return of Tobias.
The Seven Words of the Saviour on the Cross.
The Creation of the World.
The Four Seasons.
13 Cantatas, for 3 and 4 voices.

In English.

Selection of 150 Original Songs.
216 Scotch Songs, with symphonies and accompaniments.

Works written by Haydn, during his residence in London. Copied from his Journal.

    Orfeo, opera seria.
6 Symphonies.
    Sinfonia concertante.
    The Tempest, a chorus
3 Symphonies.
    Air for David, Sen.
    Macone for Gallini.
6 Quartetts.
3 Sonatas for Drodevif. (Broderip)
3 Sonatas for P.
3 Sonatas for M. Jonson.
1 Sonata in F minor.
1 Sonata in G.
    The Dream.
1 Compliment for Harrington.
6 English Songs.
100 Scotch Songs.
50 Ditto.
2 Divertimentos for the Flute.
3 Symphonies.
4 Songs for F.
2 Marches.

1 Air for Mistress P.
1 God save the King.
1 Air, with orchestra accompaniment.
Invocation to Neptune.
1 Canon. The Ten Commandments.
1 March. The Prince of Wales.
2 Divertimentos for several voices.
24 Minuets and German airs for dancing.
12 Ballads for Lord A.
Different songs.
Canons.
1 Song with orchestra accompaniment for Lord A.
4 Country dances.
6 Songs.
Overture for Covent Garden.
Air for Madame Banti.
4 Scotch Songs.
2 Songs.
2 Country dances.
3 Sonatas for Broderich. (Broderip)

CANON CANCRIZANS
a 3 voce.
HAYDN.

Thy Voice O Har-mo-ny is di-vine

See page 196.

The music may be read backwards by shining it on this side-

THE LIFE

OF

MOZART.

Venice, July 22, 1814.

YOU are desirous, my friend, of some information respecting the Life of Mozart. I have enquired for the best memoir of that celebrated man, and have had the patience to translate for you, the Biographical notice published by M. Schlictegroll. I now present you with it: excuse its simplicity.

THE LIFE

OF

MOZART,

TRANSLATED

FROM THE GERMAN OF M. SCHLICTEGROLL.

CHAPTER I.

HIS CHILDHOOD.

THE father of Mozart had the greatest influence upon the singular destiny of his son, whose dispositions he developed, and perhaps modified: it is therefore necessary, in the first place, to say a few words concerning him.

Leopold Mozart was the son of a bookbinder of Augsburg. He pursued his studies at Salzburg; and, in 1743, was admitted into the number of the musicians of the prince-archbishop of that city. In 1762, he became sub-director of the prince's chapel. As the duties of his office did not take up the whole of his time, he employed a part of it in giving lessons on the violin, and teaching the rules of musical composition. He published "An Essay on teaching the Violin with accuracy," which met with good success. He married *Anna Maria Pertl;* and it has been remarked, as a circumstance worthy the attention of an exact observer, that this couple, which gave birth to an artist so happily organised for musical harmony, were noted in Salzburg for their uncommon beauty.

Of seven children sprung from this marriage, two only lived; a daughter, Mary Ann; and a son, of whom we are now to speak.

John-Chrysostom-Wolfgang-Theophilus Mozart, was born at Salzburg, on the 27th of January, 1756. A few years afterwards, his father discontinued giving lessons in the town, and determined to devote all the time which the duties of his office left at his disposal, to the superintendance of the musical education of his two children.

The daughter, who was rather older than Wolfgang, made great proficiency, and shared the public admiration with her brother, in the excursions which she afterwards made with her family. She married, in the sequel, a counsellor of the prince-archbishop of Salzburg, preferring domestic happiness to the renown of distinguished talent.

Mozart was scarcely three years old when his father began to give lessons on the harpsichord to his sister, who was then seven. His astonishing disposition for music immediately manifested itself. His delight was to seek for *thirds* on the piano, and nothing could equal his joy when he had found this harmonious chord. The minute details into which I am about to enter, will, I presume, be interesting to the reader.

When he was four years old, his father began to teach him, almost in sport, some minuets, and other pieces of music, an occupation which was as agreeable to the master, as to the pupil. Mozart would learn a minuet in half an hour, and a piece of greater extent in less than twice that time. Immediately after, he played them with the greatest clearness, and perfectly in time. In less than a year, he made such rapid progress, that, at five years old, he already invented little pieces of music which he played to his father, and which the latter, in order to encourage the rising talent of his son, was at the trouble of writing down. Before the little Mozart acquired a taste for music, he was so fond of all the amusements of his age, which were in any way calculated to interest him, that he sacrificed even his meals to them. On every occasion he manifested a feeling and affectionate heart. He would say ten times in a day to those about him, *" Do you love me well?"* and whenever in jest they said *No*, the tears would roll down his cheeks. From the moment he became acquainted with music, his relish for the sports and amusements of his age vanished, or to render them pleasing to him, it was necessary to introduce music in them. A friend of his parents often amused himself in playing with him: sometimes they carried the play-things in procession from one room to another: then, the one who had nothing to carry, sung a march, or played it on the violin.

During some months, a fondness for the usual studies of childhood gained such an ascendancy over Wolfgang, that he sacrificed every thing, even music, to it. While he was learning arithmetic, the tables, the chairs, and even the walls, were covered with figures which he had chalked upon them. The vivacity of his mind led him to attach himself easily to every new object that was presented to him. Music, however, soon became again the favourite object of his pursuit. He made such rapid advances in it, that his father, notwithstanding he was always with him, and in the way of observing his progress, could not help regarding him as a prodigy. The following anecdote, related by an eye-witness, is a proof of this.

His father, returning from the church one day with a friend, found his son busy in writing. "What are you doing there, my little fellow?" asked he. "I am composing a concerto for the harpsichord, and have almost got to the end of the first part."—"Let us see this fine scrawl,"—"No, I have not yet finished it." The father, however, took the paper, and shewed his friend a sheet-full of notes, which could scarcely be decyphered for the blots of ink. The two friends at first laughed heartily at this heap of scribbling, but, after a little time, when the father had looked at it with more attention, his eyes were fastened on the paper; and, at length, overflowed with tears of joy, and wonder, " Look, my friend," said he, with a smile of delight; " every thing is composed according to the rules: it is a pity that the piece cannot be made any use of, but it is too difficult: nobody would be able to play it."—It is a concerto, replied the son, and must be studied till it can be properly played.—" This is the style in which it ought to be executed." He accordingly began to play, but succeeded only so far as to give them an idea of what he had intended. At that time, the young Mozart firmly believed that to play a concerto was about as easy as to work a miracle, and, accordingly, the composition in question was a heap of notes, correctly placed, but presenting so many difficulties, that the most skilful performer would have found it impossible to play it.

The young composer so astonished his father, that the latter conceived the idea of exhibiting him at the different courts of Germany. There is nothing extraordinary in such an idea in this country. As soon, therefore, as Wolfgang had attained his sixth year, the Mozart family, consisting of the father, the mother, the daughter, and Wolfgang, took a journey to Munich. The two children performed before the elector, and received infinite commendations. This first expedition succeeded in every respect. The young artists, delighted with the reception they had met with, redoubled their application on their return to Salzburg, and acquired a degree of execution on the piano, which no longer required the consideration of their youth, to render it highly remarkable. During the autumn of the year 1762, the whole family repaired to Vienna, and the children performed before the court.

The emperor Francis I., said, in jest, on that occasion, to little Wolfgang: "It is not very difficult to play with all one's fingers, but to play with only one, without seeing the keys, would indeed be extraordinary." Without manifesting the least surprise at this strange proposal, the child immediately began to play with a single finger, and with the greatest possible precision, and clearness. He afterwards desired them to cover the keys of the piano-forte, and continued to play in the same manner, as if he had long practised it.

From his most tender age, Mozart, animated with the true feeling of his art, was never vain of the compliments paid him by the great. He only performed insignificant trifles when he had to do with people unacquainted with music. He played, on the contrary, with all the fire, and attention, of which he was capable, when in the presence of connoisseurs; and his father was often obliged to have recourse to artifice, and to make the great men, before whom he was to exhibit, pass for such with him. When Mozart, at the age of six years, sat down to play in presence of the emperor Francis, he addressed himself to his majesty, and asked: " Is not M. Wagenseil here? We must send for him: he understands the thing." The emperor sent for Wagenseil, and gave up his place to him, by the side of the piano. " Sir," said Mozart, to the composer, " I am going to play one of your concertos; you must turn over the leaves for me."

Hitherto, Wolfgang had only played on the harpsichord, and the extraordinary skill which he displayed on that instrument, seemed to exclude even the wish that he should apply to any other. But the genius which animated him, far surpassed any hopes that his friends could have dared to entertain: he had not even occasion for lessons.

On his return from Vienna to Salzburg with his parents, he brought with him a small violin, which had been given him during his residence at the capital, and amused himself with it. A short time afterwards, *Wenzl,* a skilful violin player, who had then just begun to compose, came to Mozart, the father, to request his observations on six trios, which he had written during the journey of the former to Vienna. Schachtner, the archbishop's trumpeter, to whom Mozart was particularly attached, happened to be at the house, and we give the following anecdote in his words:

"The father," said Schachtner, "played the bass, Wenzl the first violin, and I was to play the second. Mozart requested permission to take this last part; but his father reproved him for this childish demand, observing, that as he had never received any regular lessons on the violin, he could not possibly play it properly. The son replied, that it did not appear to him necessary to receive lessons in order to play the second violin. His father, half angry at this reply, told him to go away, and not interrupt us. Wolfgang was so hurt at this, that he began to cry bitterly. As he was going away with his little violin, I begged that he might be permitted to play with me, and the father, with a good deal of difficulty, consented. Well, said he to Wolfgang, you may play with M. Schachtner, on condition that you play very softly, and do not let yourself be heard: otherwise, I shall send you out directly. We began the trio, little Mozart playing with me, but it was not long before I perceived, with the greatest astonishment, that I was perfectly useless. Without saying any thing, I laid down my violin, and looked at the father, who shed tears of affection at the sight. The child played all the six trios in the same manner. The commendations we gave him made him pretend that he could play the first violin. To humour him, we let him try, and could not forbear laughing on hearing him execute this part, very imperfectly, it is true, but still so as never to be set fast."

Every day afforded fresh proofs of Mozart's exquisite organization for music. He could distinguish, and point out, the slightest differences of sound, and every false or even rough note, not softened by some chord, was a torture to him. It was from this cause that during the early part of his childhood, and even till he had attained his tenth year, he had an insurmountable horror for the trumpet, when it was not used merely as an accompaniment. The sight of this instrument produced upon him much the same impression as that of a loaded pistol does upon other children, when pointed at them in sport. His father thought he could cure him of this fear, by causing the trumpet to be blown in his presence, notwithstanding his son's entreaties to be spared that torment; but, at the first blast, he turned pale, fell upon the floor, and would probably have been in convulsions, if they had not immediately ceased.

After he had made some proficiency upon the violin, he occasionally made use of that of Schachtner, the family friend whom we have just mentioned, which he highly esteemed, because he drew from it sounds extremely soft. Schachtner, one day, came to the house, while the young Mozart was amusing himself with playing on his own violin. "What is your violin doing?" was the child's first enquiry; and he then went on playing fantasies. After a few moments pause, he said to Schachtner, "Could not you have left me your violin, tuned as it was when I last used it? It is half a quarter of a note below this." They at first laughed at this scrupulous exactness; but the father, who had often observed his son's extraordinary memory for sounds, sent for the violin, and to the great astonishment of all present, it was half a quarter of a note below the other, as Wolfgang had said.

Though the child every day beheld new proofs of the astonishment, and admiration, inspired by his talents, it neither rendered him proud, nor self-willed: a man in talent, in every thing else he was an obedient and docile child. Never did he appear dissatisfied with any thing that his father ordered. Even after playing the whole of the day, he would continue to do so, without shewing the least ill-humour, when his father desired it. He understood, and obeyed the slightest signs made by his parents, and carried his obedience so far as to refuse the sweetmeats which were offered him, when he had not their permission to accept them.

In the month of July, 1763, when he was in his seventh year, his family set out on their first expedition beyond the boundaries of Germany; and it is from this period that the celebrity of the name of Mozart in Europe is to be dated. The tour commenced with Munich, where the young artist played a concerto on the violin, in presence of the elector, after an extempore prelude. At Augsburg, Manheim, Francfort, Coblentz, Brussels, the two children gave public concerts, or played before the princes of the district, and received every where the greatest commendations.

In the month of November they arrived at Paris, where they remained five months. They performed at Versailles, and Wolfgang played the organ of the king's chapel before the court. They gave in Paris two grand public concerts, and universally met with the most distinguished reception. They were even so far honoured as to have their portraits taken : the father was engraved between his two children, from a design of Carmontelle's. It was at Paris that Mozart composed and published his two first works, one of which he dedicated to the princess *Victoire*, second daughter of Louis XV., and the other to the countess de Tessé.

In April, 1764, the Mozarts went to England, where they remained till about the middle of the following year. The children performed before the king, and, as at Versailles, the son played the organ of the royal chapel. His performance on the organ was thought more of, at London, than his exhibitions on the harpsichord. During his stay there, he and his sister gave a grand concert, all the symphonies of which were his own composition.

It may be supposed that the two children, and especially Wolfgang, did not stop at a degree of proficiency which every day procured them such flattering applause. Notwithstanding their continual removals, they practised with the greatest regularity, and Wolfgang began to sing difficult airs, which he executed with great expression. The incredulous, at Paris and at London, had put him to the trial with various difficult pieces of Bach, Handel, and other masters; he played them immediately, at first sight, and with the greatest possible correctness. He played, one day, before the king of England, a piece full of melody, from the bass only.* At another time, Christian Bach, the queen's music-master, took little Mozart between his knees, and played a few bars.

---

* What Mozart here did, by the aid of his natural genius only, performers in general are directed to do by means of figures placed over the notes, which indicate the harmony to be played by the right hand. This method of expressing by figures the various combinations of sound, is denominated thorough bass.

To do this with accuracy is become a desideratum in music, for, as the early harmonists had no idea of many of the combinations which are found in the works of modern authors, their scheme of figuring is found totally inadequate to the present state of musical science.

In consequence of this deficiency, the nomenclature of the art has been loaded with the barbarous terms of *chords by supposition, retardation, suspension; diminished, superfluous, anomalous, spurious,* &c; and the science of thorough bass is become a labyrinth of inextricable perplexity.

To get rid of this confusion, we must simplify the art, by establishing the principle, that all combinations of the musical scale are admissible into the harmonic code. It

Mozart then continued, and they thus played alternately a whole sonata, with such precision, that those who did not see them thought it was executed by the same person. During his residence in England, that is, when he was eight years old, Wolfgang composed six sonatas which were engraved at London, and dedicated to the queen.

---

will then be an easy operation to refer the different mixtures to one of the following classes.

    The Common Chord
    The Chord of the 7th
    The Extreme flat 7th
    The 13th, including the sharp 7th, 9th, and 11th
    The 35th or Ultimate Chord.

By the *Ultimate Chord*, we mean that in which all the tones, and semi-tones, of the scale are comprehended. It is formed by alternately placing a minor third upon a major, and may be resolved into pure harmony, by the intervention of the chord of the 7th.

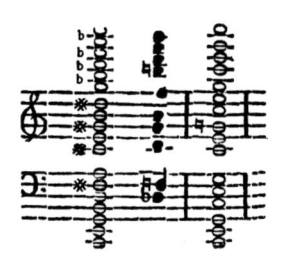

G.

In the month of July, 1765, the Mozart family returned to Calais, from whence they continued their journey through Flanders, where the young artist often played the organs of the monasteries, and cathedral churches. At the Hague, the two children had an illness which endangered their lives, and from which they were four months in recovering. Wolfgang composed six sonatas for the piano-forte during his convalescence, which he dedicated to the princess of Nassau-Weilbour. In the beginning of the year 1766, they passed a month at Amsterdam, from whence they repaired to the Hague, to be present at the installation of the prince of Orange. Mozart composed for this solemnity a *quodlibet* for all the instruments, and also different airs and variations for the princess.

After having performed several times before the Stadtholder, they returned to Paris, where they staid two months, and then returned to Germany, by Lyons and Switzerland. At Munich, the elector gave Mozart a musical *theme,* and required him to develope it, and write it down immediately, which he did in the prince's presence, without recurring either to the harpsichord or the violin. After writing it, he played it: which excited the greatest astonishment in the elector and his whole court. After an absence of more than three years, they returned to Salzburg, towards the end of November, 1766, where they remained till the autumn of the following year, and this tranquillity seemed further to augment the talents of Wolfgang. In 1768, the children performed at Vienna, in presence of the emperor Joseph II., who commissioned Mozart to compose the music of an opera buffa—the *Finta Semplice*. It was approved of by Hasse, the maître de chapelle, and by Metastasio, but was never brought on the stage.

On many occasions, at the houses of the professors Bono, and Hasse, of Metastasio, of the duke of Braganza, of prince Kaunitz, the father desired any Italian air that was at hand to be given to his son, who wrote the parts for all the instruments in presence of the company. At the dedication of the church of The Orphans he composed the music of the mass, the motet, and a trumpet duet, and directed this solemn music, in presence of the imperial court, though he was at that time only twelve years old.

He returned to pass the year 1769 at Salzburg. In the month of December, his father took him into Italy, just after he had been appointed director of the archbishop of Salzburg's concert. We may imagine the reception given in that country to this celebrated child, who had excited such admiration in the other parts of Europe.

The house of count Firmian, the governor-general, was the theatre of his glory at Milan. After having received the poem of the opera to be performed during the carnival of 1771, and of which he undertook to write the music, Wolfgang quitted that city in the month of March, 1770. At Bologna, he found an enthusiastic admirer in the celebrated Father Martini, the same person of whom Jomelli came to take lessons. Father Martini, and the Bologna amateurs, were transported at seeing a child of thirteen, whose small stature made him appear still younger, develope all the subjects of fugues proposed by Martini, and execute them on the piano-forte, without hesitating, and with the greatest precision. At Florence, he excited similar astonishment by the correctness with which he played, at sight, the most difficult fugues and themes, proposed to him by the marquis de Ligneville, a distinguished amateur.

We have an anecdote respecting him, during his residence at Florence, which does not immediately relate to music. He became acquainted, in that city, with a young Englishman, of about his own age, whose name was Thomas Linley. He was a pupil of Martini, and played on the violin with admirable skill, and gracefulness. The friendship of the two boys became quite ardent, and, on the day of their separation, Linley gave his friend Mozart some verses, which he had procured for the purpose, from the celebrated Corilla. He accompanied him to the gate of the town, and their parting was attended with a copious effusion of tears.

In the passion-week, the Mozarts repaired to Rome, where, as may be supposed, they did not fail to hear the celebrated *Miserere*, performed in the Sixtine chapel, on the evening of Ash-Wednesday. As it was said, at that time, that the pope's musicians were forbidden to give copies of it, under pain of excommunication, Wolfgang determined to commit it to memory, and actually wrote it all down on his return to his inn. The service being repeated, on Good-Friday, he again attended with his manuscript in his hat, and had thus an opportunity of making some corrections. The story was much talked of in Rome, but the thing appeared so incredible, that in order to ascertain its truth, the child was engaged to sing this *Miserere* at a public concert. He executed it to perfection, and the amazement of Cristofori, who had sung it at the Sixtine chapel, and who was present, rendered the triumph of Mozart complete.

The difficulty of what he thus accomplished is much greater than may at first be imagined. But, for the sake of explanation, I shall enter into a few details respecting the Sixtine chapel, and the *Miserere*.

In this chapel, there are usually not less than thirty-two voices, without an organ, or any other instrument to accompany or support them. The establishment reached its highest perfection about the commencement of the eighteenth century. Since that time, the salaries of the singers at the pope's chapel having remained nominally the same, and consequently being really much diminished, while the opera was rising in estimation, and good singers obtained premiums, before unknown, the Sixtine chapel has gradually lost the talents it originally possessed.

The *Miserere*, which is performed there twice in passion-week, and which produces such an effect upon strangers, was composed, about two hundred years since, by Gregorio Allegri, a descendant of Antonio Allegri, better known by the name of Correggio.

At the moment of its commencement, the pope and cardinals prostrate themselves. The light of the tapers illumines the representation of the last judgment, painted by Michael Angelo, on the wall with which the altar is connected. As the service proceeds, the tapers are extinguished, one after the other, and the impression produced by the figures of the damned, painted with terrific power, by Michael Angelo, is increased in awfulness, when they are dimly seen by the pale light of the last tapers. When the service is on the point of concluding, the leader, who beats the time, renders it imperceptibly slower; the singers diminish the volume of their voices, and the sinner, confounded before the majesty of his God, and prostrated before his throne, seems to await in silence his final doom.

The sublime effect of this composition depends, as it appears, on the manner in which it is sung, and the place in which it is performed. There is a kind of traditional knowledge, by which the pope's singers are taught certain ways of managing their voices, so as to produce the greatest effect, and which it is impossible to express by notes.* Their

---

* One thing of great importance to the effect of a musical composition, for the expression of which no written characters were formerly employed, is accent.

By accent, in music, is to be understood, the manner in which sounds are uttered, without reference to their loudness, or softness, or to their pitch in the musical scale. The same *note* may be struck on a drum, with a glove, or with a stick, but the *accent* of it will be different. The *note* of a harpsichord-wire is the same with that of a piano-forte, but the *accent* is not so, the sounds of the one being produced by a quill, those of the other by a hammer.

The natural accent of all the instruments is different, but the performer is enabled to vary it at pleasure, by certain methods of playing. This is particularly the case with the violin, on which every variety of accent may be produced by means of the bow. We recommend the treatise of M. Baillot, on this subject, to every student.

As no characters have yet been adopted that will sufficiently express these varieties, it is evident that the kind of accent given to any note, will depend on the taste and fancy of the performer, and it will not therefore appear surprising, that the effect of the same music should often be very different, as in the case of the *Miserere*.

But though the *species* of the accent is left thus undecided, its *place* depends on certain laws, derived from the singing possesses all the qualities which render music affecting. The same melody is repeated to all the verses of the psalm, but the music, though similar in the masses, is not so in the details. It is accordingly easy to be understood, without being tiresome. The peculiarity of the Sixtine chapel, consists in accelerating or retarding the time in certain expressions, in swelling or diminishing the voice according to the sense of the words, and in singing some of the verses with more animation than others.

The following anecdote will shew still more clearly the difficulty of the exploit performed by Mozart in singing the *Miserere*.

---

same principles as those which regulate the cadences of poetry, and the euphony of language in general,—namely, that the ear requires the observance of a certain proportion in the distances at which the emphatic notes or words recur.

These proportions will vary, according to the time of the music, and the species of versification; and, hence arises the difficulty of translating the words of a piece of vocal music, without destroying that *unity of accent* which should always subsist between them. G.

It is related that the emperor Leopold I. who not only was fond of music, but was himself a good composer, requested of the pope, through his ambassador, a copy of the *Miserere* of Allegri, for the use of the imperial chapel at Vienna. The request was complied with, and the director of the Sixtine chapel caused a copy to be written out, which was immediately transmitted to the emperor, who had in his service the first singers of the day.

Notwithstanding their talents, the *Miserere* of Allegri produced, at Vienna, no more effect than the dullest common chant, and the emperor and his court were persuaded that the pope's maître de chapelle, desirous of keeping the *Miserere* to himself, had eluded his master's orders, and sent an inferior composition. A courier was immediately dispatched to complain to the pope of this want of respect, and the director was dismissed without being allowed to say a word in his own justification. The poor man, however, prevailed on one of the cardinals to intercede for him, and to represent to his holiness that the manner of performing the *Miserere* could not be expressed in notes; but required much time, and repeated lessons from the singers of the chapel, who possessed the traditional knowledge of it. The pope, who knew nothing of music, could scarcely comprehend how the same notes should not be just as good at Vienna, as at Rome. He, however, allowed the poor maître de chapelle to write his defence to the emperor, and, in time, he was received again into favour.

It was this well-known anecdote, which occasioned the people of Rome to be so astonished when they heard a child sing their *Miserere,* correctly, after two lessons. Nothing is more difficult than to excite surprise in Rome, in any thing relating to the fine arts. The most brilliant reputation dwindles into insignificance in that celebrated city, where the finest productions of every art are the subjects of daily, and familiar, contemplation.

I know not whether it arose from the reputation which it procured him, but it appears that the solemn and affecting chant of the *Miserere,* made a deep impression in the mind of Mozart, who shewed, ever afterwards, a marked preference for Handel, and the tender Boccherini.

CHAPTER II.

SEQUEL OF THE CHILDHOOD OF MOZART.

FROM Rome, the Mozarts went to Naples, where Wolfgang played on the piano-forte at the *Conservatorio alla pietà*. When he was in the middle of his sonata, the audience took it into their heads, that there was a charm in the ring which he wore. It became necessary to explain to him the cause of the disturbance which arose, and he was at last obliged to take off this supposed magic circle. We may imagine the effect produced on such an auditory, when they found that after the ring was taken off, the music was not the less beautiful. Wolfgang gave a second grand concert, at the house of prince Kaunitz, the emperor's ambassador, and afterwards returned to Rome. The pope desired to see him, and conferred on him the cross and brevet of a knight of the Golden Militia *(auratæ Militiæ Eques)*. At Bologna, he was nominated, unanimously, member and master of the Philharmonic Academy. He was shut up alone, agreeably to usage, and in less than half an hour he composed an antiphony for four voices.

Mozart's father hastened his return to Milan, that he might attend to the opera which he had undertaken. The time was advancing, and they did not reach that city till the close of October, 1770. Had it not been for this engagement, Mozart might have obtained what is considered in Italy the first musical honour,—the composition of a serious opera for the theatre of Rome.

On the 26th of December, the first representation of the *Mithridates* took place, at Milan. This opera, composed by Mozart, at the age of fourteen, was performed twenty nights in succession; a circumstance which sufficiently indicates its success. The manager immediately entered into a written agreement with him for the composition of the first opera for the year 1773. Mozart left Milan, which resounded with his fame, to pass the last days of the carnival at Venice, in company with his father. At Verona, which he only passed through, he was presented with a diploma, constituting him a member of the Philharmonic Society of that city. Wherever he went in Italy, he met with the most distinguished reception, and was generally known by the name of The Philharmonic Knight: *Il Cavaliere Filarmonico*.

When Mozart returned with his father to Salzburg, in March, 1771, he found a letter from count Firmian, of Milan, who commanded him, in the name of the empress Maria Theresa, to compose a dramatic cantata on occasion of the marriage of the arch-duke Ferdinand. The empress had chosen the celebrated Hasse, as the oldest professor, to write the opera, and she was desirous that the youngest composer should undertake the cantata, the subject of which was *Ascanius in Alba*. He undertook the work, and in the month of August, set out for Milan, where, during the solemnities of the marriage, the opera and the serenade were performed alternately.

In 1772, he composed for the election of the new archbishop of Salzburg, the cantata entitled *Il sogno di Scipione;* and at Milan, where he passed the winter of the year following, he wrote *Lucio Silla,* a serious opera, which had twenty-six successive representations. In the spring of 1773, Mozart returned to Salzburg, and during some excursions which he made in the course of this year to Vienna and Munich, he produced various compositions of merit, as, *La Finta Giardiniera,* an opera buffa, two grand masses for the elector of Bavaria's chapel, &c. In 1775, the archduke Maximilian spent some time at Salzburg, and it was on this occasion that Mozart composed the cantata entitled *Il Re Pastore.*

The early part of the life of Mozart is the most extraordinary: the details of it may interest the philosopher, as well as the artist. We shall be more concise in our account of the remainder of his too short career.

CHAPTER III.

ARRIVED at the age of nineteen, Mozart might flatter himself that he had attained the summit of his art, since of this he was repeatedly assured, wherever he went;—from London to Naples. As far as regarded the advancement of his fortune, he was at liberty to choose among all the capitals of Europe. Experience had taught him that he might every where reckon on general admiration. His father thought that Paris would suit him best, and accordingly, in the month of September, 1777, he set out for that capital, accompanied by his mother only.

It would have been, unquestionably, very advantageous to him to have settled there, but the French music, of that time, did not accord with his taste; and the preference shewn for vocal performances would have given him little opportunity of employing himself in the instrumental department. He had also the misfortune to lose his mother in the year after his arrival. From that time, Paris became insupportable to him. After having composed a symphony for the *Concert spirituel,* and a few other pieces, he hastened to rejoin his father in the beginning of 1779.

In the month of November, of the year following, he repaired to Vienna, whither he had been summoned by his sovereign, the archbishop of Salzburg. He was then in his twenty-fourth year. The habits of Vienna were very agreeable to him, and the beauty of its fair inhabitants, it appears, still more so. There he fixed himself, and nothing could ever prevail upon him afterwards to leave it. The empire of the passions having commenced in this being, so exquisitely sensible to his art, he soon became the favourite composer of his age, and gave the first example of a remarkable child becoming a great man.*

---

* Mozart composed the music of the opera of *Idomeneus* under the most favourable circumstances. The

To give a particular analysis of each of Mozart's works would be too long, and too difficult; an amateur ought to know them all. Most of his operas were composed at Vienna, and had the greatest success, but none of them was a greater favourite than the *Zauber Flöte,* which was performed one hundred times in less than a year.

---

elector of Bavaria, who had always shewn him distinguished favour, requested him to write this opera for his theatre at Munich, the orchestra of which was one of the best in Germany. Mozart was then in the full bloom of his genius; he was in his twenty-fifth year, and passionately enamoured of mademoiselle Constance Weber, a celebrated actress, whom he afterwards married. The family of his mistress opposed the match, on account of his unsettled habits, his having no permanent situation, and because his manners had hitherto been far from exemplary. He was desirous of shewing to this family, that though he had no settled rank in society, he nevertheless possessed the means of obtaining consideration, and his attachment to Constance supplied him with the subjects of the impassioned airs which his work required. The love, and vanity of the young composer, thus stimulated to the highest pitch, enabled him to produce an opera, which he always regarded as his best, and from which he has frequently borrowed ideas for his subsequent compositions.

Like Raphael, Mozart embraced his art in its whole extent. Raphael appears to have been unacquainted with one thing only, the mode of painting figures on a ceiling, in contracted proportion, or what is termed *fore-shortening*. He always supposes the canvas of the piece to be attached to the roof, or supported by allegorical figures.

As for Mozart, I am not aware of any department in which he has not excelled: operas, symphonies, songs, airs for dancing—he is great in every thing. Haydn's friend, the baron Von Swieten, went so far as to say, that if Mozart had lived, he would have borne away the sceptre of instrumental music, even from that great master. In the comic-opera, Mozart is deficient in gaiety. In this respect, he is inferior to Galuppi, Guglielmi, and Sarti.

The most remarkable circumstance in his music, independently of the genius displayed in it, is the novel way in which he employs the orchestra, especially the wind instruments. He draws surprising effects from the flute, an instrument of which Cimarosa hardly ever made any use. He enriches the accompaniment with all the beauties of the finest symphonies.

Mozart has been accused of taking interest only in his own music, and of being acquainted with none but his own works. This is the reproach of mortified vanity. Employed all his life in writing his own ideas, Mozart had not, it is true, time to read all those of other masters. But he readily expressed his approbation of whatever he met with that possessed merit, even the simplest air, provided it was original; though, less politic than the great artists of Italy, he had no consideration for mediocrity.

He most esteemed Porpora, Durante, Leo, and Alessandro Scarlatti, but he placed Handel above them all. He knew the principal works of that great master by heart. He was accustomed to say; " Handel knows best of all of us what is capable of producing a great effect. When he chooses, he strikes like the thunder-bolt."

He remarked of Jomelli, " This artist shines, and will always shine, in certain departments; but he should have confined himself to them, and not have attempted to write sacred music in the ancient style." He had not much opinion of Vincenzo Martini, whose *Cosa rara* was at that time much in favour. " There are some very pretty things in it," said he, " but twenty years hence, nobody will think of it."

We possess nine operas composed by Mozart to Italian words : *La Finta Semplice,* comic opera, his first essay in the dramatic department : *Mitridate,* serious opera : *Lucio Silla,* serious opera: *La Giardiniera,* comic opera : *Idomeneo,* serious opera : *Le Nozze di Figaro,* and *Don Giovanni,* composed in 1787: *Così fan tutte,* comic opera; and *La Clemenza di Tito* an opera of Metastasio, which was performed, for the first time, in 1792.

He wrote only three German operas, *Die Entführung aus dem Serail, Der Schauspieldirector,* and *Die Zauber Flöte,* in 1792.

He has left seventeen symphonies, and instrumental pieces of all kinds.

Mozart was also one of the first pianoforte players in Europe. He played with extraordinary rapidity; the execution of his left hand, especially, was greatly admired.

As early as the year 1785, Haydn said to Mozart's father, who was then at Vienna: " I declare to you, before God, and on my honour, that I regard your son as the greatest composer I ever heard of."

Such was Mozart in music. To those acquainted with human nature, it will not appear surprising, that a man, whose talents in this department were the object of general admiration, should not appear to equal advantage in the other situations of life.

Mozart possessed no advantages of person, though his parents were noted for their beauty. Cabanis remarks, that

" Sensibility may be compared to a fluid, the total quantity of which is determined; and which, whenever it flows more abundantly in any one channel, is proportionally diminished in the others."

Mozart never reached his natural growth. During his whole life, his health was delicate. He was thin and pale; and though the form of his face was unusual, there was nothing striking in his physiognomy, but its extreme variableness. The expression of his countenance changed every moment, but indicated nothing more than the pleasure or pain which he experienced at the instant. He was remarkable for a habit, which is usually the attendant of stupidity. His body was perpetually in motion; he was either playing with his hands, or beating the ground with his foot. There was nothing extraordinary in his other habits, except his extreme fondness for the game of billiards. He had a table in his house, on which he played every day by himself, when he had not any one to play with. His hands were so habituated to the piano, that he was rather clumsy in every thing beside. At table, he never carved, or if he attempted to do so, it was with much awkwardness, and difficulty. His wife usually undertook that office.

The same man, who, from his earliest age, had shewn the greatest expansion of mind in what related to his art, in other respects remained always a child. He never knew how properly to conduct himself. The management of domestic affairs, the proper use of money, the judicious selection of his pleasures, and temperance in the enjoyment of them, were never virtues to his taste. The gratification of the moment was always uppermost with him. His mind was so absorbed by a crowd of ideas, which rendered him incapable of all serious reflection, that, during his whole life, he stood in need of a guardian to take care of his temporal affairs. His father was well aware of his weakness in this respect, and it was on this account that he persuaded his wife to follow him to Paris, in 1777, his engagements not allowing him to leave Salzburg himself.

But this man, so absent, so devoted to trifling amusements, appeared a being of a superior order as soon as he sat down to a piano-forte. His mind then took wing, and his whole attention was directed to the sole object for which nature designed him, *the harmony of sounds.* The most numerous orchestra did not prevent him from observing the slightest false note, and he immediately pointed out, with surprising precision, by what instrument the fault had been committed, and the note which should have been made.

When Mozart went to Berlin, he arrived late on the evening. Scarcely had he alighted, than he asked the waiter of the inn, whether there was any opera that evening. " Yes, the *Entführung aus dem Serail*"—" That is charming !" He immediately set out for the theatre, and placed himself at the entrance of the pit, that he might listen without being observed. But, sometimes, he was so pleased with the execution of certain passages, and at others, so dissatisfied with the manner, or the time, in which they were performed, or with the embellishments added by the actors, that, continually expressing either his pleasure, or disapprobation, he insensibly got up to the bar of the orchestra. The manager had taken the liberty of making some alterations in one of the airs. When they came to it, Mozart, unable to restrain himself any longer, called out, almost aloud, to the orchestra, in what way it ought to be played. Every body turned to look at the man in a great coat, who was making all this noise. Some persons recognised Mozart, and, in an instant, the musicians and actors were informed that he was in the theatre. Some of them, and amongst the number a very good female singer, were so agitated at the intelligence, that they refused to come again upon the stage. The manager informed Mozart of the embarrassment he was in. He immediately went behind the scenes, and succeeded, by the compliments which he paid to the actors, in prevailing upon them to go on with the piece.

Music was his constant employment, and his most gratified recreation. Never, even in his earliest childhood, was persuasion required to engage him to go to his piano. On the contrary, it was necessary to take care that he did not injure his health by his application. He was particularly fond of playing in the night. If he sat down to the instrument at nine o'clock in the evening, he never left it before midnight, and even then it was necessary to force him away from it, for he would have continued to modulate, and play voluntaries, the whole night. In his general habits he was the gentlest of men, but the least noise during the performance of music offended him violently. He was far above that affected or mis-placed modesty, which prevents many performers from playing till they have been repeatedly entreated. The nobility of Vienna often reproached him with playing, with equal interest, before any persons that took pleasure in hearing him.

CHAPTER IV.

An amateur, in a town through which Mozart passed in one of his journies, assembled a large party of his friends, to give them an opportunity of hearing this celebrated musician. Mozart came, agreeably to his engagement, said very little, and sat down to the piano-forte. Thinking that none but connoisseurs were present, he began a slow movement, the harmony of which was sweet, but extremely simple, intending by it to prepare his auditors for the sentiment which he designed to introduce afterwards. The company thought all this very common-place. The style soon became more lively; they thought it pretty enough. It became severe, and solemn, of a striking, elevated, and more difficult harmony. Some of the ladies began to think it quite tiresome, and to whisper a few criticisms to one another: soon, half the party were talking. The master of the house was upon thorns, and Mozart himself, at last perceived how little his audience were affected by the music. He did not abandon the principal idea with which he commenced, but he developed it with all the fire of which he was capable; still he was not attended to. Without leaving off playing, he began to remonstrate rather sharply with his audience, but as he fortunately expressed himself in Italian, scarcely any body understood him. They became however more quiet. When his anger was a little abated, he could not himself forbear laughing at his impetuosity. He gave a more common turn to his ideas, and concluded with playing a well known air, of which he gave ten or twelve charming variations. The whole room was delighted, and very few of the company were at all aware of what had passed. Mozart, however, soon took leave, inviting the master of the house, and a few connoisseurs, to spend the evening with him at his inn. He detained them to supper, and upon their intimating a wish to hear him play, he sat down to the instrument, where, to their great astonishment, he forgot himself till after midnight.

An old harpsichord tuner came to put some strings to his travelling piano-forte. " Well, my good old fellow", says Mozart to him, " what do I owe you ? I leave tomorrow." The poor man, regarding him as a sort of deity, replied, stammering and confounded, ": Imperial Majesty ! ...... Mr. the maître de chapelle of his imperial majesty ! ... I cannot . . . It is true that I have waited upon you several times. . . . . You shall give me a crown."—"A crown !" replied Mozart, "a worthy fellow, like you, ought not to be put out of his way for a crown ;" and he gave him some ducats. The honest man, as he withdrew, continued to repeat, with low bows, " Ah ! Imperial Majesty !"

Of his operas, he esteemed most highly the *Idomeneus,* and *Don Juan.* He was not fond of talking of his own works; or if he mentioned them, it was in few words. Of *Don Juan* he said one day, " This opera was not composed for the public of Vienna, it is better suited to Prague; but, to say the truth, I wrote it only for myself, and my friends."

The time which he most willingly employed in composition, was the morning, from six or seven o'clock till ten, when he got up. After this, he did no more for the rest of the day, unless he had to finish a piece that was wanted. He always worked very irregularly. When an idea struck him, he was not to be drawn from it. If he was taken from the piano-forte, he continued to compose in the midst of his friends, and passed whole nights with his pen in his hand. At other times, he had such a disinclination to work, that he could not complete a piece till the moment of its performance. It once happened, that he put off some music which he had engaged to furnish for a court concert, so long, that he had not time to write out the part which he was to perform himself. The emperor Joseph, who was peeping every where, happening to cast his eyes on the sheet which Mozart seemed to be playing from, was surprised to see nothing but empty lines, and said to him : " Where's your part?"— " Here," replied Mozart, putting his hand to his forehead.

The same circumstance nearly occurred with respect to the overture of *Don Juan.* It is generally esteemed the best of his overtures; yet it was only composed the night previous to the first representation, after the general rehearsal had taken place. About eleven o'clock in the evening, when he retired to his apartment, he desired his wife to make him some punch, and to stay with him, in order to keep him awake. She accordingly began to tell him fairy tales, and odd stories, which made him laugh till the tears came. The punch, however, made him so drowsy, that he could go on only while his wife was talking, and dropped asleep as soon as she ceased. The efforts which he made to keep himself awake, the continual alternation of sleep and watching, so fatigued him, that his wife persuaded him to take some rest, promising to awake him in an hour's time. He slept so profoundly, that she suffered him to repose for two hours. At five o'clock in the morning she awoke him. He had appointed the music-copiers to come at seven, and by the time they arrived, the overture was finished. They had scarcely time to write out the copies necessary for the orchestra, and the musicians were obliged to play it without a rehearsal. Some persons pretend that they can discover in this overture the passages where Mozart dropped asleep, and those where he suddenly awoke again.

Don Juan had no great success at Vienna at first. A short time after the first representation, it was talked of in a large party, at which most of the connoisseurs of the capital and amongst others Haydn, were present. Mozart was not there. Every body agreed that it was a very meritorious performance, brilliant in imagination, and rich in genius; but every one had also some fault to find with it. All had spoken, except the modest Haydn. His opinion was asked. " I am not," said he, with his accustomed caution, " a proper judge of the dispute: all that I know is, that Mozart is the greatest composer now existing." The subject was then changed.

Mozart, on his part, had also a great regard for Haydn. He has dedicated to him a set of quartetts, which may be classed with the best productions of the kind. A professor of Vienna, who was not without merit, though far inferior to Haydn, took a malicious pleasure in searching the compositions of the latter, for all the little inaccuracies which might have crept into them. He often came to shew Mozart symphonies, or quartetts, of Haydn's, which he had put into score, and in which he had, by this means, discovered some inadvertencies of style. Mozart always endeavoured to change the subject of conversation: at last, unable any longer to restrain himself, " Sir," said he to him, sharply, " if you and I were both melted down together, we should not furnish materials for one Haydn."

A painter, who was desirous of flattering Cimarosa, said to him once, that he considered him superior to Mozart. " I, Sir," replied he smartly ; " what would you say to a person who should assure you that you were superior to Raphael ?"

CHAPTER V.

Mozart judged his own works with impartiality, and often, with a severity, which he would not easily have allowed in another person. The emperor Joseph II. was fond of Mozart, and had appointed him his maître de chapelle; but this prince pretended to be a *dilettante*. His travels in Italy had given him a partiality for the music of that country, and the Italians who were at his court did not fail to keep up this preference, which, I must confess, appears to me to be well founded.

These men spoke of Mozart's first essays with more jealousy than fairness, and the emperor, who scarcely ever judged for himself, was easily carried away by their decisions. One day, after hearing the rehearsal of a comic opera *(die Entführung aus dem*

Serail,) which he had himself demanded of Mozart, he said to the composer : " My dear Mozart, that is too fine for my ears ; there are too many notes there."—" I ask your majesty's pardon," replied Mozart, dryly; " there are just as many notes as there should be." The emperor said nothing, and appeared rather embarrassed by the reply ; but when the opera was performed, he bestowed on it the greatest encomiums.

Mozart was himself less satisfied with this piece afterwards, and made many corrections and retrenchments in it. He said, in playing on the piano-forte one of the airs which had been most applauded; " This is very well for the parlour, but it is too verbose for the theatre. At the time I composed this opera, I took delight in what I was doing, and thought nothing too long."

Mozart was not at all selfish ; on the contrary, liberality formed the principal feature of his character. He often gave without discrimination, and, still more frequently, expended his money without discretion.

During one of his visits to Berlin, the king, Frederic William, offered him an appointment of 3,000 crowns a year, if he would remain at his court, and take upon him the direction of his orchestra. Mozart made no other reply than " Shall I leave my good emperor?" Yet, at that time, Mozart had no fixed establishment at Vienna. One of his friends blaming him afterwards for not having accepted the king of Prussia's proposals, he replied : " I am fond of Vienna, the emperor treats me kindly, and I care little about money."

Some vexatious intrigues, which were excited against him at court, occasioned him, nevertheless, to request his dismissal; but a word from the emperor, who was partial to the composer, and especially to his music, immediately changed his resolution. He had not art enough to take advantage of this favourable moment, to demand a fixed salary; but the emperor himself, at length, thought of regulating his establishment. Unfortunately, he consulted on the subject a man who was not a friend to Mozart. He proposed to give him 800 florins (about 100*l.*) and this sum was never increased. He received it as private composer to the emperor, but he never did any thing in this capacity. He was once required, in consequence of one of the general government-orders, frequent at Vienna, to deliver in a statement of the amount of his salary. He wrote, in a sealed note, as follows: " Too much for what I have done: too little for what I could have done."

The music-sellers, the managers of the theatres, and others, daily took advantage of his well-known disinterestedness. He never received any thing for the greater part of his compositions for the piano. He wrote them to oblige persons of his acquaintance, who expressed a wish to possess something in his own writing for their private use. In these cases he was obliged to conform to the degree of proficiency which those persons had attained; and this explains why many of his compositions for the harpsichord appear unworthy of him. Artaria, a music-seller, at Vienna, and others of his brethren, found means to procure copies of these pieces, and published them without the permission of the author; or, at any rate, without making him any pecuniary acknowledgment.

LETTER VI.

ONE day, the manager of a theatre, whose affairs were in a bad state, and who was almost reduced to despair, came to Mozart, and made known his situation to him, adding, "You are the only man in the world who can relieve me from my embarrassment."—"I," replied Mozart, "how can that be?"—"By composing for me an opera to suit the taste of the description of people who attend my theatre. To a certain point you may consult that of the connoisseurs, and your own glory; but have a particular regard to that class of persons who are not judges of good music. I will take care that you shall have the poem shortly, and that the decorations shall be handsome; in a word, that every thing shall be agreeable to the present mode." Mozart, touched by the poor fellow's entreaties, promised to undertake the business for him. "What remuneration do you require?" asked the manager. "Why, it seems that you have nothing to give me," said Mozart, "but that you may extricate yourself from your embarrassments, and that, at the same time, I may not altogether lose my labour, we will arrange the matter thus:—You shall have the score, and give me what you please for it, on condition that you will not allow any copies to be taken. If the opera succeeds, I will dispose of it in another quarter." The manager, enchanted with this generosity, was profuse in his promises. Mozart immediately set about the music, and composed it agreeably to the instructions given him. The opera was performed; the house was always filled; it was talked of all over Germany, and was performed, a short time afterwards, on five or six different theatres, none of which had obtained their copies from the distressed manager.

On other occasions, he met only with ingratitude from those to whom he had rendered service, but nothing could extinguish his compassion for the unfortunate. Whenever any distressed artists, who were strangers to Vienna, applied to him, in passing through the city, he offered them the use of his house and table, introduced them to the acquaintance of those persons whom he thought most likely to be of use to them, and seldom let them depart without writing for them *concertos*, of which he did not even keep a copy, in order that being the only persons to play them, they might exhibit themselves to more advantage.

Mozart often gave concerts at his house on Sundays. A Polish count, who was introduced on one of these occasions, was delighted, as well as the rest of the company, with a piece of music for five instruments, which was performed for the first time. He expressed to Mozart how much he had been gratified by it, and requested that, when he was at leisure, he would compose for him a trio for the flute. Mozart promised to do so, on condition that it should be at his own time. The count, on his return home, sent the composer 100 gold demi-sovereigns, (about 100*l*.) with a very polite note, in which he thanked him for the pleasure he had enjoyed. Mozart sent him the original score of the piece for five instruments, which had appeared to please him. The count left Vienna. A year afterwards he called again upon Mozart, and enquired about his trio. " Sir," replied the composer, " I have never felt myself in a disposition to write any thing that I should esteem worthy of your acceptance."—" Probably," replied the count, " you will not feel more disposed to return me the 100 demi-sovereigns, which I paid you beforehand for the piece." Mozart, indignant, immediately returned him his sovereigns; but the count said nothing about the original score of the piece for five instruments; and it was soon afterwards published by Artaria, as a quatuor for the harpsichord, with an accompaniment for the violin, alto, and violoncello.

It has been remarked, that Mozart very readily acquired new habits. The health of his wife, whom he always passionately loved, was very delicate. During a long illness which she had, he always met those who came to see her, with his finger on his lips, as an intimation to them not to make a noise. His wife recovered, but, for a long time afterwards, he always went to meet those who came to visit him with his finger on his lips, and speaking in a subdued tone of voice.

In the course of this illness, he occasionally took a ride on horseback, early in the morning, but, before he went, he was always careful to lay a paper near his wife, in the form of a physician's prescription. The following is a copy of one of these: " Good morning, my love, I hope you have slept well, and that nothing has disturbed you : be careful not to take cold, or to hurt yourself in stooping : do not vex yourself with the servants : avoid every thing that would be unpleasant to you, till I return : take good care of yourself: I shall return at nine o'clock."

Constance Weber was an excellent companion for Mozart, and often gave him useful advice. She bore him two children, whom he tenderly loved. His income was considerable, but his immoderate love of pleasure, and the disorder of his affairs, prevented him from bequeathing any thing to his family, except the celebrity of his name, and the attention of the public. After the death of this great composer, the inhabitants of Vienna testified to his children, their gratitude for the pleasure which their father had so often afforded them.

During the last years of Mozart's life, his health, which had always been delicate, declined rapidly. Like all persons of imagination, he was timidly apprehensive of future evils, and the idea that he had not long to live, often distressed him. At these times, he worked with such rapidity, and unremitting attention, that he sometimes forgot every thing that did not relate to his art. Frequently, in the height of his enthusiasm, his strength failed him, he fainted, and was obliged to be carried to his bed. Every one saw that he was ruining his health by this immoderate application. His wife, and his friends, did all they could to divert him. Out of complaisance, he accompanied them in the walks and visits to which they took him, but his thoughts were always absent. He was only occasionally roused from this silent and habitual melancholy, by the presentiment of his approaching end, an idea which always awakened in him fresh terror.

His insanity was similar to that of Tasso, and to that which rendered Rousseau so happy in the valley of Charmettes, by leading him, through the fear of approaching death, to the only true philosophy, the enjoyment of the present moment and the forgetting of sorrow. Perhaps, without that high state of nervous sensibility which borders on insanity, there is no superior genius in the arts which require tenderness of feeling.

His wife, uneasy at these singular habits, invited to the house those persons whom he was most fond of seeing, and who pretended to surprise him, at times when, after many hours' application, he ought naturally to have thought of resting. Their visits pleased him, but he did not lay aside his pen; they talked, and endeavoured to engage him in the conversation, but he took no interest in it; they addressed themselves particularly to him, he uttered a few inconsequential words, and went on with his writing.

This extreme application, it may be observed, sometimes accompanies genius, but is by no means a proof of it. Who can read Thomas's emphatic collection of superlatives? Yet this writer was so absorbed in his meditations on the means of being eloquent, that once, at Montmorency, when his footman brought him the horse on which he usually rode out, he offered the animal a pinch of snuff. Raphael Mengs also, in the present age, was remarkable for absence, yet he is only a painter of the third order; while Guido, who was always at the gaming table, and who, towards the conclusion of his life, painted as many as three pictures in a day, to pay the debts of the night, has left behind him works, the least valuable of which is more pleasing than the best of Mengs, or of Carlo Maratti, both of them men of great application.

A lady once said to me, " Mr. —— tells me that I shall reign for ever in his heart, —that I shall be sole mistress of it. Assuredly I believe him, but what signifies it, if his heart itself does not please me?" Of what use is the application of a man without genius? Mozart has been, in the eighteenth century, perhaps the most striking example of the union of the two. Benda, the author of Ariadne in the isle of Naxos, has also long fits of absence.

CHAPTER VII.

It was in this state of mind that he composed the *Zauber Flöte*, the *Clemenza di Tito*, the *Requiem*, and some other pieces of less celebrity. It was while he was writing the music of the first of these operas, that he was seized with the fainting fits we have mentioned. He was very partial to the Zauber Flöte, though he was not quite satisfied with some parts of it, to which the public had taken a fancy, and which were incessantly applauded. This opera was performed many times, but the weak state in which Mozart then was, did not permit him to direct the orchestra, except during nine or ten of the first representations. When he was no longer able to attend the theatre, he used to place his watch by his side, and seemed to follow the orchestra in his thoughts. " Now the first act is over," he would say—" now they are singing such an air," &c; then, the idea would strike him afresh, that he must soon bid adieu to all this for ever.

The effect of this fatal tendency of mind was accelerated by a very singular circumstance. I beg leave to be permitted to relate it in detail, because we are indebted to it for the famous *Requiem*, which is justly considered one of Mozart's best productions.*

---

* This great work is a solemn mass in D minor for the burial of the dead, hung round with the funereal pomp and imagery which the forebodings of the author inspired. At its opening, the ear is accosted by the mournful notes of the *Corni di bassetto*, mingling with the bassoons in a strain of bewailing harmony, which streams with impressive effect amidst the short sorrowful notes of the accompanying orchestra.

The *Dies irae* follows in a movement full of terror and dismay. The *Tuba mirum*, is opened by the sonorous *tromboni*, to awaken the sleeping dead. Every one acquainted with the powers of this instrument acknowledges the superiority of its tones for the expression of this sublime idea.

Rex tremendae Majestatis, is a magnificent display of regal grandeur, of which none but a Mozart would have dared to sketch the outline. It is followed by the beautiful movement *Recordare*, which supplicates in the softest inflexions. The persuasive tone of the Corni di bassetto is again introduced with unexampled effect.

One day, when he was plunged in a profound reverie, he heard a carriage stop at his door. A stranger was announced, who requested to speak to him. A person was introduced, handsomely dressed, of dignified, and impressive manners. " I have been commissioned, Sir, by a man of considerable importance, to call upon you."—" Who is he ?" interrupted Mozart.—" He does not wish to be known"—" Well, what does he want?"— "He has just lost a person whom he tenderly loved, and whose memory will be eternally dear to him. He is desirous of annually commemorating this mournful event by a solemn service, for which he requests you to compose a *Requiem.*" Mozart was forcibly struck by this discourse, by the grave manner in which

---

It is too evident where the pen of our author was arrested; and this wonderful performance is very absurdly finished by repeating some of the early parts of the work to words of a very contrary import. *The Lux æterna,* is a suject worthy of the pen of Beethoven, and it is to be hoped he will yet finish this magnificent work, in a style worthy of its great projector. G.

it was uttered, and by the air of mystery in which the whole was involved. He engaged to write the *Requiem*. The stranger continued, "Employ all your genius on this work; it is destined for a connoisseur."—" So much the better,"—" What time do you require?"—" A month."—" Very well: in a month's time I shall return.—What price do you set on your work?"—" A hundred ducats." The stranger counted them on the table, and disappeared.

Mozart remained lost in thought for some time; he then suddenly called for pen, ink, and paper, and, in spite of his wife's entreaties, began to write. This rage for composition continued several days; he wrote day and night, with an ardour which seemed continually to increase; but his constitution, already in a state of great debility, was unable to support this enthusiasm: one morning, he fell senseless, and was obliged to suspend his work. Two or three days after, when his wife sought to divert his mind from the gloomy presages which occupied it, he said to her abruptly: "It is certain that I am writing this *Requiem* for myself; it will serve for my funeral service." Nothing could remove this impression from his mind.

As he went on, he felt his strength diminish from day to day, and the score advanced slowly. The month which he had fixed, being expired, the stranger again made his appearance. "I have found it impossible," said Mozart, "to keep my word"—"Do not give yourself any uneasiness," replied the stranger; "what further time do you require?" —" Another month. The work has interested me more than I expected, and I have extended it much beyond what I at first designed."—" In that case, it is but just to increase the premium; here are fifty ducats more."—" Sir," said Mozart, with increasing astonishment, " who, then, are you?"—" That is nothing to the purpose; in a month's time I shall return."

Mozart immediately called one of his servants, and ordered him to follow this extraordinary personage, and find out who he was; but the man failed for want of skill, and returned without being able to trace him.

Poor Mozart was then persuaded that he was no ordinary being: that he had a connection with the other world, and was sent to announce to him his approaching end. He applied himself with the more ardour to his *Requiem,* which he regarded as the most durable monument of his genius. While thus employed, he was seized with the most alarming fainting fits, but the work was at length completed before the expiration of the month. At the time appointed, the stranger returned, but Mozart was no more.

His career was as brilliant as it was short. He died before he had completed his thirty-sixth year; but in this short space of time he has acquired a name which will never perish, so long as feeling hearts are to be found.

Monticello, August 29, 1814.

My dear Friend,

It appears that the only works of Mozart known at Paris, are *Figaro, Don Juan,* and *Così fan tutte,* which have been performed at the Odeon.

The first reflection which offers itself on Figaro, is that the sensibility of the musician, has led him to convert into serious passions, the transient inclinations which, in the piece of Beaumarchais, amuse the agreeable inhabitants of the chateau of Aguas-Frescas. In the latter, count Almaviva has a fancy for Susanna—nothing more; and is far from feeling the passion which breathes in the air,

> Vedrò mentr'io sospiro
> Felice un servo mio!

And in the duet

Crudel! perchè finora?

we certainly do not recognise the man who says, in act iii, scene 4, of the French play, "How is it that I am so taken with this whim? I have been on the point of abandoning it twenty times over.—Strange effect of irresolution! if I was determined to have her, I should be a thousand times less desirous of her." How was it possible for the musician to give this idea, which, nevertheless, is very natural? How can a man be witty in music?

We feel, in the comedy, that the inclination of Rosina for the little page might become serious. But the state of her feelings, her reflections on the scanty portion of felicity allotted us by fate, all that agitation of mind which precedes the greater passions, is infinitely more developed by Mozart, than by the French author. We have scarcely terms to express this state of mind, which is perhaps better to be described by music, than by words.

The airs sung by the countess, therefore, represent an entirely new character: and the same may be said of that of Bartholo, so well marked in the grand air :

<blockquote>La Vendetta! la Vendetta!</blockquote>

The jealousy of Figaro, in the air,

<blockquote>Se vuol ballar, signor Contino,</blockquote>

is far removed from the frivolity of the French Figaro. In this sense, it may be said that Mozart has disfigured the piece as much as possible. I am not sure that music could be made to represent French gallantry and trifling, in all the characters through four whole acts;—it requires decided passions—joy, or sorrow. A smart repartee produces no effect upon the feelings, suggests no subject for meditation. When Cherubino leaps out of the window, " The rage for leaping may be catching," says Figaro; " remember the sheep of Panurge." This is delightful; but if you dwell on it for a moment, the charm disappears.*

---

* The allusion is to a story in Rabelais in which the author ridicules the servility of the courtiers. Panurge,

I should like to see the " Noces de Figaro," set to music by Fioravanti. In Mozart, the true expression of the French piece is nowhere to be found, except it be in the duet

> Se a caso madama,

between Susanna and Figaro; and even here he is too much in earnest when he says:

> Udir bramo il resto.

Lastly, to complete the transformation, Mozart concludes the *Folle Journée* with the finest church chant that it is possible to hear;—that which follows the word " Perdono," in the last finale.

He has entirely changed the picture of Beaumarchais. The wit of the original is preserved only in the situations; all the characters are altered to the tender and impassioned. The page is only just sketched in

---

king of the Isle of Lanterns, has a flock of sheep, which, on seeing him dance, begin all to do the same, *par courtoisie.* T.

the French piece; his whole soul is displayed in the airs,

> Non so più cosa son,
>
> Voi che sapete cosa è amore;

and in the duet with the countess, at the conclusion, when they meet in the dark walks of the garden, near the grove of chesnut-trees.

The opera of Mozart is a sublime combination of spirit, and melancholy, of which we have no other example. The delineation of sad and tender sentiments is liable to become tiresome: but here, the brilliant wit of the French author, which appears in all the situations, effectually prevents the only defect which was in danger of occurring.

To be in the spirit of the original, the music should have been written conjointly by Cimarosa and Paesiello. Cimarosa only could have imparted to Figaro the brilliant gaiety and confidence which belongs to him. Nothing can be more completely in this character than the air,

> Mentr'io era un fraschetone
> Sono stato il più felice;

which it must be confessed is feebly given in the only gay air of Mozart's piece:

> Non più andrai farfallone amoroso.

The melody of this air is even rather commonplace; it is the expression which it gradually assumes that constitutes its whole charm. As for Paesiello, we need only bring to mind the quintetto in the *Barbiere di Siviglia*, where he says to Basil,

> Andate a letto,

to be convinced that he was exactly fitted to depict situations purely comic, and in which there is no warmth of sentiment.

As a work of pure tenderness and melancholy, entirely free from all unsuitable admixture of the majestic and tragical, nothing in the world can be compared to the *Nozze di Figaro*. I have pleasure in imagining this opera to be performed by one of the Monbelli as the Countess, Bassi as Figaro, Davidde or Nozzari as Count Almaviva, Madame Gaforini as Susanna, the other Monbelli as the Little Page, and Pellegrini as Doctor Bartholo.

If you were acquainted with these delightful voices, you would share the pleasure of this idea with me; but, in music, we can only talk to people of their recollections.

I might, with a multiplicity of words, succeed in giving you an idea of the Aurora of Guido, in the Rospigliosi palace, though you should never have seen it; but I should be tedious as a writer of poetical prose, if I were to give you the same detailed account of the Idomeneus, or the Clemenza di Tito, as I have done of Figaro.

It may be said, with truth, and without being chargeable with those delusive exaggerations to which one is perpetually liable, in speaking of a man like Mozart, that, absolutely, nothing is comparable to the Idomeneus. I do not fear to say, contrary to the opinion of all Italy, that to me, the first serious opera extant, is not the Horatii, but the Idomeneus, or the Clemenza di Tito.

Majesty, in music, soon becomes tiresome. The art is incompetent fully to give the spirit of Horatius, when he says,

Albano tu sei, io non ti conosco più;

and the patriotic feeling which is displayed in the whole of that character, while tenderness alone animates those of the *Clemenza*. What can be more affecting than Titus saying to his friend,

> Confidati all'amico: io ti prometto
> Che Augusto nol saprà?

His generous forgiveness at the conclusion, where he says,

> Sesto, non più: torniamo
> Di nuovo amici,

brings tears into the eyes of the most hardened traitors, as I have myself witnessed at Königsberg, after the terrible retreat from Moscow. On our re-entering the civilized world, we found the *Clemenza di Tito* very well got up, in that city, where the Russians had the politeness to give us twenty days rest, of which, in truth, we stood greatly in need.

To form any idea of the *Zauber Flöte*, it is absolutely necessary to have seen it. The story, which is like the wandering of a delirious imagination, harmonizes divinely with the genius of the musician. I am convinced that if Mozart had been a writer, his pen would have been employed in depicting scenes like that where the negro, Monostatos, comes in the silence of the night, by the light of the moon, to steal a kiss from the lips of the sleeping princess. Chance has produced what the lovers of music never met with, except in Rousseau's *Devin du Village*. We may say of the *Zauber Flöte*, that the same man wrote both the words and the music.

The romantic imagination of Don Juan, in which Moliere has drawn so many interesting scenes, from the murder of the father of Donna Anna, to the invitation and terrible reply of the speaking statue, is altogether suited to the talent of Mozart.

He shines in the awful accompaniment to the reply of the statue—a composition perfectly free from all inflation or bombast—it is the style of Shakespeare in music.

The fear of Leporello, when he excuses himself from speaking to the commander, is painted with true comic spirit:—a thing unusual with Mozart. On the other hand, men of feeling carry away a thousand melancholy recollections from this opera. Even at Paris, who does not remember the passage,

> Ah! rimembranza amara!
> Il padre mio dov' è?

Don Juan did not succeed at Rome;—perhaps, because the orchestra was unable to execute this very difficult music; but I doubt not that it will one day be a favourite there.

The subject of *Cosi fan tutte,* was formed for Cimarosa, and is altogether unsuitable to Mozart, who could never trifle with love, a passion that was always the happiness, or the torment, of his life. He has only given the tender part of the characters, and has entirely omitted the drollery of the satirical old sea-captain. He has sometimes escaped by the aid of his sublime science in harmony, as in the trio at the conclusion.

> Tutte fan così.

Mozart, philosophically contemplated, is still more astonishing, than when regarded as the author of sublime compositions. Never was the soul of a man of genius exhibited so naked, if we may be allowed the expression. The corporeal part had as little share as possible in that extraordinary union called Mozart. To this day the Italians designate him by the appellation of " *quel mostro d'ingegno,*"—that prodigy of genius.

LETTER

ON THE GENIUS

OF

METASTASIO.

Varese, October 24, 1812.

My Friend,

The generality of men have little regard for gracefulness. Vulgar minds esteem only what they fear. Hence arises the universal passion for military glory, and the partiality for tragedy at the theatre. In literature, such persons are most pleased with what appears difficult; and it is the general prevalence of this taste, which has prevented Metastasio from obtaining a reputation more correspondent with his merit. At the Museum, every body understands the Martyrdom of St. Peter by Titian, few feel the St. Jerome of Correggio:

they require to be taught that this beauty, so graceful, is beauty. On this subject, women, who are less habitually swayed by interested considerations, are much better judges than men.

The object of music is to give pleasure; and Metastasio was the poet of music. His natural tenderness of feeling led him to avoid whatever would have given the slightest pain to the spectator. He has abstained from describing poignant distress, even of sentiment merely. His pieces never terminate tragically; never do they exhibit the gloomy realities of life, or those chilling suspicions, which infuse their poison into the most tender passions.

He was sensible that if the music of his operas was good, it would agreeably divert the mind of the spectator, by leading him to think of what he most loves. He, therefore, continually repeats whatever is necessary to be known of his characters, in order to understand what they are singing. He seems to say to the spectator, " Enjoy yourself, I will not even give you the trouble of attending. Do not concern yourself about the plot of the piece; forget the theatre altogether. Make yourself happy in your box; give yourself up to the tender sentiment which my hero expresses." His characters retain scarcely any thing of the dull reality of life. He has created a set of beings possessed of a spirit, and genius, which men of the most fortunate constitution of mind experience only in some fortunate moments;—St. Preux entering the chamber of Julia.*

Your rational people, who are not offended by the severity of Tacitus, or Alfieri,—who, scarcely sensible to music at all, do not even suspect the object of this charming art; who, insensible to the thorns which, in real life, pierce the feeling heart at every moment, or what is worse, re-plunge it in dull reality; —these people, I say, have, in Metastasio, called that a want of truth, which is, in reality, consummate art. It is as if we should censure the sculptor of the Belvedere Apollo,

---

* Nouvelle Héloïse.

for having omitted the muscular details, seen in the Gladiator and other statues, which represent only men. All that can be said is, that the pleasure arising from an opera of Metastasio, cannot be felt in the country situated between the Alps, the Rhine, and the Pyrenees. I can fancy an intelligent Frenchman, well acquainted with every subject that usually engages the attention of a man of the world, entering the delightful *loggie* of the Vatican, adorned by Raphael with those charming *arabesques*, which are, perhaps, the purest and most divine productions ever inspired by genius and love. Our Frenchman will be offended with the want of probability: these cupids riding on chimæras, these female heads on lions' bodies, will appear absurd to him. There is nothing like these to be found in nature, he will say, in a dogmatical tone. It is true;—and it is equally so that you are not capable of entering into the pleasure, mingled, perhaps, with a little folly, which a man born under a happier sky enjoys, after a burning day, in taking ices in the evening at the villa of Albano.

He is in the company of charming women; the heat of the day has inclined him to a delicious languor. Reclining on a sofa, he traces on a ceiling, resplendent with the richest colours, the charming forms which Raphael has given to these beings, which, as they resemble nothing that we have seen elsewhere, call up none of those common ideas which disturb the felicity of these rare and delightful moments.

I am of opinion also, that the gloominess of the Italian theatres, and their boxes, which resemble saloons, greatly aid the effect of music. How many amiable women are there in France, who understand English, to whom the word *love* has a charm, which the word *amour* no longer possesses. The reason is, that the word *love* has never been pronounced before them by beings unworthy of feeling the sentiment. Nothing tarnishes the brilliant purity of *love,* while the couplets of the vaudeville have for ever spoiled the idea of *amour.*

Those who can enter into these distinctions, will admire the arabesques of Raphael, and the brilliant and un-terrestrial beings which Metastasio has pourtrayed.

He banishes, as far as possible, every thing which would remind us of the melancholy reality of life. He employs the passions only so far as they are necessary to interest us: nothing is stern, or harsh; his very dignity is voluptuous.

Music, in which he delighted, and for which he always wrote, though so powerful in expressing the passions, is incapable of delineating character. Accordingly, in the verses of Metastasio, the Roman, and the Persian, touched by the same passion, speak the same language, because they will do so in the music of Cimarosa. In like manner, the virtues of patriotism, devoted friendship, filial love, chivalrous honour, which are all to be found in history, or society, acquire with him an additional charm; we feel ourselves transported into the land of Mahomet's houris.

These ideal pieces, which in fact ought not to be read, but only heard with music, the cold critics of a certain nation have examined as tragedies. These wise-acres, like their illustrious Italian predecessor Crescimbeni, who, in his "Course of Literature," has taken the *Morgante maggiore,* a poem of the lowest buffoonery, or even something more, for a serious work;—these poor gentlemen, who ought to have followed some more substantial employment, have not even been aware that Metastasio was so far from seeking to inspire terror, that he even refrained from depicting what was merely odious. On this account, he ought to be patronized by every government desirous of encouraging a taste for pleasure among its subjects. To suppose that things might be managed better; to find fault with the existing state of affairs — how shocking! — how unpolite!— would you render us distrustful, and miserable?

The poor critics aforesaid, have been mightily offended at Metastasio's frequent transgression of the rule concerning unity of place. They could not imagine that the Italian poet, so far from being desirous of observing this rule, had laid down one for himself, directly contrary, which was, to change the scene as frequently as possible, that the splendour of the decorations, which in Italy are very beautiful, might give new pleasure to the gratified spectator.

Metastasio, in transporting us, for our gratification, so far from real life, was under the necessity, in order that his characters might be interesting from their resemblance to ourselves, of observing nature scrupulously in the details. In this respect he has rivalled Shakespeare, and Virgil, and far surpassed Racine, and every other poet.*

It was, I think, in 1731, that Pergolese went to Rome to write the music of the *Olimpiade:* which did not succeed. As Rome is, in Italy, the capital of the arts, and the tribunal most competent to sit in judgment on them, this failure greatly distressed him. He returned to Naples, where he composed

---

* The author has here quoted a whole scene from the Olympiad, in support of his assertion, which, as being interesting only to the Italian reader, I have omitted.   T.

some pieces of sacred music. In the mean time, his health daily declined; he had been, for four years, afflicted with a spitting of blood, which was insensibly wearing him away. His friends persuaded him to take a small house at *Torre del Greco,* a village situated on the sea-shore, at the foot of Vesuvius. It is said, at Naples, that persons labouring under complaints of the chest, recover, or decline, with peculiar rapidity, in that place.

Pergolese left the solitary retirement of his cottage once a week, to superintend the performance of the pieces he composed at Naples. He wrote, at Torre del Greco, his famous *Stabat Mater,* the cantata of Orpheus, and the *Salve Regina,* which was the last of his works.

In the beginning of 1733, his strength being entirely exhausted, he ceased to live, and the gazette which announced his death was the signal of his glory. His operas, so lately neglected, were performed in every theatre of Italy. Rome desired, once more, to see his Olimpiade, which was got up with the greatest magnificence. The greater the indifference that had been shewn towards this sublime work, during the author's life-time, the more enthusiastically were its beauties admired after his death.

In this opera, the chef-d'œuvre of Italian music for expression, nothing can exceed the scene between Megacles and Aristea. Act. ii. scene 9. *Al fin, siam soli,* &c. The air

Se cerca, se dice,

is known by heart all over Italy, and this, perhaps, is the principal reason why the Olimpiade is no longer acted. No manager would venture to give an opera, the principal air of which was already in the recollection of all his audience.

In the Olimpiade, music is a language, the expression of which has been added by Pergolese to that of the common language spoken by the characters of Metastasio. But this language of Pergolese, which is capable of conveying the slightest shades of emotion inspired by the passions :—shades which ordinary language might attempt in vain to depict, loses all its enchantment in a rapid pronunciation. He has, therefore, given the explanation between Megacles and Aristea in simple recitative, and has reserved all the energy of his divine language for the air

Se cerca, se dice,

which is, perhaps, the most affecting thing he ever wrote.

It would have been contrary to the genius of the art to have sung the whole scene. The circumstances which render it a duty in the unhappy Megacles to sacrifice his mistress to his friend, could not well be described in any kind of air.

But though the verses

Se cerca, se dice
L'amico dov' è?
L'amico infelice
Respondi, morì.

Ah no! sì gran duolo
Non darle per me;
Rispondi, ma solo,
Piangendo partì.

Che abisso di pene!
Lasciare il suo bene,
Lasciarlo per sempre,
Lasciarlo così, *

should be declaimed by the first actor in the world,—with whatever pathos he might pronounce them, he could speak them but once. He could paint only one of the thousand ways in which the heart of the unfortunate Megacles is torn. Every one has a confused idea of the various and impassioned feelings with which, at the moment of so cruel a separation,

---

* O! should she seek, or ask thee where
   Thy hapless friend is fled;
Return this answer to the fair:
   My hapless friend is dead.

Yet, ah! let not such grief torment
   The tender mourner's breast:
Reply but this: from hence he went,
   With anguish sore opprest.

What deep abyss of woe is mine!
   From her I love to part!
And thus for ever to resign
   The treasure of my heart!

HOOLE.

a man would be likely to say to the friend whom he leaves with a mistress he so passionately loves.

> Ah no! sì gran duolo
> Non darle per me;
> Rispondi, ma solo,
> Piangendo partì.

The unhappy lover will pronounce these verses, at one time, with extreme emotion, at another, with resignation and courage: now, with a faint hope of better fortune, and again, with all the gloom of despair.

He will not be able to speak to his friend of the distress in which Aristea will be plunged, when she recovers her senses, without thinking of the situation in which he will himself be placed, in a few moments; accordingly, the words

> Ah no! sì gran duolo
> Non darle per me,

are repeated five or six times by Pergolese, and each time with a different expression. It is impossible for human sensibility to surpass the picture which this great composer has given of the situation of Megacles. We feel that such a scene could not long be endured. The music would exhaust both the actor and the spectator; and this, my friend, will account for the extasy with which a well-sung air is applauded in Italy. A fine singer confers on them the greatest of benefits; he gives to a whole theatre a divine pleasure, of which the least negligence, or want of feeling on his part, would have deprived them. Never, perhaps, did one man give greater pleasure to another than Marchesi, in singing the rondo in the *Achille in Piro,* of Sarti.

Mia speranza! io pur vorrei.

This happiness is not merely imaginary; it is matter of history. To find its equal, we must go out of real life; we must look into romance: we must represent to ourselves the baron d' Étange, taking St. Preux by the hand, and bestowing on him his daughter.*

Thus it appears, that with seven or eight short verses, with which the poet has supplied

---

* Nouvelle Héloise.

the musician, after having introduced an interesting scene, the latter is able to melt a whole audience. He will express, not only the principal passion of the character, but others, also, of the various emotions with which his heart is agitated in speaking to her whom he loves. Where is the man, who, on parting from the woman he adores, does not say, over and over, *adieu, adieu.* It is the same word which he repeats, but where is the being so unfortunate as not to know, from experience, that, every time, it is pronounced in a different manner. In these seasons of pain, or felicity, the heart changes every moment.

Now it is clear, that common language, which is nothing more than a series of conventional signs to express things generally known, has no term to express certain emotions, which perhaps not more than twenty persons, in a thousand, have ever experienced. Persons of feeling were therefore unable to communicate, and to describe their impressions. Seven or eight men of genius in Italy discovered, about a century ago, this language so much needed. But it has the defect of being unintelligible to the nine hundred and eighty, who have never felt what it describes. These people are in the same situation, with regard to Pergolese, as we should be with respect to a savage *Miami*, who should describe a tree peculiar to America, which grows in the vast forests he traverses in hunting. We hear nothing but an unintelligible noise, which would soon tire us, were the savage to prolong his narration.

To speak still more plainly. If, when we are yawning, we see symptoms of the most lively pleasure in the person who sits by our side, we shall seek to depress this impertinent felicity, in which we have no share; and judging of him, very naturally, by ourselves, we shall deny the reality of the thing, and shall endeavour to turn this pretended rapture into ridicule.

Nothing, therefore, is more absurd, than discussion about music. We either feel it, or we do not, and this is all. Unfortunately for the interests of sincerity, it has become the fashion to be fond of it. That dry old fellow Duclos,* on setting out for Italy, at the age of sixty, thinks himself obliged to tell us that he is passionately fond of music. What an idea!

This language, then, for which it is so fashionable to have a liking, is naturally very indefinite. It required a poet to guide our imaginations, and Pergolese, and Cimarosa, have had the good fortune to find a Metastasio. This language addresses itself directly to the heart, without passing, so to speak, through the understanding; it produces, at once, pain, or pleasure. It was, therefore, necessary that the poet of music should preserve the most perfect clearness in the dialogue; which Metastasio has accordingly done.

Music increases the ideal beauty of every character which it touches. Beaumarchais

---

* Duclos wrote on various subjects of history, and the belles lettres, and is mentioned with eulogium by Palissot and La Harpe. He died in 1772. T.

has drawn Cherubini in a charming manner. Mozart, employing a more powerful language, has put into his mouth the airs

and
>Non so più cosa son
>Cosa faccio,
>
>Voi che sapete
>Che cosa è amore;

and has left the French dramatist far behind. The scenes of Moliere enchant the man of taste, but though this great genius has written many things which music cannot reach, it may be questioned whether he has produced any thing equal, in comic effect, to Cimarosa's airs

>Mentre io era un fraschetone,
>Sono stato il più felice;
>
>Quattro baj e sei morelli;

and
>Le orecchie spalancate.

Observe, that the comic music of Cimarosa produces its effect in spite of the words, which, three times out of four, are the most absurd possible. They, however, almost always possess a decided character of distress, or happiness, or ridiculous buffoonery, full of spirit and humour, which is precisely what music requires. It is an art, which will not admit of the sentimental refinement of the amiable Marivaux.* I should bring the whole of the *Serva maestra* of Pergolese in illustration, if it were known at Paris; but as I am prevented from referring to that delightful music, let me be permitted to quote one of the most agreeable men that France has produced. When the president de Berville was at Bologna, in 1740, he wrote a letter to a friend at Dijon, containing the following passage, which he certainly never supposed would appear in print:

...... "But one of the first, and most important of his duties (speaking of the cardinal Lambertini, archbishop of Bologna, afterwards pope Benedict XIV.) is to go three times a week to the opera. It is not

---

* The French say of an affected, sentimental style, "*C'est du Marivaudage*," in allusion to the writer here mentioned. T.

performed in the city; that would be too vulgar, nobody would go to it; but being at a village, four leagues from Bologna, it is the fashion to be exact. The beaux and belles, from all the neighbouring towns, repair thither, in their berlins and four, as to a rendezvous. It is almost the only opera open in Italy at this season. For a country exhibition, it is very tolerable. Not that the chorusses, dances, dialogue, or actors, are supportable; but the Italian airs are so beautiful, that, after hearing them, one desires nothing more. There are, moreover, a comic actor and actress, who perform a farce between the acts, with such native humour, that nothing can be imagined equal to it. It is not true that a man may die of laughing, otherwise I should certainly have lost my life in that way, in spite of the vexation I felt at it, for preventing me from hearing, as I wished, the celestial music of this farce. It is composed by Pergolese. I bought, on the spot, the original score, which I intend to take with me to France. The ladies are quite at their ease at this entertainment, and converse, or to speak more properly, call to the opposite boxes; they get up, and clap their hands, crying *bravo! bravo!* The gentlemen are more moderate. They content themselves, when an act has pleased them, with bawling till the piece recommences. At midnight, when the opera is over, the audience return home in small parties, or stay to take supper in some snug retreat."

In these delightful compositions, whether tragic or comic, the air, and the singing, commence with the display of the passion. As soon as this appears, the musician takes possession of it: whatever is merely preparatory is thrown into recitative.

When the part of the actor becomes animated, the recitative has an accompaniment, as in the beautiful recitative in the second act of Pyrrhus, which Crivelli sings:

> L'ombra d'Achille
> Mi par di sentire;

or that of Caroline, in the second act of the Matrimonio segreto:

> Come tacerlo puoi?

When the actor has fully entered into the passion, the air commences.

It is singular, that the poet is allowed to be eloquent and explicit only in the recitatives. As soon as the passion shews itself, the musician demands only a small number of words: he charges himself with the expression.

If I were to shew my letter to the agreeable society, which I am going to join this evening, at the *Madonna del Monte,* every body, my dear Louis, would know the touching airs to which I refer. How different is it where you are!

O! fortunatos nimium, sua si bona norint!

What fools we are to be always finding fault and vexing ourselves—to busy ourselves about political matters in which we have no concern. Let the emperor of China hang the philosophers: let the constitution of Norway be wise or foolish, what is it to us? How absurd to take upon us the cares of greatness, and only its cares! The time which you waste in these vain discussions, is deducted from the sum of your life; old age is coming on, and your bright days are fleeting away.*

> Cosi trapassa, al trapassar di un giorno,
> Della vita mortal il fior, e'l verde:
> Nè perchè faccia indietro April ritorno,
> Si rinfiora ella mai, nè si rinverde.
> TASSO.

> So, swiftly fleeting with the transient day,
> Passes the flower of mortal life away!
> In vain the spring returns, the spring no more
> Can waning youth to former prime restore.
> HOOLE.

Ergo, says our philosopher, *let us enjoy ourselves with the ladies in the parlour.* (See page 485.)

> . . . . Amiamo or quando
> Esser si puote riamato amando.

There are persons who infer from the shortness of life that it ought not to be wasted in frivolous pursuits. T.

DANTE was endowed by nature with a profound cast of thought; Petrarch, with an agreeable one. She bestowed on Bojardo, and Ariosto, imagination; on Tasso dignity; but none of them possessed the clearness and precision of Metastasio; none arrived, in their department, at the perfection which Metastasio has attained in his.

Dante, Petrarch, Ariosto, Tasso, have left their successors some possibility of imitation. A few men, of distinguished talents, have occasionally written verses which those great men themselves would not perhaps have disavowed.

Several of the sonnets of Bembo approach those of Petrarch. Monti, in his *Basvigliana*, has some *terzine* worthy of Dante. Bojardo has found in Agostini, if not his equal in imagination, at least a successful imitator of his style. I could quote some octaves which, for richness, and felicity of versification, immediately remind us of Ariosto. I know a still greater number, the harmony and majesty of which, would perhaps have deceived Tasso himself. But notwithstanding the repeated attempts that have been made for near a century, to produce an *aria* in the style of Metastasio, Italy has not yet seen two verses that could deceive us for a moment. He is the only one of her poets, who, literally speaking, has been hitherto inimitable.

How many replies have been written to the *Canzonetta a Nice!* Not one of them will bear reading; and, in my opinion, there exists nothing comparable to it, in any language, not even in Anacreon, or Horace.

The clearness, the precision, the dignified facility which characterize the style of this great poet,—qualities so indispensible in words that are to be sung—have, moreover, the singular effect of rendering his verses extremely easy to retain in the memory. We remember, without effort, this divine poetry, which, though written with the most scrupulous correctness, bears not the slightest marks of constraint.

The *Canzonetta a Nice* pleases the same feelings as are charmed by the small Magdalen of Correggio, at Dresden, and which has been so well copied by the burin of Longhi.

It is difficult to read the Clemenza di Tito, or the Giuseppe, without tears; and Italy possesses few things more sublime than certain passages in the characters of Cleonice, Demetrius, Themistocles, and Regulus.

I know of nothing in any language that can be compared to the cantatas of Metastasio. One is tempted to quote them all.

Alfieri has surpassed every other poet in pourtraying the heart of a tyrant, because, if he had been possessed of rather less honesty, I think he would, on the throne, have made a sublime tyrant himself. The scenes of his Timoleon are very fine;—I feel them to be so. The manner is totally different from that of Metastasio, but I am of opinion that posterity will not consider it superior. We think too much of the style in reading Alfieri. The style, which, like a transparent varnish, ought to cover the colours, to heighten their brilliancy, but not to change them, usurps, in him, a part of our attention.

But who thinks of the style in reading Metastasio. We are carried away by it. He is the only foreign writer in whom I have found the charm of La Fontaine.

The court of Vienna, for fifty years, did not celebrate a birth-day, or a marriage, without requiring a cantata from Metastasio. What subject can possibly be more dry! With us, the poet is only expected not to be detestable. Metastasio is divine; abundance springs from the bosom of sterility.

Observe, my friend, that the operas of Metastasio have charmed not only Italy, but all that is intellectual in every court of Europe, merely by the observation of the following simple, and commodious rules.

In every drama six characters are required, all lovers, in order that the musician may have the advantage of contrasts. The three principal actors, namely, the *primo soprano*, the *prima donna*, and the *tenore*, must each sing five airs: an impassioned air *(aria patetica,)* a brilliant air *(aria di bravura,)* a tranquil air *(aria parlante,)* an air of a mixed character; and, lastly, an air which breathes joy *(aria brilliante.)* It is requisite that the drama should be divided into three acts, and not exceed a certain number of verses; that each scene should terminate with an air; that the same personage should not sing two airs in succession, and that two airs of the same character should never follow one another. It is necessary that the first and second acts should conclude with the principal airs of the piece. It is required that, in the second and third acts, the poet should reserve two suitable places, one for a *recitativo obligato,* followed by an air for display *(aria di tranbusto;)* the other for a grand duet, which must always be sung by the hero and heroine of the piece. Without attending to these rules, there can be no music. It is further understood, that the poet must give frequent opportunities for the scene-painter to display his talents. Experience has shewn that these rules, apparently so singular, and some of which have been laid down by Metastasio himself, cannot be departed from, without injuring the effect of the opera.

Finally, this great lyric poet, in producing so many wonders, was not able to make use of more than a seventh part, or thereabouts, of the words of the Italian language. It contains about forty-four thousand, according to a modern lexicographer, who has been at the pains of counting them ; and the language of the opera, admits of not more than six or seven thousand, at most. The following is an extract from a letter which Metastasio wrote to a friend, in his old age.

.... "It happens, for my sins, that the female characters of the *Re Pastore* have so pleased his majesty, that he has commanded me to write another piece of the same description for the approaching month of May. In the state in which my poor head is, at present, through the continual tension of my nerves, it is a terrible task to me to have any thing to do with those jades, the muses. But my work is rendered a thousand times more disagreeable by the restrictions of all sorts, which are imposed on me. In the first place, I am prohibited from all Greek or Roman subjects, because our chaste nymphs cannot endure those indecent costumes. I am obliged to have recourse to oriental history, in order that the women, who perform the characters of men, may be duly wrapped up from head to foot in Asiatic drapery. All contrasts between vice and virtue are of necessity excluded, because no lady will choose to appear in an odious part. I am restricted to five characters, for this substantial reason, given by a certain governor,—that persons of rank ought not to be lost in a crowd. The duration of the performance, the changes of the scene, the airs, almost the number of the words, are fixed. Tell me if this is not enough to drive the most patient man mad? You may imagine then its effect on me, who am the high-priest of misfortune in this vale of misery."

It is a curious circumstance which shews how much chance has to do with every thing, even with the decisions of that posterity, which is so often held up to us *in terrorem*, that it has been thought a favour to admit such a man as this, to the rank of the frigid lover of Laura, who has produced some fifty sweet sonnets.*

Metastasio, who was born at Rome, in 1698, was distinguished, at the early age of ten years, by his talents as an *improvvisatore*. A rich lawyer, named *Gravina*, who amused himself with writing bad tragedies, was taken with the boy. He began with changing his name, from Trapassi, to Metastasio, *for the love of Greek*. He adopted him, gave him a careful, and, as it happened, an excellent, education, and finally left him a part of his property.†

---

* See the opinion expressed by M. Sismondi as to the general character of Petrarch's sonnets. *Litterature du Midi.* T. II. p. 408. T.

† The circumstances which introduced Metastasio to Gravina's notice, are thus related by Carlini.

Gravina was walking near the Campus Martius one su ner's evening, in company with the abbé Lorenzini, when they heard, at no great distance, a sweet and power-

Metastasio was twenty-six years old, when his first opera, the *Didone*, was performed at Naples in 1724. In the composition of it, he was guided by the advice of the fair Marianna Romanina, who executed the part of Dido in a superior style, because she passion-

---

ful voice, modulating verses with the greatest fluency to the measure of the *canto improvviso*. On approaching the shop of Trapassi, whence the grateful melody proceeded, they were surprised to see a lovely boy pouring forth elegant verses on the persons and objects which surrounded him, and their admiration was increased by the graceful compliments which he took an opportunity of addressing to themselves.

When the youthful poet had concluded, Gravina called him to him, and with many encomiums and caresses, offered him a piece of money, which the boy politely declined. He then enquired into his situation, and employment, and being struck with the intelligence of his replies, proposed to his parents to educate him as his own child. Convinced of the sincerity of the offer, and flattered by the brilliant prospects which it opened for their son, they consented, and Gravina faithfully, and generously, fulfilled the paternal character which he had thus voluntarily undertaken.

CARLINI. *Vita di Metastasio.*

T.

ately loved the poet. This attachment appears to have been durable. Metastasio was an intimate friend of Marianna's husband, and lived many years in the family, recreating himself with fine music, and studying unremittingly the Greek poets.

In 1729, the emperor Charles VI., that great and grave musician, who, in his youth, had played so miserable a part in Spain, proposed to him to be the poet of the opera at Vienna. He hesitated a little, but at length accepted the offer.

He never afterwards left that city, where he lived to an extreme old age, in the midst of a delicate and dignified voluptuousness, with no other occupation than that of expressing, in beautiful verses, the fine sentiments by which he was animated. Dr. Burney, who saw him in his seventy-second year, thought him, even then, the gayest, and handsomest man of his time. He always declined accepting any titles or honours, and lived happy in retirement. No tender sentiment was wanting to his sensibility.

This great and happy man died on the 2d of April, 1782, having been acquainted, in the course of his long career, with all the eminent musicians who have delighted the world.

ON THE

PRESENT STATE OF MUSIC IN ITALY.

Venice, *August* 29, 1814.

You still remember, then, my friend, the letters which I wrote to you six years ago, from Vienna, and you wish that I would give you a sketch of the present state of music in Italy. The course of my ideas has much changed during this period. I am now richer, and happier, than I was at Vienna; and the time which I do not pass in society, is entirely devoted to the history of painting.

You know how much I was rejoiced, on being restored to an income barely sufficient for my support. It seems that my ambition deceived me, for out of this limited revenue, I find means to buy, every day, some precious little picture, which the great collectors have overlooked, or rather, of which they have not known the value. I saw, a few days since, at the house of a polite sea-captain, on the *Riva dei Schiavoni,* some charming little sketches, by Paul Veronese, in the same golden tone of colour which gives such animation to his larger pieces; and I am already in hope, that I shall be able to procure some similar relics of this great master, whose works are interred, with so many others, in your immense Museum. You think yourselves vastly civilized, but you have acted like barbarians, in taking these fine productions out of Italy. You did not consider, thieves as you are—that you could not carry away the atmosphere which adds so much to their beauty. You have lessened the pleasures of the civilized world. The picture which now hangs solitary, and almost unobserved, in one of the corners of your gallery, formed, when here, the glory and the conversation of a whole city. At Milan, as soon as you arrived, they began to talk to you of the " Christ crowned with thorns," of Titian. At Bologna, the first enquiry of your valet was, whether you wished to see the St. Cecilia of Raphael: even this valet would know half-a-dozen phrases of connoisseurship relative to that chef d'œuvre.

I am aware that these phrases are tiresome to the amateur, who is desirous of feeling, and judging, for himself. He is often disgusted with the Italian superlatives; but these superlatives shew the general feeling of the country, with respect to the fine arts. Tiresome as they may be to me, they perhaps awaken the love of the art in some young mechanic, who will one day be an Annibal Caracci. They are like the marks of respect paid to the marquis Wellington, when he passes through the streets of Lisbon. Assuredly, the shop-boy, who cries *e viva*, cannot judge of the military talents, and sublime prudence, of that extraordinary man; but what does it signify, these shouts are to him the recompense of his virtues, and will, perhaps, make another Wellington of the young officer who is his aide-de-camp.

At Rome, the person best known, and highest in estimation, is Canova. At Paris, the people of the quarter know M. the Duke, whose hotel is at the end of the street. Nothing more is necessary, to shew you that it is in vain that you carry off to Paris the Transfiguration, and the Apollo :—that you transfer to canvas, the Descent from the Cross, painted by Daniel de Volterra, in fresco: these works are dead to you; your fine arts want a public that can feel them.

Have your Italian opera,—have your Museum :—it is all very well. You may, perhaps, arrive in these departments, at a decent mediocrity; but you will excel only in comedy, in the lively song, in moral ridicule;

<blockquote>Excudent alii spirantia mollius æra.</blockquote>

You have your Moliere, your Collé, your Pannard, your Hamilton, your La Bruyere, your Dancourt, your " Lettres Persannes." In this delightful department, you will always be the first people in the world. Cultivate it; place your pride in it; encourage such writers; great men of this description are produced by the ground on which you tread.

Give a tolerable orchestra to your Theatre Français; purchase for it the fine scenery of the theatre de la Scala, at Milan, which is fresh painted every two months, and which you might have for the cost of the canvas. Men of taste from Naples, and from Stockholm, will meet each other in the place du Carrousel, going to your theatre to see the Tartuffe, or the Mariage de Figaro. We who have travelled, know that these pieces cannot be acted any where but at Paris.

In like manner, the pieces of Louis Caracci may be regarded as invisible, except in Lombardy. Which of your fashionable ladies has ever looked, without a yawn, at the " Calling of St. Matthew," or at the " Virgin carried to the Sepulchre," which have rather too much depth of colour. I am convinced that the worst imitations, placed in the same frames, would produce just as much effect on the genteel society of France. Now, at Rome, they will talk for a fortnight of the manner in which the fresco of the convent of San Nilo, painted by Dominichino, is going to be transferred to canvas. At Rome, it is the great artist who occupies the public attention; at Paris, it is the successful general, or the favourite minister,—Marshal Saxe, or M. de Calonne. I do not say that this is well, or ill; I merely say that it is so: and the great artist, who is jealous of his reputation, and who knows the weakness of the human heart, should live where his merits will be best appreciated, and where, for the same reason, his defects will be most severely criticised. At Rome, Signors A. B. C. D., of whom I know nothing but their charming works, may reside in a garret, without fear of disregard. The consideration of the whole city, from the pope's nephew, to the humblest abbé, will follow them, and they will be far more esteemed for having produced a fine picture, than a happy repartee. This is the atmosphere required by the artist; for he, like other men, has his moments of despondency.

Some of the most interesting conversation I meet with, is that into which I fall, on my arrival in a town, with the coach-maker from whom I hire the carriage in which I go to deliver my letters of introduction. I ask him what curiosities are to be seen, who are the most distinguished of their nobility? He commences his reply with a few invectives against the tax-gatherers; but after this tribute to his station in society, he points out to me, very clearly, the actual current of public opinion.

When I returned to Paris, your charming madame Barilli was still there. Not a word, however, did the master of my handsome hotel, in the rue Cerutti, say to me about her; and as for mademoiselles Mars and Fleury, he scarcely knew their names. Go to *Schneider's,* at Florence, the least shoe-black will say to you, " Davidde has been here these three days; he is to sing with the Monbelli; the opera, *fera furore,* will draw all the world to it; every body is coming to Florence to hear it."

You will be disappointed, my dear Louis, if ever you visit Italy, to find the orchestras so inferior to that of the Odeon; and perhaps not more than one or two good voices in a company. You will think that I have been telling you travellers' tales. No where will you meet with an assemblage like that of Paris, when you had, at the same opera, madame Barilli, mesdames Neri and Festa; and for men, Crivelli, Tachinardi, and Porto. But do not despair of your evening; the singers, whom you will think indifferent, will be electrified by a sensible and enthusiastic audience; and the fire spreading from the theatre to the boxes, and from the boxes to the theatre, you will hear them sing with an unity, a warmth, a spirit, of which you have not even an idea. You will witness moments of delirium, when both performers, and auditors will be lost in the beauty of a finale of Cimarosa. It signifies nothing giving Crivelli thirty thousand francs at Paris; you must purchase also a public, fitted to hear him, and to cherish the love which he has for his art. He gives a simple and sublime trait;—it passes unnoticed. He gives a common, and easily distinguished, embellishment, and forthwith, every one, delighted to shew that he is a connoisseur, deafens his neighbour, by clapping as if he were mad. But these applauses are without any real warmth; his feelings are unmoved; it is only his judgment which approves. An Italian gives himself up, without fear, to the enjoyment of a fine air, the first time he hears it; a Frenchman applauds with a sort of anxiety. He is afraid of having approved of what is but indifferent: —it is not till after the third or fourth representation, when it is fully determined that the air is *delicious*, that he will dare to cry *bravo!* accenting strongly the first syllable, to shew that he understands Italian. Observe how he says to his friend, whom he meets in the green room at a first representation: *How divine that is!* He affirms with his lips, but with his eye he interrogates. If his friend does not reply with another superlative, he is ready to dethrone his divinity. The musical enthusiasm of Paris admits of no discussion; every thing is either *delicieux*, or *execrable*. On the other side the Alps, every man is sure of what he feels, and the discussions about music are endless.

I thought all the great singers of the Odeon cold. Crivelli is no longer the same as he was at Naples: Tachinardi alone had some perfect passages in the *Distruzione di Gerusalemme*. This evil is not one of those which money can remedy; it results from the qualities of the French public.

Hear this same Frenchman, so cautious and fearful for his vanity in speaking of music, express his admiration of a bon mot, or a happy repartee. With what animation, with what spirit, and nicety of distinction, with what copiousness of detail, does he describe the felicity of it. If you were visionary, you would be tempted to say: This country will produce a Moliere, or a Regnard, but not a Galuppi or an Anfossi.

A young Italian prince will be a *dilettante*. He will write music, good or bad, and will fall desperately in love with some actress. If he appears at the court of his sovereign, his demeanour will be embarrassed and respectful.

A young French nobleman goes up, even to the royal bed-chamber, with an easy elegance of air. You see that he is happy, and in full possession of himself. Carelessly humming some tune, he places himself against the balustrade which separates the king's bed from the rest of the apartment. A black-looking usher comes up, and tells him that he cannot be allowed to lean there, that he *profanates* the king's balustrade.—" Ah! my friend, you are right; I will take care to *proclamate* your attention," — and he turns upon his heel with a laugh.*

I still retain, my dear Louis, the opinion I held six years ago, when I wrote to you about the great German symphonist. The cultivation of the instrumental department has ruined music. It is much more common, and much more easy, to play well on the violin, or the piano-forte, than it is to sing; and hence arises the facility with which instrumental music corrupts the taste of the lovers of vocal; as the last fifty years have abundantly shewn.

---

* In the French, the usher is made to say *profaniser*, instead of *profaner*, and the wit replies by using *preconer*, instead of *preconiser*.   **T.**

One person only, in Italy, still knows how to manage his voice—that is Monbelli; and one of the principal causes of the merit of his charming daughters, is doubtless the having had such a master.

This, which I shall always maintain to be the only true style of singing, was also followed by mademoiselle Martinez, the pupil of Metastasio, who having passed his youth, in the beginning of the eighteenth century, at Rome and Naples, with the celebrated *Romanina*, knew how the human voice should be managed so as to charm every heart.

His secret is very simple.—The voice should be good, and should display itself.*

---

* This observation is perfectly just. Where nature has supplied the materials, the application of them is easy.

The first thing requisite, is to place the voice at the back part of the throat, as is done in pronouncing the vowel A in the word *all*. This will give that fulness of tone, which constitutes, what the Italians call, a *voce di petto*, and will, at the same time, bring the vocal organs into the position most proper to acquiring a correct, and rapid execution. A second position may be formed by means of the same vowel

This is all; and for this purpose it is requisite that the accompaniment should be soft,—*pizzicatos* on the violin, and, in general, that the passages executed should be slow. As things now are, a fine voice has no chance except in the recitatives;* it is here that ma-

---

as pronounced in the word *art*, and a third, upon the sound of the dipthong *ea* in the word *Earth*.

When a facility of execution in these three positions has been acquired, the pupil may proceed to the use of words, in the utterance of which he will frequently find it necessary to deviate from the pronunciation which good speaking would dictate, in order to preserve a suitable breadth of tone.

As consonants have a tendency to shut up the mouth, they should have no more stress laid on them, than is necessary to an intelligible and clear articulation, taking care never to introduce them, till the time of the note which they finish is expired.

These few directions are sufficient for what relates to the mechanical part of singing, in which the principal thing required is regular and assiduous practice; but the higher excellencies of the art, depend on the mental constitution of the artist. G.

* The sense is not very clear in the original, "Actuellement les belles voix se sauvent dans les recitatifs;" The author's sentiment appears to be, that the music is in general played so quick, that the recitatives, in which the singer *spares himself*, are the most beautiful parts. T.

dame Catalani, and Velluti, are most beautiful. It was thus that cantatas were sung eighty years ago. Now, we execute full gallop, a *polonaise*, followed by a grand air, in which the instruments contend with the voice for mastery, or pause only for ad libitum passages, and to give the singer an opportunity to make everlasting flourishes. And this we call an opera;—and this may amuse for a quarter of an hour;—and this never drew a single tear.

The best female singers that I have heard in Italy, (observe, to save my credit, that the greatest talents may perhaps never have had the good fortune to exhibit before me;) the best female singers, I have heard in these latter days, are mademoiselle Eiser, and the two Monbelli. The former has married an agreeable poet, and no longer sings in public; the latter are the hope of the Italian Polyhymnia. Imagine the finest style, the utmost sweetness of tone, the most perfect expression; imagine madame Barilli, with a voice still more beautiful, and with all the requisite warmth of feeling. I believe that the

Monbelli sing only in the serious opera; consequently madame Barilli would have an advantage over them as the *Fanciulla sventurata* of the Nemici generosi, as the countess Almavivo of Figaro, as Donna Anna in Don Juan, &c. You should have heard the little Monbelli sing the *Adriano in Siria* at Milan: people were mad after it. Happily for you, they are still very young, and you may yet have an opportunity of hearing the youngest, who takes the male characters.

Nothing was wanting to complete the opera, but Velluti, the only good soprano, of a certain kind, that Italy possesses, to my knowledge, and the younger Davidde. The latter has a charming voice, but he is at present far inferior to the Monbelli. He has a taste for embellishment, which would just suit your Paris concerts, and I am convinced he would soon rival M. Garat in the public favour. As for the little Monbelli, all our connoisseurs would say: " Is that all?" In Italy they will probably reach the highest reputation; provided some rich man does not deprive us of them.

Madame Manfredini would delight you in the *Camilla* of Paer; she has a powerful voice. But what principally pleased me in this opera, which I saw at Turin, was the performance of Bassi, who is unquestionably the first comic singer of Italy, at the present day. You should hear him, in this opera, address his master, a young officer who is thinking of passing the night at a gloomy looking castle, in the air,

> Signor la vita è corta,
> Andiam, per carità.

He is animated, he understands stage-effect, and is fond of his profession. Added to this, he has a profound knowledge of comedy, and has even composed some agreeable pieces. I have acquired this admiration of him merely f om his performance of *Ser Marc Antonio*, at Milan. He has a good voice, and would be perfect, if he possessed the counter-tenor of your Porto. I do not know where he is at present.

But what shall we say? Upon my system, the voice is destroyed by a certain degree of passion in men, and in women, by a certain degree of personal attraction. If you say that this is one of my odd fancies, I reply, with César de Senneville, *à la bonne heure!* Be it so.*

Nozzari, whom you have seen at Paris, is the fittest person in the world for the part of Paolino, in the Matrimonio segreto. I thought it rather too high for Crivelli.

Pellegrini is a magnificent counter-tenor. He should take some lessons from the younger Baptiste, from Thenard, or Potier, or, which would be still better, from the admirable Dugazon, if you are still in possession of that delightful comic singer, whose merit you have not appreciated, grave, and important gentlemen as you are.

You are better acquainted than I am with Grassini, Festa, Neri, Sessi, who have been at Paris. You still regret madame Strina-Sacchi, so superior in the part of Caroline, in the Matrimonio segreto, and whom your

---

See Picard's Novel, *Eugene et Guillaume.*   T.

theatrical amateurs used to call, not without justice, the *Dumesnil* of the theatre Louvois.

I was much pleased with madame Carolina Bassi, whom I heard in the handsome new concert-room at Brescia; she is a very animated actress. Madame Melanotti is also of the same character. Vittoria Sessi has a very pretty figure, and a powerful voice. I have never seen madame Camporesi, who must be now at Paris. She is in high estimation at Rome.

I have no occasion to say any thing of Tachinardi, who is so excellent when he is animated; the tenor-singer Siboni treads in his steps. Parlamagni and Ranfagni are still what they were when you saw them, that is, excellent comic singers. De Grecis, and Zamboni, are good actors: the performance of the former in the *Pretendenti delusi*, which had a great run at Milan three years ago, was perfect. It is our opera of *Les Pretendus*, suitably arranged for the Italian stage, with agreeable music by Mosca. The trio,

Con respetto e riverenza,

with the air for the flute, at the end, much pleased me.

I shall say nothing of madame Catalani, nor of madame Gaforini. I have not seen the first since her *debut* at Milan, thirteen years since, and the latter, unfortunately, is married. Her style was the very perfection of comic singing. You should have seen her in the *Dama Soldato,* in *Ser Marc Antonio,* in the *Ciabatino.* A more lively, gay, animated being will never again arise for the amusement of men of taste. Madame Gaforini was to Lombardy, what madame Barilli was to Paris; the place of neither can be supplied. From the different character of the people, you will suppose that, in many respects, madame Gaforini must be the opposite of madame Barilli, and you will be right in your conjecture.

Three months ago, when a very fine singer was performing at the Conservatorio of Milan, I heard those who sat near me saying: "Is it not a pity that that admirable buffo C——, should be left to vegetate in a corner of Milan? Why do they not make him a professor at the Conservatorio, that he may give a little animation to this handsome statue?" I forget the statue's name.

People who have been at Naples, speak in the highest terms of the buffo Casacieli. I have also heard a great deal of madame Paer, and the tenor singer, Marzochi. This, my friend, is the substance of what I know about the vocal performers of Italy. I may add to those before-mentioned, madame Sandrini, with whom I was much pleased at Dresden. I omit giving an account of the theatres of Vienna; I should have too much to say about them. Ask the French officers who were there in 1809. I doubt not they will remember the tears they shed at the *Croisé*, a melo-drama equal for effect to the best romantic tragedies; as well as the inextinguishable laughter excited by the admirable performance of the dancer, Rainaldi; who, I think, played in the ballet of the Vintage. Don Juan, the Matrimonio segreto, the Clemenza de Tito, the Sargines of Paer, Cherubini's Eliska, *Lisbeth folle par amour*, and many other justly-esteemed German works, were performed in a superior style at the same time.

With respect to the composers, I consider them in general to be carried away by the taste of the times, in a wrong direction; but, without entering into an unintelligible criticism of them, I shall merely relate the facts with which I am acquainted relative to them.

Paesiello, and Zingarelli, are not of the present school; they are the remaining contemporaries of Piccini and Cimarosa.

Valentine Fioravanti, so well known at Paris by his *Cantatrici villane*, is a native of Rome, and still young. His comic operas are much admired. The *Pazzie a vicenda*, which he produced at Florence, in 1791; the *Furbo* and the *Fabro Parigino*, performed at Turin, in 1797, are his principal works.

Simone Mayer, born in Bavaria, but educated in Italy, is perhaps the most esteemed composer of the present day, and, at the same time, one of whom I can say the least. His style seems to me, of all others, the most likely to occasion the total ruin of dramatic music. He resides at Bergamo, from whence the most advantageous proposals have hitherto been unable to draw him. He is very industrious. I have seen, at least, twenty of his pieces performed. He is known at Paris by the *Finte rivali*, a comic opera, in which madame Correa performs. There are some airs in it, but not always of sufficient dignity, and great richness of accompaniment. His *Pazzo per la musica* is pretty; *Adelasia and Aleramo*, a serious opera, had a great run at Milan. Mayer makes us enjoy the immense progress which instrumental music has made since the days of Pergolese, and at the same time, causes us to regret the beautiful airs of that period.

Ferdinando Paer, of whom I unfortunately have the same opinion as of Mayer, was born at Parma, in 1774. I have heard persons of the greatest intelligence in Paris speak with encomium of his genius. He has already written thirty operas. His Camilla and Sargine, two years ago, were performed at the same time, at Naples, Turin, Vienna, Dresden, and Paris.

Pavesi and Mosca, are much liked in Italy, and have written numerous comic operas, which contain some pleasing airs, not entirely stifled by the orchestra. Both these composers are young.

The operas of Farinelli, born near Padua, are pleasing. He was brought up in the *Conservatorio de' Turchini*, at Naples, and has already composed eight or ten operas.

The highest expectations are formed of signor Rossini, a young man of twenty-five, who has just made his *debut*. It must be allowed, that his airs are surprisingly graceful, when sung by the lovely Monbelli. The chef-d'œuvre of this young man, who has a fine person, is the *Italiana in Algeri*. He seems, already, to repent himself a little. I could not discover the least genius, or originality, in the *Turco in Italia*, which has just been performed at Milan, and has failed.

I surely need not repeat that I have probably passed over in silence many names of deserved reputation in Italy, merely because I am not acquainted with them. I have never been in Sicily, and it is a long time since I was at Naples. It is in that fortunate country, that land of fire, that fine voices are produced. I formerly noticed there some customs very different from ours, and in my opinion, more amusing. They do not expose a plagiary, in that country, in a pamphlet: they take the thief in the fact. If the composer, whose work is performing, has pilfered an air, or even a few bars only, from another, as soon as the stolen passage commences, shouts of *bravo* arise from all quarters, accompanied with the name of the rightful proprietor. If Piccini has plundered Sacchini, he will be saluted incessantly with *bravo Sacchini!* If it is observed, in the course of the opera, that he has taken a little from every body, they will cry, Well done, bravo, Galuppi! bravo, Traetta! bravo Guglielmi!

If the same custom prevailed in France, how many of the operas of the Feydeau would be saluted with this sort of *bravos.* But let us not speak of the living.

Every body now knows, that the celebrated air in the Visitandines, *Enfant cheri des dames,* is Mozart's.

Duni would have heard, bravo, Hasse! for the commencement of the air: *Ah! la maison maudite!* the first fifteen bars of which, are the first, also, of the air, *Priva del caro bene.*

Monsigny would have had a *bravo, Pergolese!* for the opening of his duet, *Venez, tout nous reussit,* which is exactly the same with that of the air, *Tu sei troppo scelerato,* and another for the air, *Je ne sais à quoi me résoudre.*

Philidor would have had a bravo, Pergolese! for his air, *On me fête, on me cajole,* the accompaniment of which may be found in the air, *Ad un povero polacco;* bravo, Cocchi! for the air, *Il fallait le voir au dimanche, quand il sortait du cabaret,* which is nothing else than the air, *Donne belle che pigliate,* without alteration; bravo, Galuppi! for the cavatina, *Vois le chagrin que me devore.* Gretry would also have had a few packets addressed to him.

What is more easy than to make an excursion into Italy, where, in general, the music is not engraved, to take copies of whatever a man may hear, in the hundred theatres open every year, for the performance of music in that country, that is good, or suited to the prevailing taste at Paris; to connect the different passages by a little harmony; and then to show off in France, as a grand composer. The experiment is attended with no hazard, for a French score never passes the Alps. What favourites would Mosca's airs, in the Pretendenti delusi, *Con rispetto e rivirenza,* and the quatuor, *Da che siam uniti, parliam de' nostri affari,* have been at the Feydeau; and who would ever have known them? *

A man wants nothing, but feeling, to be sensible that Italy is the land of excellence in all the arts. There is no occasion to go into the proof of this with you, my friend: but a thousand circumstances seem to favour music more especially. The extreme heat, followed in the evening by a refreshing coolness, grateful to every thing that breathes,

---

* We think we have consulted the author's reputation in omitting here a passage in vindication of an infamous practice, once frequent in Italy, but which the universal reprobation of a more humane and enlightened age has nearly abolished. T.

renders the hour at which the theatres open, the most agreeable of the day. This hour is almost every where, between nine and ten in the evening, that is to say, four hours, at least, after dinner.

You hear the music in a favourable obscurity. Excepting on festivals, the theatre *de la Scala,* at Milan, which is larger than the opera at Paris, is only lighted by the lamps of the balustrade; in short, you are perfectly at ease, in dark boxes, which resemble small parlours.

I am disposed to think that a certain languor is necessary, thoroughly to enjoy vocal music. It is a fact, that a month's residence at Rome changes the gait of the most lively Frenchman. He no longer walks with his former sprightliness, he is in a hurry for nothing. In cold climates, exercise is necessary for circuation. In warm ones, the supreme felicity is the *divino far niente—*the delight of doing nothing.

Paris, ...

Will you reproach me, in inquiring into the present state of music in France, with speaking only of Paris? In Italy, one may mention Leghorn, Bologna, Verona, Ancona, Pisa, and twenty other towns, which are not capitals; but in France, there is no originality in the provinces. Paris, alone, in this great kingdom, can be considered with relation to music.

An unfortunate spirit of imitation prevails in the provinces, which renders them of no weight in the arts, as in many other things. At Bourdeaux, at Marseilles, at Lyons, you might fancy yourself in the Marais.* When will these cities have resolution to think for themselves, and to hiss what comes from Paris, when it does not please them? In the present state of society there, they imitate awkwardly the elegance of the capital; they

---

* The *Marais* is one of the most ancient quarters of Paris, inhabited principally by the *bourgeoisie*.   T.

are studiously simple, affectedly natural, pompously unpretending.

From Toulouse, to Lille, the young man of fashion, the nymph who wishes to be agreeable, are above all things desirous of being like the Parisians; and pedants are to be met with, even in things where pedantry would seem impossible. These people appear not to know whether they like a thing or not; they must know what is thought of it at Paris. I have often heard foreigners remark, and justly, that there is nothing in France, but Paris, or the country. Even a man of sense, if born in the provinces, will in vain attempt to resist the contagion: for a long time, his manners will be less natural than if he had been a native of Paris. Simplicity, " that straight-forward quality which prevents a man from calculating the effects of his actions,"*

---

* The quotation is from Fenelon, and is scarcely susceptible of translation. " Cette droiture d'une ame qui s'interdit tout retour sur elle, et sur ses actions." T.

is perhaps, of all things, the most uncommon in France.

To a person familiar with Paris, there is nothing new to be seen at Marseilles, or at Nantes, but the Loire, and the port, that is to say, physical objects; the moral world is the same. Whereas, fine cities like these, containing 80,000 inhabitants, the natural situation of which is so different, would be very interesting subjects for investigation, if they possessed any originality. The example of Geneva, where strangers stop much longer than at Lyons, though it is not a quarter of the size of the latter, and though the manners of the place are rather pedantic, ought to have its influence on the French city. In Italy, nothing can be more different, and, sometimes, more opposite, than towns which are situated within thirty leagues of each other. Madame Gaforini, though such a favourite at Milan, was almost hissed at Turin.

In judging of the state of music in France and Italy relatively, we must not make the comparison between Paris and Rome, or we shall again be deceived in favour of our dear country. We must consider, that, in Italy, towns which contain not more than four thousand inhabitants, as Crema, and Como, which I mention out of a hundred others, have fine theatres, and, occasionally, excellent singers. Last year, people went from Milan to hear the Monbelli at Como; which was as if the Parisians were to go to the theatre at Melun, or Beauvais. The manners of the two countries are altogether different; you would suppose you were at a thousand leagues distance.

In the largest cities of France, you meet with nothing but the shrill singing of the French comic opera. If a piece succeeds at the Feydeau, you are sure to see it acted at Lyons two months afterwards. When will the wealthy inhabitants of a town, containing a population of 100,000 souls, situated at the very entrance of Italy, take it into their heads to send for a composer, and have some music of their own?

The climate of Bordeaux, the rapid fortunes, and novel ideas, arising from commerce, added to the natural vivacity of the Gascons, ought, one should think, to produce a comedy more lively, and more fertile in events, than that of Paris. Not the least appearance of any such thing. The young Frenchman there, as every where else, studies his La Harpe, and never once thinks of laying down the book, and asking himself: Does this really please me?

What little originality there is in France, is to be met with only in those classes who are too ignorant to imitate; but the lower ranks, in that country, have no regard for music, and never will the son of a French wheelwright become a Joseph Haydn.

The opulent class learn from the journals every morning, what opinions they are to hold upon politics and literature for the rest of the day. Lastly, we may mention, as a cause of the decline of the arts in France, the *English* attention which our most intelligent and sensible men pay to politics. It is certainly an advantage to live in a free country; but, unless a man's pride be extremely irritable, or his sensibility very unfortunately placed for his enjoyment, I do not see what pleasure he can find in continually busying himself about political matters. The happiness of a man of the world, is very little increased by the way in which power is distributed in the country which he inhabits; it may be injured, but not augmented, by it.

I compare the condition of those patriots who are incessantly dwelling on the administration of the laws, and the balance of powers, in a state, to that of a man who should be in continual anxiety about the solidity of the house in which he lives. I would choose, in the first instance, a solid, and well-built habitation; but, after all, the house has only been built to live comfortably in; and it seems to me, that a man must be of a very unfortunate turn, to be troubling himself about the state of his roof, when he might enjoy himself with the ladies in the parlour;

*Et propter vitam, vivendi perdere causas.**

Thus, my friend, I have given you, according to your request, my ideas, perhaps hastily formed, of the present state of music in Italy. It is generally considered to be in a state of rapid declension, and I believe it to be so myself. I am, however, content to enjoy the declension every evening, but I devote the day to another art.

The account which I have given you, therefore, is doubtless very incomplete For instance, it has only just occurred to me that Mosca has a brother, who, like himself, is an agreeable composer.

I should much rather have talked to you about the admirable copy of the Last Supper of Lionardo da Vinci, which has been made

---

* This French political philosophy reminds one of the Fable of the Fox and Grapes.   T.

by the chevalier Bossi;—of the fine sketches made by this great painter, and amiable man, for the late count Battaglia, relative to the character of the four great Italian poets; —of the frescos of Appiani, at the royal palace, or the villa built by signor Melzi,* on the lake of Como. This would be much more to my present taste, than to write about the finest modern opera.

In music, as, alas! in many things besides, I am a man of another age.

Madame de Sévigné, faithful to her ancient predilections, liked Corneille only; and said that Racine, and coffee, would go out of fashion. I am, perhaps, equally unjust to signors Mayer, Paer, Farinelli, Mosca, Rossini, who are highly esteemed in Italy. The air,

Ti rivedrò mi rivedrai,

---

* Melzi was vice-president of the Italian Republic under Bonaparte. T.

in the Tancred of the latter, who, I am told, is very young, has certainly much pleased me. I am also always gratified with a duet of Farinelli's, beginning,

No, non v'amò,

which, in many theatres, is added to the second act of the Matrimonio segreto.

I must confess, my dear Louis, that since the time I wrote to you from my retreat at Salzburg, I have never been able to account for the little interest shewn in Italy for the works of Pergolese, and the great masters who were contemporary with him. It is almost as singular, as if we should prefer our petty writers of the present day, to Racine and Moliere. I am aware that Pergolese was born before music had attained perfection in all its branches; the instrumental department has apparently reached its height since his death. But chiaro-scuro made immense progress after the time of Raphael, yet he is still considered the first painter in the world.

Montesquieu justly observes: " If heaven were to bestow on men the piercing sight of the eagle, who doubts that the rules of architecture would be immediately changed. We should require orders differently composed."

It is evident that the Italians are changed since the time of Pergolese.

The conquest of Italy, which was effected by a series of splendid actions, first roused the people of Lombardy. In the sequel, the exploits of her soldiers in Spain and Russia, her association with the destinies of a great, though unfortunate, empire,—the genius of Alfieri, who opened the eyes of his youthful countrymen to the trifling character of the pursuits on which their ardour was wasted; every thing has awakened in this fine country,

<blockquote>Ch' Appenin parte, e'l mar circonda e l'Alpe,</blockquote>

the desire to become a nation.

I have heard that, in Spain, the Italian

troops, on some occasions, surpassed even the French veterans. Many noble characters have distinguished themselves in the ranks of that army. Judging from the conduct of a young field-officer, whom I saw wounded in the neck, at the battle of Moscow, that army possesses officers as remarkable for elevation of mind, as for military merit. I have found them, in general, unaffected in their manners, natural and profound in their way of thinking, and free from all ostentation. This was not the case in 1750.

There has, then, taken place, an important change in the inhabitants of Italy. This change has not yet had time to affect the arts. The provinces of the ancient kingdom of Italy have not yet enjoyed any of those long intervals of repose, which lead nations to seek for a variety in their sensations from the fine arts.

I have been well pleased to observe, of late years, in Lombardy, a circumstance which is not equally agreeable to all my countrymen. I mean a little aversion for France.

Alfieri laid the foundation of this sentiment, and it has been strengthened by the twenty or thirty millions which the kingdom of Italy paid every year to the French empire.

An ardent young man, just entering upon his career, and eager to distinguish himself, is checked by the admiration he cannot help feeling to be due to those who have obtained the first honours from the hands of victory before him. If the Italians admired us more, they would resemble us less in our brilliant qualities. I should not be greatly surprised, if they were now to become aware that there is no true greatness, in the arts, without originality; no national greatness, without an English constitution. Perhaps I may yet live to see the Mandragore of Machiavel, the *Commedie dell' arte,* and the operas of Pergolese, revived in Italy. The Italians will be sensible, sooner or later, that these are what constitute their glory, and foreigners will esteem them the more for it. For my own part, I confess I was quite disappointed, on going one day to the theatre at Venice, to find them performing Zaïre. The whole audience, down to the very corporal at the door, were in tears, and the actors possessed considerable merit. But when I want to see Zaïre, I go to the Theatre Français, at Paris. I was much more gratified with seeing, the next day, the *Ajo nel imbarazzo*, a comedy written by a native of Rome, and played in superior style by a fat actor, who reminded me, immediately, of Ifflaud of Berlin, and of Molé, in the serio-comic parts which he took towards the close of his career. This fat actor appeared to me worthy to be one of the triumvirate. But I sought in vain in Venice for the plays of Gozzi, and the *Commedia dell arte;* instead of these, they performed, almost every day, translations from the French theatre. The day before yesterday I escaped from the dullness of the *Jealous Wife*, to divert myself with Punch, in the piazza di S. Marco. He has really afforded me more amusement than I have found in any theatre where music is not performed.

Punch, and Pantaloon, are natives of Italy, and in spite of all our endeavours, we never excel, but in the department which nature has assigned us.

INDEX.

ACCENT, 359.
Aeras of Composers, 39. 177.
Alfieri, 444.
Ancient Concert, 192.
Artaxerxes, 30.
Assassination of Stradella, 296.

Balliot, 359.
Bach, 105.
Barilli, 88. 158. 466.
Beethoven, 2. 22. 64. 115. 205.
Bernard, 152.
Bertoni, 30.
Bobbin of Gold Thread, 243.
Billington, 18. 194.
Boschi, 58.
Branchu, 155.
Borromean Isles, 212.

Camporesi, 470.
Cabanis, 221.
Canova, 285. 455.
Capri, 267.
Carpani, 264.
Cantatrici, 320.
Carracci, 128. 155. 457.
Carissimi, 267.
Caravaggio, 128.
Catalani, 278.
Café de Foi, 76.

Cherubini, 217.
Cimarosa, 120. 171. 181. 273. 286.
Claude Lorraine, 149. 169. 240.
Clementi, 141.
Colour of the Instruments, 255.
Cosi fan Tutti, 417.
Comparison with Painters, 301.
Concert Spiritual, 185.
Corelli, 21.
Corner, 39.
Correggio. 127. 253. 267.
Counterpoint, 48. 201. 273.
Creation, 225. 238. 246.
Crivelli, 89. 95. 262. 489. 460.
Curtz, 44.

Dante, 442.
Davidde, 459.
Devil on Two Sticks, 45.
Delille, 234.
Doctors degree, 196.
Domenechino, 272. 274. 302. 457.
Don Juan, 121. 380.
Description of Canzonetts, 150.
————— Creation, 261.
————— Chaos, 247.
————— Leviathan, 258.
————— Wild beasts, 265.
————— Orpheus, 194.
————— Ariadne, 153.

INDEX. 495

Description of Sinfonia, 186.
———— Comic do. 144.
———— Quartett, 63.
———— Beethoven's do. 64.
———— Beethoven Sinf. 115.
———— Masses, 215.
———— Mount of Olives, 205
———— Mozart's Operas, 302.
———— Requiem, 403.

English Music, 165.
——— School, 171.

Flemish music, 165.
Fioravanti, 473.
Figaro, 237. 271—304. 408.
Four Seasons, 288.
Friedburg, 54.
Fugue, 13.

Gabrielli, 18.
Gaforini, 471—482.
Garal, 278.
Gassman, 21.
Garrick, 161.
German music, 164.
Gherard, 162.
Gluck, 105. 120. 126. 162 180. 239.
Guido, 205. 269. 271.

Handel, 229. 370.
Haydn's Birth-day, 308.
——— Ring, 183.
——— Picture, 195.
Harmony, 252.
Harmonic Game, 111.
Hasse, 142. 175.
Hymn at St. Paul's, 87.

Instinctive tones, 221.
Introduction to P. E, 55.
Inn, *Isola bella*, 71.

Jomelli, 113, 175.

Keys in Music, 98.
Keller, 42.

Laharp, 163. 205.
Leo, 173.
Leonardi da Vinci, 95, 204.
Lobkowitz, 264. 309.
London Captain, 188.
——— Nobleman, 187.
——— Music-seller, 190.
Lulli, 14. 16. 20.

Mat. Segreto, 85. 157. 241. 244. 270.
Martinez, 52.
Martini, 106. 113. 141. 871.
Marcello, 139. 239.
Marchesi, 18. 432.
Masses, 199. 202. 214.
Melody, 200
Marata, 139.
Mortzin, 54.
Milton, 260
Mithridates, 365.
Miserere, 356.
Murad, 299.

Neapolitan School, 171.
Nemici Generosi, 270. 272.
Nightingale, 280.
Notation, 51.

Operas, Haydn's, 145. 193.
———, Sarail, 375. 389.

Paer, 474.
Paesiello, 95. 125. 182. 216.
Paul Veronese, 454.
Perez, 175.
Pelligrini, 469.

INDEX.

Pergolese, 174. 265, 426.
Philharmonic Society, 35. 192.
Piano-Forte, 106.
Pitt, Mr. 242.
Podestra, 238.
Porpora, 39. 173.
Power of the Orchestra, 231.
Purcel, 166.

Quartetts, 62. 111. 306.

Raphael, 84. 169. 271. 422.
Reynolds, Sir Joshua, 194.
Reuter, 25. 35.
Requiem, 403.
Rossini, 475.
Rousseau, 37.

Sacchini, 116. 182. 280.
Salomon 185. 234.
Sarti 125. 181.
Scarlatti 173.
Seven Words. 132.
Spectator, 275.
Sinfonias, 62. 100. 134. 143.
―――― Conic, 143.
Singing 464.

Stradella, 295.
Swieten Von, 233. 248. 304.

Tartini, 96.
Talma, 289.
Thorny Accacia, 269.
Thorough Bass, 248.
Titian, 454.
Transfiguration, 93.
Traetta, 176. 178.
Trombone, 15.

Violin, 52. 359.
Voice, 124.
Vienna, 5.
Virgil, 170. 321.
Vigano's Ballet, 249.

Werter, 281.
Webbe, 166.
Weigl, 233.
Wellington, Duke, 455
Wind Instruments 102.

Zauber Flöte, 415.
Zingarelli 232.

Printed by W. Lewis, St. John's-square, London.